Voices of the Lost Children of Greece

Voices of the Lost Children of Greece

Oral Histories of Cold War International Adoption

Edited by Mary Cardaras

ANTHEM PRESS

Anthem Press
An imprint of Wimbledon Publishing Company
www.anthempress.com

This edition first published in UK and USA 2023
by ANTHEM PRESS
75–76 Blackfriars Road, London SE1 8HA, UK
or PO Box 9779, London SW19 7ZG, UK
and
244 Madison Ave #116, New York, NY 10016, USA

British Library Cataloguing-in-Publication Data
A catalogue record for this book is available from the British Library.

Library of Congress Cataloging-in-Publication Data
A catalog record for this book has been requested.
2022940886

ISBN-13: 978-1-83998-3-702 (Hbk)
ISBN-10: 1-83998-3-701 (Hbk)

ISBN-13: 978-1-83998-804-2 (Pbk)
ISBN-10: 1-83998-804-5 (Pbk)

This title is also available as an e-book.

"There can be no keener revelation of a society's soul than the way in which it treats its children."

—Nelson Mandela
May 1995

DEDICATED TO

Dena Poulias
She was lost, then found after 42 years. Her incredible adoption
story first inspired this collection.

Gonda Van Steen
"The Greek adoptee whisperer." She was the first one who gave us
agency and is helping us to put together the fragmented pieces of our
pasts with care, great sensitivity, kindness, and affection.

Gabrielle Glaser
With love and a generous spirit in her beautiful writing
about adoption, she has invited adoptees to lean in to their
feelings, to acknowledge that they are real, and to find comfort
in the reality that they are not alone in them.

You three are changing the lives of thousands of people.
In gratitude.

CONTENTS

FOREWORD

Antonios Sakkas/Andrew Mossin

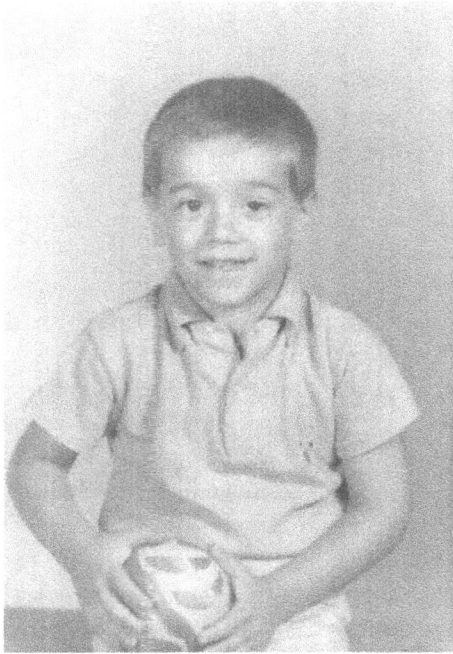

A four-year-old child lands in Chicago, having been flown from Athens in the care of her adoptive mother. As a grown woman, she cannot remember anything of these early years, yet they continue to haunt her into the present day.

A young woman recalls how as a child she found solace in Greek mythology whose stories felt more real to her than those that circulated in the household of her adoptive U.S. family.

A child is placed in a box outside the orphanage in Patras, Greece, in May 1953, only to be adopted three years later by a married couple living in San Diego. In turn, the couple would adopt three more children, among them a boy from an orphanage in Athens. Facing nightly abuse from her adoptive father for repeated bedwetting that continued until she was twelve years old, the girl fantasizes about her birth father, thinking to herself, "*My real dad would never treat me this way.*"

For another adoptee, the story of unsettlement and dislocation would begin with her being left at the same orphanage in Patras, a note attached to her infant body reading, "Her name is Despo. She was born 1/5/1958. She likes to eat."

A thirteen-year-old boy on a car ride with his father and uncle recognizes without understanding why that he is not related by blood to the people in the car with him, that he is somehow a "fraud," without a family line he can call his own.

A twelve-year-old boy growing up in the shadow of Disneyland is completing a registration form for junior high school and realizes he doesn't know the answer to the question, "What is your city of birth?" In the conversation that occurs with his parents, his father tells him, "You were adopted, we told you before." As he would remember years later, he couldn't at that moment fathom the reason anyone would want to give their child away.

Twenty-five years after being forced to give her son up for adoption, a Greek woman writes to her now-grown son a letter that will change both their lives. She was 16 at the time of her son's birth, forty-three when she would write the letter from Athens in the winter of 1984 that her son would read: "My sweet boy, my beloved child, my good boy. I would have liked to be keeping you in my arms till I die."

These are some of the voices you will meet in this book. Each exerts a pressure on the past, on memory, on the sites of loss and reunification that are recorded in these narratives. Gaps, missing recollections, disturbed understandings, re-circling, drift, aporia, virtual flickers of phenomenal experience: each of these is registered in the accounts that follow. Marianne Hirsch, in writing about Art Spiegelman's graphic memoir, *Maus*, which recounts his father's and mother's experiences in the Nazi death camps during World War II, developed the term "post-memory" to describe the memories that haunt the children of survivors. "Post-memory," Hirsch writes, "should reflect back on memory, revealing it as equally constructed, equally mediated by the processes of narration and imagination."[1] Separated by language, geography, histories, these

---

1. Marianne Hirsch, "Family Pictures: *Maus*, Morning and Post-Memory," *Discourse*, Winter 1992–93, Vol. 15, no. 2, 8–9. The term post-memory has evolved since its

Greek adoptee voices merge with their adult selves, as long before becomes present today, the sensuality of experience is reinhabited, then retold, until it acquires the astonishing feel of the true and real. What any of us was told about our origins and births, we discover, could only be partly true, partly real at best. As Hirsch goes on to say, post-memory is empty and full at the same time. It reveals itself as documentation that stands in place of experience, letters that arrive translated from another region of the world, intricate and full of meaning–yet always threatening to disappear, to fall apart in the adoptee's hands. To start as a public record and end as indecipherable symbols.

The origin point is never really the point–yet for many of us, orphaned in the ways we were and are, the birth tale is central to what we must understand and repossess of ourselves and our histories. It is the narrative and imaginal starting place for many of our memories, our later efforts to reconstruct identity in the face of initial absence and occlusion. For many of us, the way in which our identities as adopted children were initially revealed to us leaves a mark that can never be removed, even after we may have located our birth parents and reconstructed pathways to our histories with very different maps in hand. Naming forms a critical part of this process, as we learn that we once possessed different names given to us at birth or shortly after. Between the identity of the first and the second lies a history that we traverse repeatedly, living in the in-between spaces imposed by bifurcated identities. First name. Second name. The hermetic closure of one over the other, as we may not initially understand the significance of what we're being told. The poet Robert Duncan, in seeking to understand his own adoption, relates his experience of a seance in which his mother returned to him:

> My mother is alive, there, four hundred miles from here. She has dark
> hair and eyes.
> First mother. Second mother.

In Duncan's telling, he would later ask his adoptive mother of his biological mother, "What did she look like?" To which she responded, "I always kept

---

original usage to include other forms of narrative recollection not solely related to the Holocaust. I use the term here provisionally to speak of the condition of memories passed on to adoptees about their pre-adoptive lives, memories that become fused over time with the adoptees' own stories and recollections of the circumstances surrounding their adoption.

a picture of her in your room when you were little, but you never cared. Now it is lost. You remember nothing. You never cared."[2]

First memory. Second memory.

In time we find our way to the narratives that help us understand our own displacement, the ongoing feelings of exile, isolation, homelessness. Many years after I was told the stories at age 6 or 7 of my adoption by my adoptive mother, Iris—stories I would later learn bore little resemblance to the facts as I would come to know them—I began reading the work of my Greek ancestors: Homer, Plato, Aristophanes, Euripides, Sophocles. It was in *Oedipus the King* that I encountered this exchange between the blind seer of Thebes, Tiresias, and Oedipus:

Tiresias: Call me a fool, if you like, but your parents,
            who gave you life, they respected my judgment.
Oedipus: Parents?
            What do you mean?
            Who are my mother and father?[3]

"Who are my mother and father?" The question has lingered over a lifetime, each time proposing new possibilities, alternative narratives, tales that start and stop, only to begin all over again. I've recounted much of this re-searching in my memoir, *A Son from the Mountains*,[4] a book that took me nearly 20 years to complete [...] or 40 [...] or it was never completable and had to come into the world unfinished, a story that must not be passed on, must be passed on, to paraphrase Toni Morrison.[5]

Our histories are never settled; rather, they propose different routes in, potentially different outcomes. "What if [...]" becomes the axiomatic phrase for the adoptee, as they ponder the consequential steps that led to their orphaning. And they cannot let go of the perception that they bear little resemblance to those they are living among, most especially but not only their own family members. Traveling to Crete in 1990, my first trip back to Greece since my adoption in 1959, I walked through the streets

---

2. Robert Duncan, "A Sequence of Poems for H.D.'s Birthday," *Roots and Branches* (New York: New Directions, 1964) 13–15. In this same poem, Duncan recollects the origin of his name, Robert, given to him by his "new mother."

3. Sophocles, "Oedipus the King," *The Complete Sophocles. Volume 1: The Theban Plays*, translated by Stephen Berg and Diskin Clay (New York: Oxford University Press, 2011), 235.

4. Andrew Mossin, *A Son from the Mountains: A Memoir* (New York: Spuyten Duyvil, 2021).

5. Toni Morrison, *Beloved* (New York: Vintage Books, 2004), 323.

of Chania startled to see young men who resembled me: the shape and color of their eyes and hair, their dark-complected skin and long torsos. I couldn't have recognized until that moment how out of place I'd felt in my childhood home world of Washington, DC, growing up among families and other children whose faces were paler than mine, whose voices spoke an English that even years after my adoption was foreign-sounding, unfamiliar. As for my adoptive parents, Richard and Iris, emigrés from post–World War II Europe whose lineages were, respectively, Polish and British, they appeared to my young person as refractions of an inner break I couldn't yet identify but knew intimately, wordlessly: an estrangement that embodied our relations to one another throughout their lifetimes—and mine. These privations of not seeing oneself among familiars, of not being able to locate oneself in a communal world of others, often create their own irreparable gaps and lesions. A version of the "I" that is never securely at home, perpetually unsettled, adrift, seemingly cut off from the bonds of kinship and community. In but not of the world.

The work gathered here, the voices in this book, can't be said to have reached completion, even after many of these adoptees' hard-won struggles to locate birth parents and resettle understandings of their adoptive families and homeland. They are the genitive tales of individuals starting and starting over, of claiming an identifiable place and time, recognizing as they do so that memory is inherently incomplete, the work starts over again, without finality or adequate conclusion. As Angelos Sikelianos has written:

Neither forward nor back,
but here, on this spot,
without room to lie down or stretch out,
here on this same spot,
upright.[6]

First land. Second land. Let your eye travel far enough across the horizon and you will see them merge, briefly and without interruption, before separating again.

---

6. Angelos Sikelianos, *Selected Poems*, translated and introduced by Edmund Keeley and Philip Sherrard (Princeton: Princeton University Press, 1979), 67.

INTRODUCTION

Mary Cardaras

In the 1990s, when I was a journalist working in Philadelphia, I executive produced a documentary about an orphanage in Guatemala that, at the time, was one of the "go to" places where childless couples could find infants and young children to adopt. I remember helping the reporter and producer craft the storyline, deciding to begin by telling the story of Moses (yes, that Moses), who was maybe one of the first adoptees in recorded history, and what that story has meant in Judaism and in the greater historical narrative about adoption.

I worked on the story dispassionately. We had long discussions about the plucking of Guatemalan children from their rich culture and language to see them dispatched to points all over the globe. We talked about birth mothers and fathers. We talked about what could become of these children and what they might feel about their adoptions as they grew up. And yet, I failed to internalize the stories and destinies of those precious children. I failed to acknowledge, in my own heart, that I was one of them, even as I had begun my own search for biological kin, via the sluggish U.S. Postal Service, before the Internet was widely available.

My own ten-year search (to this point in the 1990s) was not yielding fruit; my biological mother, whose name was listed on my Greek birth certificate, had decided, after many letters through intermediaries back and forth, that she would not pursue and did not want a meeting with me, as I had requested. No explanation was given, just speculation about her feelings and frame of mind, but again, I failed to internalize the news. Rather than to feel about it, I abruptly abandoned my search. Obviously, I was too hurt to deal with the rejection, but failed to express it. I summarily buried my deepest feelings about the circumstances of my birth, my adoption, and what it felt like to have been born into one family and be given to and raised by another.

It was not until after both my adoptive parents had died when I allowed myself to seriously think about my early childhood again. There was an undeniable void. An emptiness. A loneliness in realizing that I have no known biological connection to anyone, not even children. My parents and grandparents had provided my adoption story and had been the ties that bound me to a family. Once they were gone, I was left untethered and wondering. Maybe even longing.

I returned to my Greek culture in 2018 and decided to attend Greek language classes at a church in Oakland, California. One of my delightful and enthusiastic classmates, who is half Greek through her mother, and in love with all things Greek, told me the story of her cousin, Dena Polites Poulias, a Greek-born adoptee of the 1950s, just like me. Dena's story was moving, utterly tragic, and unbelievable. I was compelled to write about it and did so, working closely with Dena and her family, to produce the novella, *Ripped at the Root* (published by Spuyten Duyvil Publishers, 2021).

Dena's story changed my life. Her willingness to recount the painful trajectory of her life after an adoption that never should have happened first led me to Gonda Van Steen, who exhaustively researched and wrote the essential book *Adoption, Memory, and Cold War Greece: Kid pro quo?* (University of Michigan Press, 2019).

Later, I discovered the eloquent, best-selling author and investigative journalist, Gabrielle Glaser, who produced the groundbreaking *American Baby* (Penguin Random House, 2021) about "the adoption industrial complex" in America (still very much alive), told through one painful, forced relinquishment of a child and his adoption by another family.

I have described my encounter with these three wonderful individuals as my own revelatory journey down the Yellow Brick Road. Gonda educated me about my own history for the first time and asked me to think again about my own adoption. Gabrielle encouraged me to listen to the beating of my heart, prying it open about my past in ways that I never had. And Dena showed me what courage looks like in telling the truth about her own life.

These three individuals—Gonda, Gabrielle, and Dena—spawned both the idea for this collection of essays and the shape the book has taken, which I now understand has been a long time coming. This is a unique collection from a group of adoptees who are rarely heard from. These adoptees represent the first systematic export of children, en masse, to adoption. What we have in common, and what binds us, is that we were systematically exported from our country of origin, Greece, after a tumultuous time, two wars in succession, which left the country desperate and devastated. There are thousands of us, who were sent out of our country and far away from home. The essays here are but a tiny sample. There are hundreds of other stories.

Fourteen of us share similar feelings and emotions, but our individual adoption stories are quite different. Each lived experience can only be described by the author alone. Most of the essayists are not writers. We come from many varied professions and different parts of the world. Our voices are authentic, raw, and pure, and were preserved as such without any heavy-handed editing.

As adoptees, what happened to us? What do we feel about what happened to us? What does it feel like to be adopted? How has adoption shaped and influenced our lives? What have our lives been like? What lessons and insights can we offer to other adoptees, adoptive parents, prospective adoptive parents, and all those who work in adoption or write about adoption (lawyers, elected officials, reporters, filmmakers, academics, social service workers, anthropologists, sociologists, psychologists, historians, and activists)?

It is important to remember that knowing who we are, from whom we came, and what the circumstances were of our births and early lives are fundamental to our psychological health and happiness. The acknowledgment of our stories helps to make us complete and whole, helps us to make sense of our lives. The readers of these essays are invited to bear witness to both our early lives and our lives today. There are many people who have been hurt in the process of our adoptions, some who will never recover from the trauma.

While the past cannot be changed, we can use it as a cautionary tale, a learning experience, to ensure that adoption practices, from here forward, are ethical, open, and thoughtful; that birth mothers (and fathers) are treated with care and empathy; and that a child's life should not and cannot be appropriated by anyone. Adopted children have pasts and will grow up into adults who deserve to know and to tell our own stories, fully, openly, and honestly.

On these points, we cannot equivocate; we owe each of them, at least, that.

This text can stand alone. It can also be used in tandem with various academic texts about adoption and the tangled web of problems and unintended consequences it often produces. These stories also contribute to the growing collection of personal narratives by adopted people.

First, the collection is put into historical context by Gonda Van Steen, one of the world's leading scholars in Modern Greek Studies, who has devoted many years to compiling a comprehensive database of all Greek-born adoptees. She is helping many of us discover what happened to us and to trace and sometimes find our biological kin. In addition, she is working with a number of important political and social constituencies to restore what has been lost for most of us: our complete adoption records and our Greek citizenship, which we regard as our birthright.

In addition to my own essay, "Maria/Mary," I have written the last chapter, which notes a global movement for the millions of adoptees who seek biological kin, who demand open adoption records, who plead for no more secrets in adoption, not ever, and who advocate for justice in all matters of identity, which is the birthright of every child.

At the heart of the book, however, are the essays themselves. They preserve this particular, relatively brief period in history through the testimonies of the people who actually lived it. Many of us still experience the repercussions of our adoption journeys, which began as infants and children. Many have found their first families. Others are still searching and, for them, time is running out. Their contributions to the pantheon of adoption literature, stories, books, and movies demonstrate that there are no better accounts than first person accounts. With this collective volume, we amplify the *Voices of the Lost Children of Greece*, who are, in fact, lost no more.

This volume serves as testament to that fact.

Chapter 1

ADOPTION'S UNFINISHED BUSINESS

Gonda Van Steen

At dinner a man got drunk,
and over the wine charged me with not being my father's child.
I was riled, and for that day
scarcely controlled myself; and on the next I went to
my mother and my father and questioned them; and they made
the man who had let slip the word pay dearly for the insult.
So far as concerned them I was comforted, but still
this continued to vex me, since it constantly recurred to me.

—Sophocles, *Oedipus Tyrannus*, 779–786, trans. Hugh Lloyd-Jones

It has become impossible to ignore the organized mass adoptions of Greek children to the USA during the two decades that followed the end of the Greek Civil War of 1946–1949. This movement must be characterized less as a byproduct of the Greek Civil War and more as a Cold War phenomenon, when Greek agency, let alone children's agency, was at a historic low—and U.S. demands marked a new postwar high. This mass adoption phenomenon, which involved some 4,000 children, has been contested, denied, or grossly exaggerated. Recently, however, this controversial subject has also been studied and documented.[1]

We have now arrived at that critical junction where the debate can and must broaden and draw in many more interlocutors. The debate must be led by the Greek-born adopted persons themselves, who are finding each other via social media and communicate more frequently and more productively than ever before.

---

1. See Gonda Van Steen, *Adoption, Memory, and Cold War Greece: Kid pro quo?*, Ann Arbor: University of Michigan Press, 2019.

That is why the collection that you have picked up is so important: it is the first anthology of Greek adoption stories written by Greek international adoptees and compiled by the scholar and journalist Mary Cardaras, herself a Greek-to-American adoptee. This book is nothing short of a path-breaking initiative, given that no previous collection of such Greek adoptee stories, written by the people themselves, exists anywhere, whether in Greece or in the English-speaking world. These stories then strike home the experience of international adoption, whose impact is lifelong but is not properly measured, let alone acknowledged.

Remarkably, more than half a century after the voyage of no return, the voices of the adoptees who "lived it," as the Greeks would say, have yet to be heard. But times have changed dramatically since 1949, and the voices of international adoptees from anywhere living just about everywhere have only grown louder. The Korean adoptees to the United States have led the way, which is not unrelated to their very large numbers. Others chime in regularly, with blogposts and other forms of expression. It is not at all a hyperbolic prediction to state that the international adoptee voices, at large and out loud, will shape the 2020s conversation on cross-border adoption. It is about time. For the Greek adoptees born in the 1940s, it is definitely *about time*. This book empowers the Greek adoptee voices, registers their experiences, lets them make their claims—all long overdue. The seventy-year-long path to this achievement has not been an easy one.

For unraveling the fabric of Greek family life, and the myth of the Greek mother singularly devoted to child-rearing, this Greek child export phenomenon presents a difficult history but one that certainly merits further exploration. This scarcely-talked-about phenomenon may well have remained absent from nearly all official Greek histories, even from more progressive social histories and histories dealing with other large postwar movements of Greek children. But the topic has never been absent from popular public memory or from more intimate family conversations. Covering an era when archival documentation *is* available (be it scarce), this adoption movement and Greek adoption altogether have remained some of the last social taboos that need to be broken.

I pose the bold question of whether, after granting agency to women, we are now ready to also give agency back to the children. The question is urgent now: the older Greek adoptees, who no longer speak Greek for having lived abroad for decades, have a lot to share but have yet to gain formal representation in the Greek sociopolitical and state system. Their demands for easier access to their birth and adoption records are entirely legitimate, as is the demand of some for Greek citizenship as a second citizenship. But the ultimate demand is for the basic recognition that these Greek child exports were carried out, and then conveniently forgotten, leaving the adoptees to fend for themselves for more than half a century.

The making and presentation of this collection ensure that the Greek-born adopted persons and those with experience of adoption, or rather adoptee-hood, can reflect on the enduring nature of adoption and adapting, on the writing process that tries to capture it, and on the big and small challenges that transcultural adoptions still present.

The authors raise all the critical, big-picture questions: What made this writing happen and why now? How would you define the "unfinished business" of adoption? Does it relate to the lack of birth and adoption records? The lack of truth? Is it a matter of institutional challenges or of psychological and even medical concerns? What has changed recently in the adoption discussion? What is changing for you? What remains to be debated and fought for? But more important may well be the personal questions and details, the suppressed incidents, that relate individual history to Greek and global history—and mindset: What to make of these international adoptions? Could and should my adoption have been avoided? How come these intercountry adoptions still happen despite the known drawbacks? What could be the alternatives, then and now? What does the "what if" hold?

Intercountry Adoption from Greece: A Historical Overview

First, however, let me provide a Greek overseas adoption history in a nutshell. The Greek adoption movement with destination "rich America" had been negotiated since 1948 and was well underway by 1950. The first half of the 1950s saw adoptions that addressed the needs of children, typically called "orphans" or even "war orphans" (in the aftermath of World War II and the ensuing Greek Civil War). The first wave of Greece's history of "adopting out" to the United States built on WWII relief efforts, postwar family migration or reunification, and the common goal to resettle stateless and "displaced persons" (as per the well-known 1948 US Displaced Persons Act and the 1953 Refugee Relief Act and its successors). Models and also legal provisions for European adult migration and refugee care were developed in the turbulent 1940s. Models for child migration and overseas childcare by way of "supply-driven" intercountry adoption soon followed. A precursor to formal or legal adoptions was the system of symbolic adoptions, whereby families in more prosperous countries committed to financially and morally supporting children from poorer countries. These families did so from afar, by sending money, letters, and care packages.[2] Such symbolic and remote fostering arrangements, however, which were often called "adoptions," did not alter the child beneficiaries' family or legal status, whereas intercountry adoption re-created the child's personal and legal identity and, subsequently, its nationality.

Jewish child survivors of WWII and the Holocaust were among the first to be united or reunited with relatives in the United States or in other countries. Many were formally adopted by American relatives (from 1946 on); older teenagers could, by 1948, decide to move to the newly formed state of Israel.[3] By the late 1940s, too, the United States was negotiating special immigration provisions for children fathered by American servicemen stationed abroad, focusing first on Germany and Austria, and, by the early 1950s, on Japan and Korea. Evangelical Christian adoptions became widespread in most Asian intercountry adoption flows, following the rationale that "mixed-race" children needed to be rescued from the patriarchal societies that marginalized them. Greece never saw an American presence on the scale of what Korea, for instance, experienced. Therefore, the logic of saving "mixed-race" children, "rejected" by their local societies, did not apply to Greece. But, in the fervor of Cold War anticommunism, the categories were easily confused.

Beth Cohen established 1946 as the starting date of the legal adoptions of Jewish children by American, mostly related, families (2018, 8). The first Greek-to-American adoptions were being formally discussed from 1948 onward, along with other adoptions from the countries named above. Even though the Greek adoptions did not stem from a catastrophe comparable to the Holocaust or to the fate of the "fatherless," "mixed-race" children, the first petitions for sponsorships or adoptions from war-torn Greece again originated in kinship networks already established in the United States. The war-infused ideology of saving "orphaned" and "abandoned" or "relinquished" children was thus re-applied and kept blurring otherwise important geographical, historical, and cultural distinctions (including diverging definitions of what overseas adoption legally entailed). This ideal of rescuing Greek "war orphans" (whether the war had long ended or not) took hold with the best intentions but not necessarily

---

2. Van Steen, *Adoption*, 93–95. The Greek Civil War had left thousands of orphaned children in a war-torn country, many of whom had relatives in the United States. Greek Americans were, therefore, the first addressees of Greek appeals for assistance. Greek Americans stepped up to commit to informal or symbolic adoptions and later also to formal adoptions.

3. See Beth B. Cohen, *Child Survivors of the Holocaust: The Youngest Remnant and the American Experience*, New Brunswick, Camden, and Newark, NJ: Rutgers University Press, 2018.

with positive outcomes. International adoption of any country's children can hardly be equated with a postcrisis return to normalcy. In the case of Greece, it attests to America's undue influence in the process of postwar state-(re)building. For a Greece committed to postwar economic reconstruction and to balancing transatlantic relations, the US-bound adoption traffic became one of the ideological but all-too-real battlefields of the emerging Cold War.

The first Greek American charitable group to commit to rescuing "orphans" was the American Hellenic Educational Progressive Association (AHEPA) (founded in 1922 in Atlanta, Georgia).[4] From the late 1940s on, the AHEPA preoccupied itself with adapting the patterns of adult migration to child migration. Through the late 1950s, the AHEPA tried hard to establish a monopoly on Greek intercountry adoptions, much like Catholic charitable foundations were doing in Italy and later in Ireland or like Evangelical Christian organizations in Korea and Japan.[5] Greece of the mid-1950s was penetrated also by the International Social Service (ISS), competing with the AHEPA, and by local lawyers who had started to specialize in foreign adoptions. The Greek Queen Frederica was instrumental in trying to legitimize otherwise contested royal welfare institutions. She played a role but by no means the largest one. So did a few other middlemen who developed an international adoption business. The competition between the AHEPA and the ISS was especially

---

4. A 100th-anniversary volume on the history of the AHEPA is being prepared by Alexander Kitroeff, who has also discussed Greek-to-American adoption traffic in his recent article "Greece's Forgotten Cold War Orphans and America's Complicity," *The Pappas Post*, May 5, 2021, https://www.pappaspost.com/greeces-forgotten-cold-war-orphans-and-americas-complicity/.

5. A much-anticipated book by Maria Laurino will treat Italian-to-American adoptions at length. See also Silvia Cassamagnaghi, "Emigration for Adoption: The National Catholic Welfare Conference and the Adoption of Italian Children in the United States," in *Italianness and Migration from the Risorgimento to the 1960s*, edited by Stéphane Mourlane, Céline Regnard, Manuela Martini, and Catherine Brice, 119–129, Cham, Switzerland: Palgrave Macmillan (Springer Nature Switzerland AG), 2022; Paul J. Redmond, *The Adoption Machine: The Dark History of Ireland's Mother and Baby Homes and the Inside Story of How Tuam 800 Became a Global Scandal*, Kildare, Ireland: Merrion Press/Irish Academic Press, 2018; most recently, Claire McGettrick, Katherine O'Donnell, Maeve O'Rourke, James M. Smith, and Mari Steed, *Ireland and the Magdalene Laundries: A Campaign for Justice*, London: I.B. Tauris, 2021.
Standard histories of the Korean-to-American adoptions (and their racial dimensions) are Eleana J. Kim, *Adopted Territory: Transnational Korean Adoptees and the Politics of Belonging*, Durham, NC: Duke University Press, 2010; Arissa H. Oh, *To Save the Children of Korea: The Cold War Origins of International Adoption*, Stanford, CA: Stanford University Press, 2015.

fierce, each vying for a greater slice of the adoption pie, but pursuing these adoptions with very different philosophies and practices. For one, the ISS was not seeking any financial gain. By 1962, however, many intermediaries retreated because the tide had turned, and the widespread practice of adopting out to couples who were not Greek or Greek American had encountered ardent domestic Greek resistance.

Time and again, extensive research and documentation lead to an interpretive framework that ties postwar intercountry adoption to foreign relations, Cold War power dynamics, inadequate social infrastructure, and lack of professional expertise. Through the 1950s, the flow of adoptees was controlled at the source by a small circle of Greek state bureaucrats, orphanage directors, local mayors, doctors, lawyers, judges, Greek American community leaders, and even travel agents, with little direct interference from the Greek government or oversight from American federal or state authorities. The adoption protocols and methods used ranged from legal and slow-moving to hasty, dubious, and plain illegal practices, with the ISS alone insisting on proper casework. Desiderata and other criteria for adopting, such as home studies, background investigations and references, and social worker visits and follow-up checks throughout a probationary period, became decisive requirements in Greek overseas adoptions only from the 1970s on, by which time the profession of social worker had gained greater recognition as well.

Together, these Greek third parties and lax governments unwittingly created the movement of international adoption that is still with us today, complete with all the weaknesses of such a hurried new system: hastily taken decisions, shoddy record-keeping, lack of oversight and follow-up, lack of accountability years later. The ISS adoption dossiers are a bright exception, even if many of their placements abroad should still not have happened. Compare these practices with those of the AHEPA lawyers, whose records either "disappeared" or were otherwise lost. The AHEPA presidents and lawyers were the first to feel the pulse of international adoption from Greece and to notice how "market dynamics" were rapidly changing, from a supply-driven to a demand-driven adoption flow. By early May 1959 and with the "Scopas scandal," they were also the ones responsible for the first major scandal of the kind that has rocked intercountry adoption to this day and that inevitably raises charges of cross-border child trafficking.[6] A typical international adoption scandal, of the type that reoccurs with some frequency, operates on the following premises:

---

6. See Gonda Van Steen, "Of Foundlings and 'Lostlings': When the Scopas Scandal Rocked the Unstable Foundations of the First 1950s Intercountry Adoptions," *Annales de démographie historique*, special issue on the history of adoption, "Formes adoptives (XVIe–XXe siècles)," 141, no. 1 (2021), 123–155.

monetary gain, lack of due diligence, "lost" or falsified paperwork, deceived birth families, uninformed adoptive families, innocent children—all covered by the mantle of "confidentiality," the child's "best interests," rigid statutes of limitations, and the inexorable passing of time.

Greek-born adoptees arrived in the United States in four distinct waves. A first wave of mainly kin migration preceded the landmark US Refugee Relief Act of 1953 (Public Law 203, section 5 (a)): this first wave lasted from 1950 through the late summer of 1952, and it counted more than one thousand cases, among them many young relatives of Greek American couples adopting from the home country. Many came as sibling groups, with at least one older sibling whose memory kept the others connected to their roots. The members of this first wave tend to *not* look for their origins in Greece: they likely knew them all along, and the extended family's experience was often steeped in Civil War trauma.

The temporary provisions of the Refugee Relief Act raised the Greek adoption movement's second wave: they allowed more than 500 Greek children to enter the States between 1953 and 1956 (but in reality between late spring 1954 and fall 1956). This second wave was marked by the novelty of "stranger" adoptions of far younger children: infants and toddlers went to unknown new parents in the States by way of a prevailing system of adoptions by proxy. They met at the airport (most often in New York) with overjoyed but often underprepared adoptive parents who were of diverse ethnic and religious backgrounds—no longer were the Greek Americans in the majority. Technically, the age limit on the eligible children was set at ten, which meant that plenty of Greek eight- to ten-year-olds were adopted out overseas as well. Such was the growing demand for white adoptable children that the United States permitted American prospective parents to petition for up to two children per citizen couple, and the US legislature even raised the age limit on the adoptees to age fourteen in the next phase. Again, exceptions could be granted for the purpose of keeping siblings together. Needless to say, older children come with histories, memories, likes and dislikes that are much more outspoken than those of newborns. But the hopeful American parents were told and believed that children were blank slates, and that all they needed to provide was ample love. The love that conquers all was supposed to come from the unknown American couple, while the unwed young mother was told that her love was not good enough, and that, if she truly loved her child, she would need to give it up to a "proper" family.[7] Few young mothers realized that they would never see

---

7. The coercive rhetoric with which vulnerable single mothers were beleaguered merits further study. Families, village and church communities, and also hospital personnel and social workers joined in the effort of relentless persuasion bordering

their children again. Even fewer were aware that this separation would leave lifelong emotional scars, for mother and child alike. Professional counseling did not exist or was not deemed necessary.

The handling of these Greek-to-American adoptions resembles that of other early Cold War adoption movements, which share the following important characteristics as they moved from humanitarian initiatives to practices of family-building: (a) the intercountry adoptions were seen as part of migratory flows, and the rules that governed them were conceptualized as immigration law, not as actual adoption legislation, with all the special care the latter would have required; (b) voluntary organizations and agents with political, ethnic, and religious interests played critical roles in the design of the first "emergency" migratory dispensations and moved toward rapid implementation of the new and untested schemes, with far more idealism than expertise; (c) the exaggerated push for "speed" resulted in haphazard procedures and sloppy record-keeping, and drove such risky practices as adoption by proxy; (d) the rhetoric of "urgency" perpetuated also the language and imagery of the "rescue" of "war orphans," long after the war had ended and referring to children who had at least one living parent; (e) that verbal and visual rhetoric also negated the fact that hundreds of children were brought into the United States from countries that had traditionally fostered very different conceptions of child-rearing and adoption, as in Greece where postwar child-rearing was still grounded in a more communal model, that of the extended family and/or the village, and where traditional "simple" adoptions did not cut off the children from their first families, from their original names, identities, cultures, and nationalities.

To most of the older adoptees, the most blatant act of insensitive erasure was being renamed to suit the purposes and predilections of the new family. Many Greek adoptees were promptly named after their new fathers or

---

on coercion (and occasionally crossing the line into illegal practices). As scores of recent news reports show, the birth mother-victims of these forced adoptions are now speaking out in Ireland, Canada, the United States, the United Kingdom, Australia, and the Netherlands—to name just a few leading countries. The Greek birth mothers, however, have now reached an age at which this revolution may well come too late. Many of them still carry the shame and few are willing to talk about this sensitive subject, let alone seek the redress they are owed. Our effort is also about empowering them.

mothers, in a symbolic act of the newly minted parents exerting ownership. The case described below highlights an irrational rush to overwrite adoptee identity:

New York: Greek orphan M., 10, of Serres, Greece, gets welcoming kisses on arrival here 12/30[/57] via TWA from her new foster mother ... and her foster brother, Nicholas, Jr., 12. Young Nicholas, also a Greek orphan, arrived in this country in 1954. Mrs. [...] said that the girl's name would be changed to Diane, because Nicholas wanted a sister named Diane.[8]

The adoptive parents, typically white middle class to well-to-do couples, adopted these children sight unseen, based on a selection made from photographs and what little information was entered into the child's record. Many of the youngest children are the relinquished babies of young, unmarried Greek mothers whose family or support network had crumbled under the weight of punitive social taboos and who, after a lot of agonizing, saw no other solution than to give up the child "for a better life." These adoptions left the birth mothers as victims as well, even as the process did everything to erase their existence: closed records, confidentiality clauses, "lost" lawyers' files, etc. The AHEPA was the lead middleman in this process but competition for infants, especially, was fierce, as intermediaries tried to fill the huge American demand for white, healthy babies "without a past," who were—and still are—expected to assimilate quickly and easily. Screening processes were minimal at best, with the ISS at least attempting to establish more professional practices. Follow-up on the adopted children, let alone on the birth mothers, was close to nonexistent. The vulnerabilities in such a system were huge, and yet many of its features continued to apply for decades. And what if things went wrong? There was no safety net in place for the child, as these sealed-records overseas adoptions meant a path of no return. But I will let the adopted persons speak to those experiences, as most of the authors in this volume belong to either this wave or the beginning of the next.

The number of 1,360 adoption cases of the third wave, from 1957 to 1962, surpassed those of the first (1,246) and the second wave (500+ cases). The "full," "stranger" adoptions of Greek children continued at record speed, and the competition stiffened because the brokers had understood that there was money to be made. Childless American couples

---

8. See UP Telephoto caption, December 30, 1957.

were willing to pay any price for a healthy, white newborn with which they could build their "as if" family, while enjoying the credit of having "saved" one or two "orphans" from "poor," "communist-struck" Greece (an anachronism but who was checking?). It did not matter that most of the children for adoption were not technically orphans, and certainly not "war orphans," and many of them did not need "saving," either. Their own mothers could have built lives with these children if only society had supported them, if only society, on both ends of the Atlantic, had not been so keen to exploit the shame of "illegitimacy" for self-serving purposes. These children could also have been adopted in Greece, but restrictive age requirements stood in the way, as did the eagerness of the orphanages (technically, the *vrefokomeia*) to attract donations in US dollars. The rhetoric hardly changed, but at last a few scandals threw the Greek-to-American baby traffic off course, and quietly diverted it to less intimidating recipient countries, such as the Netherlands and Sweden. The Greek-born adopted persons of this and the second wave are very engaged with the stories—and the lies—surrounding their adoptions. Were they truly "foundlings" or just made to look like foundlings on paper, to speed up the adoption process in Greece? Many of them have fully committed to searching for their roots, which is a quest for truth and recognition as much as for blood-related family and a deeper sense of belonging.

Added together, the numbers amount to an approximate grand total of 3,200 Greek-to-American adoptions that took place between 1950 and 1962, or during the first thirteen years following the end of the Greek Civil War.[9] I have dubbed this long decade the "kid pro quo" phase, the era of children as "payment in kind," of the Greek-to-American adoptions, because they are marked by the protracted vulnerabilities of Greek families, especially women and children, while the country itself remained heavily dependent on US aid. If I open up the time frame even further, to 1975, I may count a fourth wave of 932 Greek-to-American adoptions, even though most of the children adopted out between 1963 and 1975 went to migrating Greeks or Greek Americans or to families that had been made aware of some of the children's special needs (as per the evolving Greek legal and institutional stipulations).[10] This last number is dwarfed by the nearly 15,000 children adopted out by South Korea to the States during the same thirteen-year period. That development explains why most Americans think

---

9. Van Steen, *Adoption*, 77, 264; Richard H. Weil, "International Adoptions: The Quiet Migration," *International Migration Review* 18, no. 2 (1984), 280, his table 1.

10. Weil, "International Adoptions," 283, his table 2.

of international adoption as Korean-to-American adoption, and therefore transracial adoption. But, historically speaking, the Greek-to-American adoptions *preceded*, and then coincided with, the first placements from Korea and, up through 1962, even proportionally outnumbered them.[11]

Thus, a total of nearly 4,000 Greek children were adopted out to the United States, and most of them to non-Greek-American families. Many Greek-born children went to military families, New York Jewish families, Mormon families, families in Texas, etc. etc. Today they are everywhere, and they represent every and any location, religion, educational background, profession, and health condition. Greece handled an additional 600 Greek-to-Dutch adoptions from 1956 on and at least 40 Greek-to-Swedish adoptions, which are perhaps least known of all.[12] But numbers mean very little in light of the actual experiences. And while the researcher can count, the adopted person can recount. It is in that direction that we turn our attention next.

There Is Power in Telling Your Story

"The older we got, the harder it was to adopt a child in this country," said [the adoptive father]. "But we knew we had lived long enough to rear children—so we sidestepped child welfare obstacles in the United States and tried Europe."
—The Amarillo Globe-Times (Amarillo, Texas), June 29, 1960

Voices of the Lost Children of Greece represents an important collective writing project that speaks to the objectives of interdisciplinary and critical adoption history in new and unexpected ways: the individual stories attest to the various adoption networks that placed nearly 4,000 Greek children in the United States, in a movement accelerated by the aftermath of the Greek Civil War and by the new conditions of the global Cold War. In a second, reconfigured adoption landscape, as described above, Greek-born children were sent out for adoption in the Netherlands and in Sweden (1960s–1970s). In the rapidly

---

11. For the numerical and other details of this argument that pertain to the time span of 1948 (1950)–1962, see Van Steen, *Adoption*, 77–86. The numbers are borne out by my compilation of data from adoptees' testimonies and personal archives. This extensive database, cross-checked against the New York Passenger Lists and other resources on Ancestry.com (in association with the National Archives at New York City), allows me to draw chronological as well as numerical conclusions. I thank Merrill Jenkins, a contributing author to this volume, for partnering with me to master this critical part of our research.

12. Van Steen, *Adoption*, 61–62, 64, 79–80, 82, 108, 130, 171, 225, 264, 273.

developing field of the history of adoption, this book uncovers the personal histories and family politics, as well as the grave social taboos that undergirded the mass adoptions of young children from war-torn 1950s Greece and beyond—the "undesirables" of a recent but forgotten past. This book further demonstrates that, far from being a personal or a peripheral matter, intercountry adoption of the Cold War era was central to the experience and constitution of the sociopolitical realms of the postwar "West."

The era of 1950–1975 looms large as another chapter of the modern Greek past that has not been integrated well into the standard scholarly narratives. Research on Greece's postwar and post–Civil War human rights record, in particular, is still heavily dependent on personal memoirs/memories and on dispersed archival collections. Our collective writing project is, therefore, analytically vital to a better understanding not just of Greek, American, and Western political priorities but also of urgent concerns of social justice, human rights, and child welfare. The testimonies, set against their larger historical and ideological backdrop, focus on the rights and fates of Greek-born adoptees who were sent to the United States and the "West" in an unwritten "exchange" agreement compensating for economic and military aid. The Greek-to-American adoptions and, regrettably, also their transactions and transgressions, provided the blueprint for the first large-scale international adoptions, well before these became a mass phenomenon typically associated with Asian children. Thus, *Voices of the Lost Children of Greece* is a hard-hitting book that further examines Greece at the fulcrum of the postwar international child "exports." But this volume is also a multivocal companion book to any intercountry adoption history, because the same patterns and experiences recur across space and time.

Voices of the Lost Children of Greece states a cultural as well as a historical critique but also a call to action. It deconstructs one of the most tenacious cultural representations upholding the interest in transnational adoption to this day: the myth of humanitarian rescue. Since the late 1940s, this resilient and self-serving myth has shown its capacity to close down a part of the Greek (and broader Cold War) past that merits further scholarly and also public attention. The first flow of the Greek-to-American adoption movement was conditioned by postwar geopolitical strategies. It fueled and was fueled by a humanitarianism of a neo-colonial make, complete with an undying rhetoric: "poor Greek war orphans" were "saved" by the "benevolent" but rich and powerful Cold War patrons. Amid the baby boom, the United States soon responded to childless couples' calls for infants with yet more Greek and other foreign adoptions. Greece's Cold War reconstruction economy, that is, its prolonged dependency on American aid and goodwill, lies at the core of the Greek overseas adoption practice, which became an easy proxy or substitute for building a domestic welfare system. *Voices of the Lost Children of Greece* is the first book to give voice and body to the crude biopolitics underpinning the Greek adoption movement, which traced the path for subsequent cross-border adoption flows, whose long-term consequences, psychological as well as communal, have only recently become the object of discussion and study.

Methodologically speaking, *Voices of the Lost Children of Greece* is a critical life-writing project initiated by fifteen of the 4,000 Greek adoptees who were sent to the United States, the Netherlands, and Sweden in the 1950s through mid-1970s. The fate of these Greek-born children who were adopted out across-borders has only recently received attention but, prior to that, not even their number was firmly established. Contributing to the aftershocks of loss and displacement has been the Greek adoptees' realization that their history has not been properly documented and that their personal dossiers are often long lost. However, the faces of the actual adoptees must emerge from behind the numbers and the analyses, which should not empty out personal-historical particularities.

With this call at its core, this life-writing project focuses on Greece as a case study, but a case study that appeals to everyone affected by adoption. About fifty percent of the general population is either directly or indirectly affected by adoption. In some circles or countries, that percentage is even higher. Every extended Greek family seems to have been close at some point in history to the phenomenon of either international or in-country adoption, sometimes to both. *Voices*, then, draws on psychology and sociology, with references to mid-twentieth-century history and society, to bring personal accounts and testimonies to the forefront. It features various forms of life-writing that have been contributed by the adoptees themselves and also by other members of the "adoption triad" (the birth parents and adoptive parents in addition to the adoptee) or, rather, the adoption "constellation," including the committed researchers. The goal of this adoptee-centric writing project is to contribute to our knowledge in adoption studies but also to provide deeper qualitative insight and greater authenticity. Through the voices of many different stakeholders in the Greek adoption phenomenon, *Voices* aims to produce a social history in its most fine-grained, intimate form, which compels us to revisit Cold War America and Europe and to rethink their history and consequences.

Voices studies and engages with the Greek and international adoptees in the long, fraught business of becoming—an ongoing challenge, given the scant nature of the records, which lasts up to the present day. How does one become someone, or someone else, halfway around the world? How does one heal from the shock of a radical uprooting? Can one forget when the lack of answers about what happened and how it happened is ever-present? And what if the absence of paperwork is burdened also by the lingering suspicion of illegality? The Greek adoptees have not yet mobilized in ways comparable to the vocal Korean adoptee rights movement, but the lack of records and especially the "policy" of amnesia on the part of the Greek state have been salient and painful for them. Amid the recent genealogical turn and the mass public enthusiasm for DNA testing, uncovering the hidden, silenced side of genealogy that adoption still represents is an urgent matter. The various, versatile chapters of this new book explore the raw memory of the past and especially the space of the individual, whose voice should never have been drowned out. *Voices* aims to establish a more interactive and up-to-date framework for examining the adoptions of Greek-born and other adoptees, which still need to be further explored from a more psychological and psychosocial perspective. Our critical approach prompts creativity to meet criticism. But *Voices* rightly downplays the authoritative voice of the observer-historian to invite other people's voices, including their images, documents, and journal entries.

Accessing forgotten layers of the Greek diasporic or migratory history, our life-writing project on the Western-bound "exports" of "surplus" Greek children informs our broader critique of the human cost of political and economic dependencies on the Western capitalist model. A study of the cross-border adoption traffic from Cold War Greece by way of the adoptee voices and family narratives prompts us to think about this migration flow in the very current terms of dislocation, the separation of children from their parents, the threat of traumatic displacement or disruption, unaccompanied and unprotected minors moving toward an ambiguous, ever-contingent "American" identity, which will not be subsumed into the hardening rhetoric of American "homeland security." *Voices* makes us reassess also how boundary shifts between public and private initiatives occur and how individual lives may be subjected to the extremes of prolonged secrecy and extravagant publicity, often simultaneously. In the United States as the prime receiving country of the Cold War period, the adoption experience has only gradually been reshaped into a more diversified history, in which the subjective and the cultural prevail over the political. But a major concern has remained and is at this book's core: *how* to tell the fine-grained history and individual stories of the Greek adoption phenomenon, allowing, as per the adoptees' wishes, the modern, creative forms to be as important as the contents. The originality of *Voices* stems from its concerted effort to reconceptualize its topic across different media within the private as well as the cultural sphere. Here, the personal and the cultural texts, of any kind, are not viewed in isolation but are embedded in a web of interrelations, not unlike the Cold War adoption networks themselves.

Voices may thus serve as a point of reference for developing a greater historical and cultural sensibility. Our writing here, including my style of introducing the history, genre, and method, incorporates succinct forms of witness testimonies and samples of broader cultural representations of the Greek adoptions. With that background firmly in place, however, we can then delve into the archive of the emotions and bring the people involved into clearer focus (while protecting their anonymity, if they so wish). Personally, I am eager to give faces and voices to those affected, and to do so in an innovative style of writing and presenting. Our collective new project pursues a different type of scientific knowledge—insights that emerge from and with the Greek adoptees and again enrich the history of adoption and recent adoption studies.

Since its emergence two decades ago, the subfield of the history(ies) of international adoption flows has tried hard to step out of national frameworks, and it has championed transnational, transcultural, and multidirectional approaches to intercountry adoption. My engagement with the Greek adoptee experiences may seem to bring back a nationally oriented approach, but my broader concern with the adoptees' "Western" living experiences widens the horizon. The seemingly personal history of the foreign-born adoptees is also the history of some of the defining aspects of mid-twentieth-century America and Western and Northern Europe. It discloses the ways in which foreign adoption has inscribed itself in the collective memory of the Cold War. While adoption itself may be at the heart of personal and local histories, the issue of foreign adoption is by no means limited to the familial sphere but extends to national and global levels. Also, it has become an international research focus calling for the exchange of personal as well as scholarly insights, which may only be strengthened by the voices of the former-child participants in adoption themselves.

We need the Greeks and scores of others to become stakeholders in children's placements and adoptions, to reassess migrations then and now. I hope to see the relative reticence on the Greek side dissipate, and to see productive community development increase. A more acute sense of public accountability must work not only discursive shifts but also policy reform. The Greek adoptees want easier access to their birth and adoption records and many want the Greek state to restore their Greek citizenship (as a second or dual citizenship).[13] Adoptee solidarity may help some people to heal from their wounds, but it is not enough if it cannot affect change.

---

13. For a broader contextualization of these demands, see the opinion piece co-authored by Mary Cardaras and Gonca Van Steen (June 16, 2021), "Bring them Back!," *The Pappas Post*, online at https://pappaspost.com/opinion-bring-them-back/. See also Van Steen (January 26, 2022), "Επώδυνος Ελληνισμός, The Greek Diaspora in Pain: From Adoption Allure to Adoptee Activism," position essay in *Ergon: Greek/American Arts and Letters*, edited by Y. Anagnostou, online at https://ergon.scienzine.com/article/editorials/from-adoption-allure-to-adoptee-activism.

The Greek-born adoptees have turned *en masse* to social media (mainly Facebook groups) to link with one another and to voice communal concerns. Their longing for a shared relational space and for "a connection with people like me" has been acute. They participate in a new information interchange with adoptees across the globe, regardless of their place of origin or destination. They have left behind the digital traces of their searches in various online networks. The new technologies that they have been exploring together, such as DNA testing sites and databases, have been exerting their impact on root searches and reunifications.[14] International family search consultancies and other online reunion forums cannot, at this time, be very helpful to the Greek-born adoptees, even as their stories and advertisements continue to gratify sentimental needs. The bulk of the Greek public records and genealogy resources have not yet been digitized.[15] Also, the Greek language, in its various forms of the past decades, including its handwritten forms, constitutes a significant barrier and limits access as well. Feelings of isolation have been strong among the Greek-to-American adoptees, who were cut off from their birth culture and first language.[16] It is this lack of a land of origin, the absence of a more material identity, that has pulled many Greek adoptees together in a virtual community that must substitute for more substantive ties to the homeland. But adoptee community cannot really serve as a surrogate for a birth family and a land of roots. Newcomers to the active online networks react with excitement to finding a peer group and often define new friends using the language and labeling of the family-by-adoption (as in "my orphanage sister," "my orphan brother," "we've now adopted each other"). "For the first time, I heard and saw other adoptees state what I had only ever been thinking about," one person concurs, "I feel indebted to my 'support group' of adoptees

---

14. I realize how dated or quaint these lines may sound in a few years or decades from now. But, in 2022, commercial DNA testing is only now becoming more popular and more affordable in Greece. Up until a few years ago, direct-to-consumer mailing of commercial DNA test kits was not legally supported in Greece, whose laws mandated appropriate genetic counseling before taking any predictive, carrier and predisposition genetic tests. The well-known DNA testing companies did not accept credit cards linked to addresses in Greece. This landscape has changed dramatically in the course of just a few years, while DNA testing has also gained huge popularity among Greeks of the worldwide diaspora. Of course, modern genetic home detective work may come with unforeseen outcomes.

15. An exception is Greek Ancestry (www.greekancestry.net), a for-profit genealogy resource site founded in 2020 and managed by Gregory Kontos.

16. The feelings are poignantly expressed by Mary Cardaras (June 7, 2021), "Demanding What Belongs to Us: Our Greek Identity," *The Pappas Post*, online at https://pappaspost.com/demanding-what-belongs-to-us-our-greek-identity/.

and yet, for the first time, too, I don't have to show gratitude." Together the Greek-born adoptees maintain online platforms, where they conduct common explorations of family and rootedness. They cultivate a worldwide connectivity that is rife with kinship metaphors, joining a quest not only for personal origins but also for one another's origins and experiences.

Social media do not satisfy in full the Greek adoptees' hunger for connection, but they offer up an informal data economy and a forum for exchanging names, places, and circumstances. The adoptees socialize but also open up spaces for critical thinking and advocacy, restoring some power to the public sphere. Many participate in current, broader debates about cross-border adoption and communicate with adoptees from other countries. Some posts on social media engage in sweeping expressions of Greek nationalism, even in the absence of diaspora-homeland encounters to ground them. Scores of adoptees plan visits to Athens and remote little Greek towns and villages. The typical Greek festivals that so many American diaspora communities organize are, despite their tremendous popularity, hardly the places for adoptees to get their Greek culture fix. Greek salad is not a gateway to re-culturation. The "realness" of being Greek-born but left unrecognized clashes here with a Greekness that sometimes feels fake for trying too hard. Some adoptees move beyond diaspora patriotism and nationalism and plan reunion activities, bringing more of them together. Planning get-togethers leads to further participant involvement and increased adoptee networking, to everyone's great satisfaction. The group behind *Voices* will be planning a book launch party!

The initial healing has come from the adoptees' own initiative to bond and also from the first acknowledgment given to this adoption history on television and in printed media. Notably, however, no edited volume or anthology of stories has ever been published that reflects on the collective identity of the intercountry Greek adoptees, comparable to, for instance, Cerrissa Kim's et al., *Mixed Korean: Our Stories*, a 2018 anthology, or Lynelle Long's 2017 volume, *The Colour of Time*, or the pioneering 2001 collection, *The Colour of Difference*, edited by Sarah Armstrong and Petrina Slaytor. No collective volume or personal memoir has ever made a political statement about the Greek adoptions as edgy and unapologetically as that of *Outsiders Within: Writing on Transracial Adoption* (2006, republished 2021), by Jane Jeong Trenka et al., while also delivering a bold artistic statement. Some vocal Greek stories have appeared in Marina Van Dongen's *De adoptiemonologen, The Adoption Monologues* (2013). I hope to see more Greek adoptees take the lead in collecting and editing their stories. Telling adoption stories in print is a twenty-first-century phenomenon, more at home even in the second decade of this century than in the first, more at ease also in the company of other, similar narratives, especially when these narratives are told by transracial adoptees.

As communication technologies and publications advance and more participants embrace them, the adoptees together can counter a powerful stereotype, the one that dismisses their lived experience as its own brand of expertise. Historically, adoptees have been confined to the role of recipients of knowledge; they have not been given credit for actually producing knowledge. The Greek adoptees have been one heterogeneous group among many who have not been deemed valid producers of knowledge, especially when in the company of adoptive parents and adoption practitioners. On the recent and sudden death of one of the Greek-to-American adoptees in May 2021, I was stunned to see the obituary mark her as the adopted child of her American parents, with wording to contribute to the greater glory of the parents. The adoptee herself was a dynamic businesswoman, who had made a name for herself in local and regional charitable work. Did she really have to be labeled as an adopted child after her passing at age 66?!

Along with the shared exercise of writing, the intense connectivity of the virtual family of Greek adoptees offers resources for the self-making of the individual and of the group, beyond informational and material preoccupations. Together, we hover over a landscape of past memory, active imagining, and anticipation for the future. As I was frequently asked to observe, translate, befriend, guide a root trip, or deliver a piece of detective work, I rediscovered the Greek-born adoptees as a people of anticipation, as protagonists of a self-organizing movement of anticipation, and the strength of this anticipation seems inexhaustible.

Voices, then, represents the writing project that was long-awaited but never carried out before: it collectively breaks the silence; it boldly engages with the fates of the Greek children themselves, who lingered in oblivion; it acknowledges the traumatic experiences and lasting scars of those children-now-adults, who were "adopted out" at the first opportunity, in exchange for handsome sums of hard currency. This book will likely leave a few people and parties upset, but it is and will continue to be based on a judicious use of personal testimonies and contributions—areas in which the editor has gained a lot of writing and publishing experience. Also, while the discourses on both the Greek Civil War and the Cold War have been thoroughly masculinized, this pairing of subjective story with objective analysis may bolster an emerging trend to finally devote more attention to women and children in times of conflict and want. The testimonies of the once-children show the ways in which individual memories affect narration, research, and art. These stories then place the children first, but, nonetheless, write the personal into the national and the national into the global.

Gonda Van Steen, Koraes Chair of Modern Greek and Byzantine History, Language and Literature, King's College London, *gonda.van_steen@kcl.ac.uk* and *gondavs@gmail.com*

Selected Bibliography and Suggestions for Further Reading

Adoption & Culture. Journal of the Alliance for the Study of Adoption and Culture (2007–).

Armstrong, Sarah, and Petrina Slaytor, eds. *The Colour of Difference: Journeys in Transracial Adoption.* Sydney: The Federation Press, 2001.

Balcom, Karen A. *The Traffic in Babies: Cross-border Adoption and Baby-selling between the United States and Canada, 1930–1972.* Toronto: University of Toronto Press, 2011.

Bennett, Judith A., and Angela Wanhalla, eds. *Mothers' Darlings of the South Pacific: The Children of Indigenous Women and U.S. Servicemen, World War II.* Honolulu: University of Hawai'i Press, 2016.

Bon Tempo, Carl J. *Americans at the Gate: The United States and Refugees during the Cold War.* Princeton and Oxford: Princeton University Press, 2008.

Briggs, Laura. *Somebody's Children: The Politics of Transracial and Transnational Adoption.* Durham, NC, and London: Duke University Press, 2012.

Cardaras, Mary, and Gonda Van Steen. "Bring Them Back!" *The Pappas Post,* June 16, 2021, https://pappaspost.com/opinion-bring-them-back/.

Casavantes Bradford, Anita. *Suffer the Little Children: Child Migration and the Geopolitics of Compassion in the United States.* Chapel Hill, NC: The University of North Carolina Press, 2022.

Cassamagnaghi, Silvia. "Emigration for Adoption: The National Catholic Welfare Conference and the Adoption of Italian Children in the United States." In *Italianness and Migration from the Risorgimento to the 1960s,* edited by Stéphane Mourlane, Céline Regnard, Manuela Martini, and Catherine Brice, 119–129. Cham, Switzerland: Palgrave Macmillan (Springer Nature Switzerland AG), 2022.

Choy, Catherine Ceniza. *Global Families: A History of Asian International Adoption in America.* New York and London: New York University Press, 2013.

Danforth, Loring M., and Riki Van Boeschoten. *Children of the Greek Civil War: Refugees and the Politics of Memory.* Chicago and London: The University of Chicago Press, 2012.

Dubinsky, Karen. *Babies without Borders: Adoption and Migration across the Americas.* New York: New York University Press, 2010.

Fieldston, Sara. *Raising the World: Child Welfare in the American Century.* Cambridge, MA, and London: Harvard University Press, 2015.

Glaser, Gabrielle. *American Baby: A Mother, a Child, and the Shadow History of Adoption.* New York: Viking, 2021.

Heijun Wills, Jenny, Tobias Hübinette, and Indigo Willing, eds. *Adoption and Multiculturalism: Europe, the Americas, and the Pacific.* Ann Arbor: University of Michigan Press, 2020.

Herman, Ellen. *Kinship by Design: A History of Adoption in the Modern United States.* Chicago and London: The University of Chicago Press, 2008.

Kim, Cerrissa, Katherine Kim, Sora Kim-Russell, and Mary Kim-Arnold, eds. *Mixed Korean: Our Stories. An Anthology.* Bloomfield, IN: Truepenny Publishing, 2018.

Long, Lynelle, ed. *The Colour of Time: A Longitudinal Exploration of the Impact of Intercountry Adoption in Australia.* Compiled with the assistance of ISS Australia and PARC. Sydney: ISS Australia, Inscope Books, 2017.

McGettrick, Claire, Katherine O'Donnell, Maeve O'Rourke, James M. Smith, and Mari Steed. *Ireland and the Magdalene Laundries: A Campaign for Justice.* London: I. B. Tauris, 2021.

McKee, Kimberly D. *Disrupting Kinship: Transnational Politics of Korean Adoption in the United States.* Urbana, IL: University of Illinois Press, 2019.

Neagu, Mariela. *Voices from the Silent Cradles: Life Histories of Romania's Looked-After Children.* Bristol, UK: Policy Press, Bristol University Press, 2021.

Oh, Arissa H. *To Save the Children of Korea: The Cold War Origins of International Adoption.* Stanford, CA: Stanford University Press, 2015.

Park Nelson, Kim. *Invisible Asians: Korean American Adoptees, Asian American Experiences, and Racial Exceptionalism.* New Brunswick, NJ, and London: Rutgers University Press, 2016.

Rossini, Gill. *A History of Adoption in England and Wales, 1850–1961.* Barnsley, South Yorkshire, UK: Pen and Sword Books, 2014.

Scutaru, Beatrice, and Simone Paoli, eds. *Child Migration and Biopolitics: Old and New Experiences in Europe.* London: Routledge, 2020.

Theodoropoulou, Maria (Mary). *Μαρία 43668.* Athens: Nikas Books, Elliniki Paideia, 2006. Second edition and English translation *Abandoned 43668… Maria.* Athens, 2019.

Trenka, Jane Jeong, Julia Chinyere Oparah, and Sun Yung Shin, with contributions by Heidi Lynn Adelsman et al. *Outsiders within: Writing on Transracial Adoption.* Cambridge, MA: South End Press, 2006. Republished Minneapolis, MN: University of Minnesota Press, 2021.

Van Steen, Gonda. "'Are We There Yet?' The Greek Adoptees' Road of Return—An Essay." In *Ergon: Greek/American Arts and Letters,* edited by Y. Anagnostou (July 7, 2018), http://ergon.scienzine.com/article/essays/are-we-there-yet.

Van Steen, Gonda. *Adoption, Memory, and Cold War Greece: Kïd pro quo?* Ann Arbor: University of Michigan Press, 2019. Greek translation *Ζητούνται παιδιά από την Ελλάδα: Υιοθεσίες στην Αμερική του Ψυχρού Πολέμου* (translator Ariadni Loukakou). Athens: Potamos, 2021.

Van Steen, Gonda. "Of Foundlings and 'Lostlings': When the Scopas Scandal Rocked the Unstable Foundations of the First 1950s Intercountry Adoptions." *Annales de démographie historique,* special issue on the history of adoption, "Formes adoptives (XVIe–XXe siècles)," 141, no. 1 (2021), 123–155.

Van Steen, Gonda. "Επώδυνος Ελληνισμός, The Greek Diaspora in Pain: From Adoption Allure to Adoptee Activism." Position essay in *Ergon: Greek/American Arts and Letters,* edited by Y. Anagnostou (January 26, 2022), https://ergon.scienzine.com/article/editorials/from-adoption-allure-to-adoptee-activism.

Winslow, Rachel R. *The Best Possible Immigrants: International Adoption and the American Family.* Philadelphia: University of Pennsylvania Press, 2017.

Yngvesson, Barbara. *Belonging in an Adopted World: Race, Identity, and Transnational Adoption.* Chicago and London: The University of Chicago Press, 2010.

Greek-to-American Adoption Narratives

Balch, Amalia Gouvitsas, and Elaine McAllister. *Lost Child of Greece: One Orphan's Incredible Journey Home.* Newton, KS: Mennonite Press, 2021.

Cardaras, Mary. "Demanding What Belongs to Us: Our Greek Identity." *The Pappas Post* (June 7, 2021), https://pappaspost.com/demanding-what-belongs-to-us-our-greek-identity/.

Cardaras, Mary. *Ripped at the Root: An Adoption Story Based on True Events.* New York: Spuyten Duyvil, 2021.

Diamond, Kathryn S. *The Other Half of the Same Story: A Modern Greek Tragedy.* Manalapan, FL, 2020.

Dionou, C. Dionysios. *Twentieth-Century Janissary: An Orphan's Search for Freedom, Family, and Heritage.* USA: Xlibris, 2011.

Giangardella, Joanna S. *The Girl from the Tower: A Journey of Lies.* Lexington, KY: Create Space Independent Publishing Platform, 2011. Second edition, 2017.

Heckinger, Maria. *Beyond the Third Door. Based on a True Story.* Vancouver, WA, 2019.

Johnson, Deborah. "Addendum by Deborah Johnson." In *Welcome Home! An International and Nontraditional Adoption Reader,* edited by L. Linzer Schwartz and F. W. Kaslow, 50–54. Binghamton, NY: Haworth Clinical Practice Press, 2003.

Kelmis, Maria. *Golden Strangers: An Adoption Memoir.* Bloomington, IN: Author House, 2012.

Moessinger, Naomi. "From Couple to Family." In *Welcome Home! An International and Nontraditional Adoption Reader,* edited by L. Linzer Schwartz and F. W. Kaslow, 35–50. Binghamton, NY: Haworth Clinical Practice Press, 2003.

Mossin, Andrew. "From *The Day After The Day After*." In *Ergon: Greek/American Arts and Letters,* edited by Y. Anagnostou (2019), https://ergon.scienzine.com/article/memoir/day-after-the-day-after.

Mossin, Andrew. *A Son from the Mountains: A Memoir.* New York: Spuyten Duyvil, 2021.

Greek-to-Dutch Adoption Narratives

De Boer, Antoinette. *De vondeling van Kreta. The Foundling from Crete.* Overveen, the Netherlands, 2019.

Rijnsdorp, Sonia. *Een kist met geheimen. A Box of Secrets.* Zoetermeer, the Netherlands: Lecturium, 2017.

Touwen, R. Bastiaan. *Grieks bloed. Greek Blood.* The Netherlands, 2014.

Van Dongen, Marina, ed. *De adoptiemonologen. The Adoption Monologues.* Schiedam, the Netherlands: Scriptum [some Greek adoption stories juxtaposed with others], 2013.

Chapter 2

FULL CIRCLES AND BEYOND

Maria

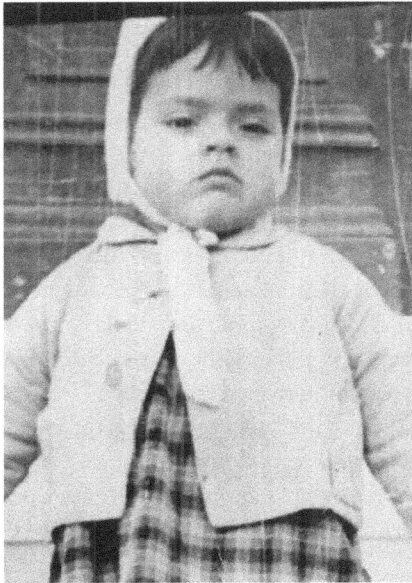

I am Maria.

On May 13, 1953, ten days after I was born, I was placed in the baby box just outside the orphanage in Patras, Greece. The orphanage became my home for three years until I was adopted by Richard and Ellen Pace of San Diego, California.

Meeting the Paces for the first time was a bit of a spectacle where almost nothing went as planned. Within minutes of meeting me, Ellen had a pretty good idea of the challenges she would face. I was going to be a handful! I had communication issues, food issues, and trust issues. My response to most things directed at me was to scream at the top of my lungs in Greek, much to Ellen's consternation. But in six months, the communication issues were resolved, and the food issues were beginning to improve. My trust issues were negotiated by keeping everything I owned in plain view. I could finally call something "mine" and it was a very special feeling.

Richard was a history professor and Ellen an executive assistant at a mortgage company. Ellen was a Scandinavian beauty who grew up in a loving home with parents who adored her and nurtured her academic and musical talents in every way. In stark contrast, Richard was a tall, handsome Texan raised by two mentally unstable parents. His father drank too much and was home too little and his mother beat him every day for insignificant infractions. As a high school student, he endured a traumatic shock when his father took his own life in his law office. Such destructive child-rearing left Richard ill-equipped for life as a husband and father.

After the war, Richard and Ellen moved from Bisbee, Arizona, to San Diego, California, where they purchased a home and started planning a family. For years they tried to have a child, but Ellen could not get pregnant. Richard's patience was exhausted, so he blamed Ellen for their fertility problems. Twelve years later, there was still no baby and they had all but given up hope. A fertility test finally provided the answer. Dad was sterile! With their dream of having a biological child shattered, they looked at adoption as their final chance to have children. As part of the war relief effort, Greece had made orphans available for adoption overseas, and the United States, a contributor to the war relief aid, became the first recipient country. In a desperate move of self-preservation, Dad embraced adoption, but he secretly remained *reluctant* about the idea. His motivation to adopt had little to do with loving children; it was a last-ditch effort to conceal his infertility and save his marriage.

Richard and Ellen waited nearly two years for me but had no idea I'd be so malnourished and weak upon arrival. In their wildest dreams they never thought they'd have to teach a three-year-old how to chew solid food. It was a dramatic reminder of how dire things were in Greece. But they learned fast. Within two years, Ellen and Richard adopted three more children: fraternal twins from a local mother and a five-year-old boy, Michael, from the Athens Municipal Orphanage. With every new child arriving, the financial and emotional pressure on Dad increased and life in the Pace household suffered. My parents went from no children to a station wagon full of four in the blink of an eye. Money dried up as Mom's career changed from administrative assistant to mommy, and their new home had become too small. I know they were trying to make up for lost time, but what were they thinking? I don't have the answer, but it was a recipe for disaster.

Before my young eyes, Dad slowly changed into a tormented adult. The stress of day-to-day life in the Pace household caused me to wet the bed until I was 12 years old. I tried everything from staying awake as late as possible to not drinking anything after 6:00 p.m., but I still was not able to control it. I missed out on the slumber parties and the camping trips that my friends took for granted. Mom's excuses for me declining these events were awkward, and they made me feel even more alone. I was responsible for a lot of extra laundry in the Pace home, but Mom never complained or made me feel bad. What gave me pause was not being ridiculed or punished by Dad the next morning. I wondered, *had he been a bedwetter, too?*

As Dad unraveled further, the beatings began. He had come full circle. The abused child had become the abusive parent. Those were the times I fantasized about the circumstances of my birth. Some fantasies were about my birth mother, but I fantasized about my biological father more than most. *Who and where was he? Did he know about me? My real Dad would never treat me this way,* I thought. In my favorite fantasy, Dad was Aristotle Onassis who had a love child with Maria Callas that he could not acknowledge. That explained my love of singing, but not the lack of an operatic voice.

During my teens, the family was in complete turmoil as the twins had now become full-blown drug addicts. Expelled from schools and in trouble with the law, they both spent time in jail. Their behavior added immeasurable stress to an already hellish situation, and I felt more isolated than ever. My self-esteem was nonexistent to the degree that I could not look people in the eye. I had no control over my life and trusted no one. Home life was an embarrassment that I was afraid others would learn about. So, I reinvented myself and became a master of avoidance and excuses. For the life of me, I never understood why Dad made Michael and me his targets and left the twins alone. We excelled in music, academics, and sports, and yet we suffered the most from Dad's behavior. One day a friend who was familiar with our family dynamics made a shrewd statement: "Considering how the twins turned out, you and Michael should be the poster children for foreign adoptions. If only your dad had known how to appreciate you."

Life with Dad was not easy for Mom either. He never hit her, but easily intimidated her with his size and disposition. He shattered her dreams of having babies and the social life that would normally come with academia. When Dad started teaching, he did not embrace college life. Work was work and he wanted no part of socializing with his colleagues. He made that decision on her behalf as well, without asking. The closest Mom ever got to college life was typing up Dad's exams. For such a warm, outgoing person, the isolation must have been soul-crushing. If she was angry, frustrated, or hurt, she never showed it while we were around. Mom paid a heavy price for the family she wanted. Resigned to her lot, she gave up on her dreams and turned her energy to taking care of her family as best she could. When I asked Mom why she stayed with Dad, her answer sounded almost trite, "You have to make do with the cards you are dealt and that's what I did." *Was it really that simple for her, or was it her way to deflect pain and hold her head high?*

The day after my 20th birthday, Dad and I had a terrible argument. I don't remember what we fought about but the conversation ended when Dad yelled, "You'd be dead in some gutter if we hadn't adopted you." I could take it no more. I called him a horrible name, told him I was leaving, and moved into an apartment within a week. That comment changed my life with repercussions I could not foresee. I went from wanting my own child rather than adopting, to being unable to have a child and choosing not to adopt. In hindsight, I have regretted the decision not to have children, but at the time it made perfect sense.

Dad passed away in 1983 after a ten-year battle with cancer. He fought hard but decided to take matters into his own hands when he knew there was no more hope. When Mom called and told me Dad had died, I was not completely surprised by her call. But I was not expecting to hear that he had taken his own life in the backyard. I sobbed for three hours over his death and have not shed a tear since. I understood Dad's decision to end his suffering but the way he carried it out was thoughtless and self-serving. *How could he put Mom through such a gruesome ordeal?* I sympathized with Mom's decision not to have a funeral for Dad. Being the center of attention at an affair like that was too much for her. Even more painful was the prospect of a funeral with no one in attendance.

With Dad gone and Mom on her own, I finally felt the freedom to take the trip I'd always dreamed of, to Greece. I researched organized tours because I thought it was a smart way to familiarize myself with the country. As luck would have it, a friend gave me a brochure about the Ionian Village tour that made several stops in the coastal city of Patras. I wanted to visit the city where I was born, so I wrote a check and signed up. Returning to Greece as an adult was not about looking for family. I just wanted to see my first hometown and the place where I spent my earliest years.

Our tour group arrived in Patras in the summer of 1984, and I was excited to see the bustling downtown and major seaport. While others shopped and dined, I strolled from the flower clock into the downtown area. It was a surreal experience dropping into what could have been my Greek life. It was impossible to stop myself from examining every face I passed hoping to find someone who looked like me. As I walked past the shops, school, and hospital that I would have frequented, I caught myself taking in the sights as if looking through my mother's eyes. *Had my mother been sitting and resting on this bench? Was this the grocery store where she shopped? Where was she and what happened to her?*

My next task was to find the orphanage or at least the location where it had been. While asking for directions I learned the original structure had been replaced after more than 100 years. Located in the city's heart, the new building sat on a hill overlooking the sea. Facing the gate, I said a silent prayer hoping that the records from the original orphanage had been saved.

Entering the courtyard, I was met by the director, Mr. Alivizatos, who was thrilled that an adoptee from the 1950s had returned to Greece to find answers. My heart skipped a beat with his reply to my question about the records. "Everything: ledgers, notes, icons, and clothing was saved from the first orphanage." In his office, he showed me the oversized ledger for 1953 and opened it to May 13, the day I was left in the baby box. Right there in faded blue ink was the nurse's entry documenting my arrival in the baby box. What I was not expecting to see at the bottom was a note with my birth mother's name, Hariklea.

Before I learned her name, it was as if the first three years of my life did not exist. Growing up, I had never thought of myself as being *born* to anyone, only *adopted* by someone. That was no longer true: I was *born* to Hariklea Voukelatos. She had given me the name Maria for protection, baptized me, and left me in a safe place. That knowledge instantly changed my perception of my insecure self: I was loved and cared for by my birth mother!

It was years before I realized how auspicious my timing was. I was granted full access to my records and even given my pick of original orphanage photos. Sadly, all that changed when a baby scandal was uncovered in the 1990s. Since then, adoptees who have traveled to Greece have often been met with closed doors and dead ends, which resulted in unimaginable heartache for parents and siblings separated for life. When I compare my search to that of other adoptees, I feel a bit guilty. I had the type of access that many adoptees can only dream of, and it hurts to see dear friends hit roadblock after roadblock.

The rest of my tour of Greece exceeded every expectation, but I couldn't get back to Patras fast enough after it was over. Luckily for me, one of our tour guides was returning to Patras and offered to help me navigate the city. Over morning coffee, we studied my adoption documents and Hariklea's note. He told me there was a Patras neighborhood called Synora where people from the Ionian islands with surnames like Voukelatos lived. Well, it was certainly worth a look, so we hopped in the car and drove to a part of Patras I had never seen.

We turned down an empty street and parked in the middle of the block. Starting at the corner house, we began knocking on doors. At the third door, a middle-aged woman answered and told us she knew Hariklea. She was alive and working nearby today. She worked for the city cleaning the public restrooms. If we wanted, we could go there and see her now. I was speechless and could barely catch my breath! *My birth mother was alive and living in Patras! There must be some mistake. You don't find your birth mother after 30 years by knocking on three doors!*

We found the bathrooms halfway down a steep street filled with eateries. I saw a figure moving about inside, but it was difficult to see much. My friend entered as I watched from nearby. I heard the woman before I saw her. Agitated and upset, she made quite a scene insisting she was not the Hariklea we were looking for. We believed her and began our retreat up the hill when the woman asked for a phone number and said she'd call with information that could help us. Thinking we'd hit another dead end we made our way back to my friend's house.

In the afternoon, Hariklea called and asked to meet at a specific table in Plateia Psilalonia, a public square shaded by trees. From the dense foliage surrounding us, it was clear she wanted privacy. But her secrecy worried me, and I began to sweat. Silently Hariklea appeared through the bushes and sat down. Without any introduction, she looked directly into my eyes and stated, "Είμαι η μητέρα σου και αυτό είναι ακριβώς σαν τις ταινίες." Translation: "I am your mother, and this is just like the movies." The comment was insightful and a bit humorous, too. *The woman we had met earlier was my birth mother and she had been in Patras all this time!*

When I could finally speak, I took a couple of deep breaths and whispered the words I had waited a lifetime to say: "You never came back for me. Please help me understand what happened to you." In between sips of water and wiping her brow Hariklea shared her story with us. She was born on the small Ionian island of Lefkada, located off the western coast of Greece. Raised by a brutal father, who killed her mother, she learned at a young age that women were commodities to be used by men as they saw fit. At seven, Hariklea contracted polio that paralyzed her right foot and was nursed back to health by the village women.

A neighbor who was her father's best friend and business partner forced himself on her when she was just a teenager. She was raped. There is no other way to say it. Crippled, unmarried, and pregnant at fifteen, Hariklea did not have the benefit of her mother's love and guidance. She was disowned and banished from her village when only 16 years old. Forced to move to Patras, she spent two months on the streets until she gave birth to me on May 3, 1953. I have often wondered how Hariklea felt carrying a child conceived in such a violent manner. Other women have been utterly broken by lesser events. Was I the last connection to her village life? Did her Orthodox faith provide the strength to carry on? Regardless of the answer, I am in utter amazement of her unfathomable grit and resolve!

A friend provided refuge in her home, but it wasn't long before Hariklea realized she could not take care of me. With no job or family support, she had no other option but to place me in the local orphanage until her situation improved. Three years later her circumstances were no better, and she lost me through an adoption to the United States.

Through tears of regret Hariklea finished by whispering, "It broke my heart, but I agreed to let you go so you could have a better life. All these years I knew I had a daughter in America, and I have never forgotten about you. I have prayed my entire life that you would come to Greece and find me because I knew I'd never be able to come to America and look for you. After you left, I took a job in a furniture factory where I met a good man and had another daughter, Katina. My husband died when she was just ten. I have been working for the city of Patras and raising my daughter alone since then."

That day was the start of an extraordinary relationship with Hariklea that spanned more than three decades. It took us awhile to warm to one another. I suspect it was harder for me because it was never my intention to search for my birth mother. I already had a wonderful Mom. But as I learned more of Hariklea's story, my heart ached for what she had been through and my admiration for her grew.

There was the stern and bossy Hariklea, who loved her family fiercely, and there was the broken Hariklea, who still suffered soul-crushing guilt over losing me. Every visit to Greece I arrived with a new journal and a list of questions. I hoped Hariklea or my half-sister, Katina, would have answers for me. As Hariklea revealed more of her story, it helped me piece together the how's and why's that weigh on so many of us adoptees. These were the times when the three of us shared funny, poignant moments as we grew to trust each other like family.

It took years before Hariklea talked to me about her island of Lefkada. She still had two brothers living there, but they had not spoken since Hariklea left Nikolis 45 years earlier. When I asked the name of her village, she clammed up and shook her head. All she admitted was that its name started with an "N." Her curt response only piqued my interest more; there were more pieces of the puzzle to be found on Lefkada!

In 1996, my friend Bev and I took a trip to Lefkada. Known for some of the finest beaches and textiles in Greece, it was a stunning island. We played tourists for a few days and then set our sights on finding Hariklea's village. With God's grace, a fork in the road, and the letter "N," we found tiny Nikolis clinging to a steep mountainside. My cousin Stathis was sitting in front of the village store at exactly the right time and is responsible for connecting me with two of my uncles, Thodoris and Nikos. They were more than a little shocked to see the child that Hariklea was carrying when she left the island. No one thought I had survived. Now they heard that the grown woman standing in front of them was their niece. It must have been like seeing a ghost from the past. We shared a meal that started with a bit of tension but ended with Thodoris welcoming me to the family. Since then, I've made several trips back to Nikolis where I helped by taking the goats out to pasture, feeding the livestock, and making feta cheese.

After a life-changing week on Lefkada, Bev and I drove to Patras to spend time with Hariklea. I waited until we got settled and were enjoying cold drinks on the balcony before I told her that we had visited Lefkada and found Nikolis. When she heard my news, she was surprised but not upset with me. I think she may even have felt a bit relieved. Hariklea understood my desire to connect with the rest of my family, and I think she wanted the same connection for herself as well. I don't know who made the first move, but after finding my Nikolis family members, the communication between Hariklea and her brothers was reestablished with phone calls and later by visits. Now, as the brothers had reason to pass through Patras, they made sure to visit their sister in the city. The Voukelatos family was reunited after 45 years apart.

It was the summer of 2007. I was happy to be back in Greece after two years away. My usual itinerary involved spending a couple of days in Athens with my cousins before I took the bus to Hariklea's home in Patras. Midmorning on my first day, we met at a beachfront coffee bar. I was happy that several of my cousins spoke English, making our conversations effortless as we caught up on each other's lives. After about an hour, cousin Zoe phoned Hariklea to tell her that I had arrived and would see her on Monday. I had an inkling something was up when their conversation lasted longer than necessary. Even so, I was not prepared for Zoe's announcement: "Maria, Hariklea has made other plans for your weekend. She wants you to come to Patras today because she wants to go home to Nikolis, and you are going to take her there. Hariklea left Nikolis as a frightened, pregnant teenager. Now she is an old woman who wants to see her childhood home one last time before she dies. When you arrive in Patras, Hariklea will have a car ready for the drive to Lefkada. You will stay with my father Thodoris, who built a new home just outside of Nikolis." Zoe's comment was met with dead silence. Her announcement caught me so off guard that it took a minute to realize the enormity of what Hariklea had requested. We sat in silence, each of us trying to get our heads around what this meant to the family. But cousin Eve cut to the chase, "Your mother was only sixteen years old when she was forced to leave Nikolis because of you. Now 54 years later she can return to Nikolis because of you." In two short sentences, Eve had articulated the irony of Hariklea's request. It was poignant and profound. I had come full circle, but it did not compare to helping Hariklea complete hers.

In less than an hour, I was on a bus heading to Patras. I had no idea what to expect but the abrupt changes in my plans were small compared to the total transformation of my Greek family's life. With heightened anticipation, I arrived in downtown Patras and walked to the car rental agency where I found Hariklea. She had rented a car with an anemic three-cylinder engine. Perfect for our duo, the little car suited the narrow roads and got good gas mileage. I laughed at the vehicle's splendid, purple paint job, but it was perfect for such a special occasion. That funny little car with its royal purple paint was the chariot that would deliver Hariklea back home. We stowed our bags and climbed in the car. Settled in, Hariklea looked at me and just said, *"Pameh."* "Let's go."

Driving together for hours with an unavoidable language barrier made for a challenging trip. We managed to converse about simple things: not much was said but a lot was communicated. Barreling down the road, I wondered what could be more reasonable than a mother and daughter driving home to visit the relatives. Nothing, except we were no ordinary mother and daughter and the home had remained unseen for five decades. The significance of what we were doing was not lost on us.

It was dark when we drove over the causeway and onto Lefkada island. Driving south along the coast, we came to the steep road that climbed into the foothills where Hariklea's brother Thodoris lived. Fifteen hairpin turns later, we pulled into his driveway. There were hugs and kisses all around as Uncle Thodoris and his wife Marianna came out to greet us. We settled in and spent the rest of the evening talking, laughing, and drinking Thodoris' homemade red *krasi*. I don't recall what was said as much as I remember the love I felt. Thodoris sat beside me, held my hand the entire evening and told me he loved me dozens of times. He released his grip only when it was time to refill our wine glasses. I remember thinking how lucky Thodoris' children were to have such a loving father and wished *my* dad had been more like him. I couldn't have asked for a better ending to the long day. Around midnight we went to bed. Tomorrow was going to be a historic day.

The excitement in the house was palpable as we prepared to leave early for Nikolis. I knew times had changed but what was about to happen was unprecedented. We were all expected for lunch with Uncle Nikos and his wife, Zahareena. There were four of us, so Thodoris and Marianna led the way in his truck while Hariklea and I followed in the purple chariot.

The drive was short, and no one spoke along the way. I wanted Hariklea to have time to prepare herself as we drove over the steep, windy roads that she had not seen since she was a teenager. We passed the field where her mother's dowry of nine olive trees still grew and noticed the olive press that our fathers had shared. *What must Hariklea be thinking? Is her heart filled with joy or pain as I drive past her childhood memories?*

I turned right at the sign that led travelers to either Nikolis or Manassi, and within minutes parked in front of Hariklea's old home. From the outside, the white, two-story, stucco house had not changed. The grape arbor was laden with grapes and garlic strands, and geraniums still grew in clay pots around the patio. I doubted much had changed since Hariklea had lived here.

My chest was pounding as I saw Nikos out front waiting. He helped Hariklea out of the car and greeted her tenderly. Tears welled in my eyes as Nikos cradled his sister's arm and became her cane. He led her around the outside of her home where she opened the outdoor bread oven, fingered the oregano drying on the fence, and stopped by the pens where, as a girl, she had fed the goats and the chickens. Her next stop was the long-neglected cemetery. She pushed open the old iron gate and made her way past white marble headstones dating back generations. It didn't take Hariklea long to find the two marble crosses that marked her mother's and father's grave site. After leaving Nikolis, she never saw her father alive again. Standing there resolute and silent, her father had stated that no punishment was too harsh for the woman who had brought shame to his family. He had felt entirely justified in beating his disobedient wife to death and in exiling his pregnant, but raped daughter. Only in death had her parents found peace. Only in his death could Hariklea find peace with her father. Hariklea kept her feelings to herself, but I sensed she was relieved that she had come. This visit brought long-awaited closure.

Our final stop was the house that had been both Hariklea's sanctuary and the scene of her worst nightmare. As she opened the door, I worried what demons awaited her inside. The kitchen was the same, apart from a few upgrades: a new refrigerator, stove, and washing machine. Hariklea nodded her approval as she ran her fingers over the latest appliances and countertop. Touching those things made returning home concrete for her. As Hariklea walked into the living room she paused to cross herself in front of the religious icons, but she did not linger there. If any memories of that awful day returned, her calm demeanor hid her feelings well. She made her way back to the kitchen where she sat at the table and basked in the sunlight streaming through the window. Hariklea could have sat there all day savoring the same view she loved as a girl.

Resting a spell, she took her time before she headed back outside to sit on a bench. Her gaze wandered across the valley to the olive trees tended by her family since the 1800s and up the hill to where her neighbors had lived. The home of my father, Yiorgos, was within eyesight. As we sat there looking at his house, our minds filled with compelling truths. To Hariklea, Yiorgos was a rapist who had ruined her life, betrayed everyone, and fled Lefkada like a coward. To me, he was a rapist and a coward, but also a piece of the puzzle I would never find. Hariklea commented, "Thank you, Maria, my death will be easier now because I have returned home." It filled my heart with warmth and peace. Despite all she had been through, Hariklea was still determined to live life on her terms, and I was privileged to help her complete her wish. Hariklea, like Ellen, possessed an indomitable spirit. I was fortunate to have not one, but two amazing mothers.

Looking up the road past Yiorgos' house, I saw the first of several villagers walking over to greet Hariklea. They were friends she had known when she was a young girl, who came to welcome her home. I joined the rest of the family on the patio and watched. I never tired of watching Greeks and the demonstrative ways in which they express their feelings. With hands flying as they speak, lips kissing with abandon, and loud voices, they use their entire bodies to communicate. Hariklea was excited to see her friends and greeted them warmly. Though I nearly missed it, she even smiled a couple of times.

Hariklea and I rested on the bench while Uncle Nikos and Zahareena finished preparing the table for lunch. They brought out hand-embroidered linens, china plates, and crystal glasses for this occasion. Because Hariklea was a family member, a less elegant setting would have sufficed but honoring the return of a sister deserved something special. Every delicacy Zahareena had prepared was grown no more than a stone's throw away from where we stood. The delicious aromas of village cooking filled the mountain air. As we all took our seats, I made sure I sat by Hariklea because I didn't want to miss a thing. There were kind words and lavish compliments all around as we thanked our hosts for such an elegant table and mouth-watering food.

Before we began, Nikos poured everyone a glass of his red *krasi*, raised his glass and spoke. "Today my sister has returned home after many years away. Let us thank God for reuniting our family." His comments were brief but powerful. With our glasses raised, we toasted Hariklea and welcomed her home. Overcome by such an outpouring of love, even stoic Hariklea could not hold back the liquid joy flowing down her cheeks. She was home and she was happy. Sharing this journey with her was one of the most joyful and meaningful moments of my life. Hariklea and I had literally and figuratively come full circle.

The food was delicious, and the conversation relaxed. Happiness lit up every face. Looking to my left, I noticed Hariklea had stopped eating and was deep into her own thoughts. The look on her face told me it was something important: maybe she was reflecting on the twists and turns her life had taken. Surely, she had not expected to see her brothers or her home again. I just hoped she was basking in the thrill of returning home after more than half a century. It was a lot for Hariklea to handle, so I gave her plenty of time before I asked her to put her thoughts into words. "For years I used to say, εγώ δεν έχω στον ήλιο μοίρα." ("I have no fate or fortune under the sun"). Her brother Thodoris instantly understood this very Greek expression. He choked up again and grabbed her by the hand. "But now," as Hariklea's face lit up, she said, "Fortune has smiled on me, and my sunshine is back forever."

Hariklea passed away in 2019. I had grown to love her and was deeply saddened by the news. As I was reading Hariklea's death announcement, I discovered the strength of another Voukelatos woman, Katina, my half-sister. Under the family section of the death notice, she had listed Hariklea as the mother of *two* daughters. It was a bold thing to do since very few people in Greece knew I was Hariklea's daughter. Suddenly Katina had a lot of explaining to do. I was touched beyond measure by such a gesture. She was her mother's daughter!

Beyond the Full Circles

Recent developments created new circles to be completed with my Greek family and again, serendipity was on my side. I was on Lefkada working on a film project when Mihalis, the oldest son of my father Yiorgos, reached out to my cousin Stathis, who runs a local bakery on the island. Mihalis told him that all four of his siblings had known about me for years. I didn't know if that was good or bad news, but it surely was a shock! With one phone call, Mihalis gave me five more pieces of my family puzzle. Unfortunately, we were unable to connect on that visit, but I left Greece with his phone number in my pocket. It looked like I had more unfinished family business to cover.

Back home I was filled with trepidation as I punched the numbers of Mihalis' phone. I had no idea what he knew or what to expect. It turned out I had worried over nothing: Mihalis was thrilled to hear from me. He told me his siblings wanted to hear from me as well. Mihalis and I spoke for about an hour before I hesitatingly asked him if he remembered anything about what had happened between his and Hariklea's family. He didn't mind the question but only remembered a couple of things about "The Incident," as he called it. Mihalis did not know what exactly had occurred between the two families, only that it was something bad. He woke up one morning to find his father gone and both family patriarchs standing face to face in front of his house. They were screaming and shouting. Both sides drew their guns, but no one got hurt. Yiorgos' father left the scene first, but not before he told Hariklea's father, "Do what you want to my son, but please don't hurt my other children." Yiorgos had fled to Athens never to return. His wife remained in the village with their five children. As each child finished school in Nikolis, they went to join their father in Athens to find better jobs.

When we finished, I asked Mihalis for the phone numbers of his siblings. I waited a few days to make calls to brother Nikos, my youngest paternal half-sibling, who makes his home in British Columbia, and to sister Kale, who lives in Ontario. It is somewhat ironic that both settled in Canada, while I live only two hours away from the Canadian border. Our first conversations were full of excitement as Niko and Kale were overjoyed to have a sister. We promised to stay in touch through phone calls, Facebook, and texts. I have also spoken to half-brothers Andreas and Philip, who live on Lefkada and Corfu, respectively. Both were warm and welcomed me to the family but spoke little English. I find it strange that their father never spoke one word to his children about his actions, but then his cover-up adds credence to Hariklea's accusation that he raped an innocent teenage girl. I would have been receptive to hearing his side of the story, but that opportunity was never given to us. He died in Athens at the age of 94.

Sadly, the communication between my half-siblings has cooled off a bit in recent weeks. My half-sister, Kale, read my book and was unhappy with my portrayal of her father. From my Lefkada cousin, Stathis, I learned that old village grudges do not fade or disappear with time. The Voukelatos family runs *Litharia*, a restaurant in the mountain village of Nikolis that boasts traditional Greek dishes and a view to the sea. A half-brother who no longer lives on Lefkada owns the land below the restaurant and refuses to let Stathis cut down the trees that block the entire view. His petty behavior thwarts one of the lovely features of dining alfresco at *Litharia*.

Answers Beget Questions

Writing my story fulfilled a promise I made to myself in 1984. It was not as much a desire as it was my destiny. I had to get it down on paper or the disappointment would have destroyed me from the inside out. Writing proved to be cathartic and helped me make sense of the puzzle pieces that shaped my life. It also provided valuable insights which led to thought-provoking questions.

What if I had not been adopted and had grown up in Patras with Hariklea? To compare the life, I lived to one I *might* have lived opens the door to speculating about the woulda, coulda, and shouldas in both scenarios. There were opportunities both in Greece and in America, but they were not the same.

Adopted by the Paces of San Diego, I enjoyed the benefits afforded by my father's middle-class income. I had a loving Mom in Ellen, new clothes, toys, and trips but everything came at a terribly high cost. I arrived in America through a proxy adoption program in the 1950s. I'm sure the motives for such adoptions were noble in the beginning, but as time passed, they proved problematic. Overwhelmed by orphaned babies and young children in the postwar era, intermediaries made no attempts to screen out unsuitable parents like Dad. The consequence of that decision took an emotional toll on me that left deep scars I still wrestle with today. It also sets the stage for the kind of instant, lucrative solution that eroded Greece's incentive to design alternative solutions.

If I had remained with my birth mother Hariklea, we would have struggled financially during the early years, but poor does not equal unhappy. Hariklea would have provided a safe home, of this I am certain. The state should have properly informed Hariklea and should have helped her apply for welfare assistance and for a priority place for me in a daycare. It would have made all the difference in the world if Hariklea could have kept me and her job at the furniture factory. Either way I have no doubt she would have figured something out.

As a young girl I'm sure I would have gravitated to athletics as I had done in America, but I doubt sports would have gained the lifeline status they did in the Pace household. Softball, racquetball, and competitive swimming kept me busy but none of those sports matched my love for gymnastics. I had a natural aptitude for the sport and was recognized as one of the top gymnasts in California. My historian friend swears that if I'd remained in tiny Greece, I would have won the Olympic gold medal in gymnastics representing my home country at the 1968 games!! Perhaps.

Attending college in Greece would have been free and my graduation a celebrated achievement. In the Pace household, attending college was a nonnegotiable family expectation to be fully funded by me. It took five years for me to graduate because I lived on my own and worked two jobs to pay for it.

It was my return to Greece that reunited my fractured family and returned Hariklea to Nikolis. If Hariklea had tried to raise me on her own, would she have tried to reconnect sooner with her Nikolis family? I cannot say for sure, but I'd like to think she would have tried. She would most likely have succeeded, because she had the support of a husband who had accepted me. Surely her extended family in Nikolis would have welcomed us back sooner rather than later. It's hard to imagine my life without all the aunts, uncles, and cousins I have come to love.

Am I happy I was adopted? There is no single, simple answer. Growing up in the Pace household was like living in a war zone where I spent nearly every day wishing I was either not adopted or at least not by the Paces. What helped me survive was Ellen, my adoptive Mom, brother Michael, and knowing my independence was in sight. As soon as I turned 18, I could legally leave the house and be on my own.

Despite my fractured childhood, I grew up in America where opportunities were there for the taking. I feel blessed to have been loved on both sides of the world by two magnificent mothers. I had a middle-class upbringing, became a teacher, and have been supporting myself since I was 20. I spent a lot of time and energy honing my survival skills. As an adult, I was finally afforded the chance to live my version of the American Dream. The part of my life that I was allowed to shape leaves me happy that I am here.

Chapter 3

WHAT'S IN A NAME?

Alexandra/Alexa

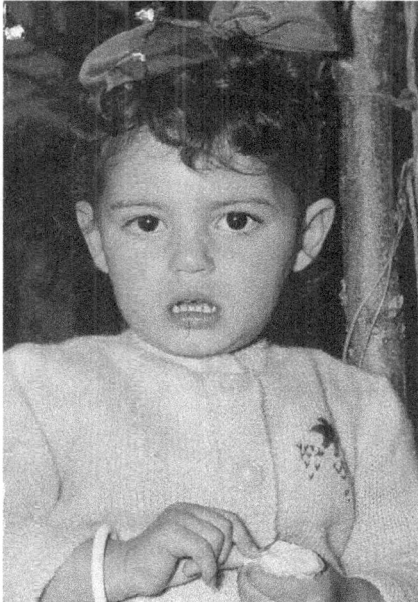

My name is Alexa.

First, it was Alexandra, then Sandra, then Sandy. I was born in 1955 and adopted from an orphanage in Greece by Greek American parents, Bess and Jim Maros, around 1959. Those four years in between my birth and adoption are lost to me, and yet they have shaped much of the person I am today. Much of my life has been spent searching for people who looked like me, felt like me, worried as much as me. I longed to belong to a family and a place I did not know. I was always trying to "fit in" and was continually disappointed at how often I did not. *Why* didn't I?

In the Beginning

I landed in Chicago, Illinois, not speaking a word of English. My adoptive mother traveled with me from Athens and later told me that on the plane I apparently hit it off with a little Italian boy my age. We didn't share a language, but enjoyed playing together. I was always glad my mom shared that little tidbit with me. In fact, any little memory she had about my adoption and insights into my young life, prior to coming to America, were always like rare gems, which I diligently pursued, held on to, and hoarded. I always wanted to learn more about who I was before becoming Sandy, the adopted daughter of Bess and Jim, who lived about 40 minutes from downtown Chicago on a tidy little block in one of the first planned suburbs in the United States. It was a place called Park Forest.

On Feeling Different and Early Fears

Being adopted means many different things to people, whether you are an adoptee or not. For me, it meant feeling just a little bit different from day one. I came to a place where I wouldn't eat the food because it wasn't familiar, let alone comforting. I didn't speak the language and found out quickly that kids made fun of you if you were different from them in any way. That went double for not speaking "American." It won't surprise you to learn that once I was able to cobble together some English, my parents could hardly squeeze a word of Greek out of me. Why use your native language when your reward for doing so was, at best, quizzical looks and, at worst, outright bullying?

Oh, yes, the bullying. My new little neighbors went out of their way to remind me that I was the newcomer, a stranger, and they made sure to make me feel like the outsider I was. They would tease me, pulling off my warm cap in the winter, throwing it into the neighborhood creek. The worst of it was luring me into one of their garages. I was so excited to be invited to a party, I thought! Instead, after I entered, they slammed the garage door shut, and quickly ditched me there. Today, we call it "ghosting," leaving someone in the dark. And I was afraid of the dark. Still am to this day.

As a child, I had a recurring dream that I would find myself in a dark place, a place where I was trapped, feeling terrified. I screamed and cried, pleading to be let out. It was always the same dream. One day I asked my mother about these nightmares. She scooped me up on her lap and told me that, for the brief period of time I was in foster care, the old lady who was my caretaker, would lock me in the closet when I was "bad." My mother explained that she was old and didn't know any better. It helped that she could provide a reason for one of my deep-seated fears. She could not, however, provide the same explanation for my feelings about not fitting in.

My hunch is that many adopted kids feel this sense of "otherness." It is hard to explain if you are not adopted. We often feel like outsiders because we *are* from someplace else. We don't come from the families we live with. We don't look like the people we are closest to And for international adoptees, we even struggled to communicate, not knowing the language we've been adopted into. New people, new family, new words, new food, new clothes, new climate, new everything. It's a lot to handle and process.

Origin Story

Because you are adopted and came from someplace else, parents often had to construct the story of how you came to be in this new place, with these new people, essentially strangers, holding you, feeding you, and loving you. The story I was told was quite dramatic, just like my wonderful, larger than life, beautiful mom, Bess.

It was a dark, stormy night. My birth parents were going out to a party. I stayed at home (no idea with whom). Guess it wasn't a village affair since they had to drive somewhere. They must have had a car. So late at night, they were driving home on the curving and twisting mountain roads. They drove off a cliff. I went to an orphanage. That was the first part of my story.

Then came the adoption story itself. My mother flew all the way to Greece to find me. She came to the Baby Center Mitera in Athens and picked me out of all the children in the world to be hers. I hugged her and showered her with kisses and started calling her mama right away, so I was told. When the visit was over, and it was time for her to leave, I started to cry and became very upset. So, my new mama did something very smart. She gave me her purse to keep, telling me that she would have to come back to get it. She was always a good deal maker and I thought it was pretty good collateral to ensure her return. She came back.

As my mother told it (and she loved to tell it), the ladies at the orphanage were floored by my resemblance to my mom-to-be and this was very important to my mother. In fact, she stressed this point throughout my life, as she told my story of how I came to be hers. And as I grew up, the resemblance became even more striking as reflected in the eyes of others who were often stunned to learn I was adopted, given how much I looked like my adoptive parents. That included my father, Jim, by the way. No surprise there because his family was from Crete and I have since learned that my biological father was from there as well.

Nurture versus Nature

We hear a lot about this. It was an especially hot topic in the 1990s. It even crept into management theory with a question—whether good managers were born that way or could be trained to be good managers. I've often wondered what part of me has sprouted from my DNA versus that which was nourished and encouraged via my upbringing. We're all some of both, I suppose. This issue transcends adoption. For me, I'm always trying to identify characteristics that may have come from my biological mother or father.

As I got older, my mother tried to help me out where she could. For example, I seemed to have some writing chops in school. My mom told me that my biological father had been the editor of a newspaper in Greece. I remember being so happy to have learned something, anything about a biological parent, and was immediately proud of a father I didn't and would never know.

The other side of the puzzle was harder. My mother noticed I could be a bit "high strung" (I wonder what that's called in boys) and could be nervous at times. One day she explained to me that my biological mother had some "problems," some issues; the kinds of things that probably prevented her from being a "good" mother. As I look back on it, I wonder what our expectations are of young girls, 14 or 15 years of age, sometimes even younger, who are impregnated, more often than not after a rape, and then evaluated in terms of their capabilities to be a mother, to be maternal.

Over time, my mom started to weave together another story that went something like this: My mother was not doing a very good job of caring for me. She was too nervous. In fact, as Bess told it, my biological mom started to "drop" me with a frequency that caused alarm. At some point, she explained, my father stepped in and took me away from my mother to place me in a "safe environment." (Absent dad as hero, I know. By the way, I don't like it and I don't buy it.)

As I learn more about Mitera, it seems that, at one time, it was a place that also took in underage girls who became pregnant. It was a home for unwed mothers and an orphanage. That means there's a reasonable chance my mother was there before giving birth to me, so the story about being dropped doesn't quite work, if this is true. On the other hand, I may have been brought there for care because of some problems in the home.

Today, I am still learning more about the institution that was instrumental to my well-being and growth as a child. As I learn more about myself, I also hope to learn more about the young girl who was my mother in Greece.

Not Caring and Then Caring

When I was a little girl, I knew I was adopted, and I knew I was loved, and I loved my parents back. That was good enough for me. Until it wasn't. I started to have questions. I wanted to know more about where I came from and from whom I came. But at the same time, I feared that asking these kinds of questions might hurt my parents. I didn't want to make to make them feel like they weren't "good enough," because I wanted to know more about my birth parents. They wouldn't understand that what I really needed was to understand more about *myself*.

Why did some things loom so large for me? Why did I have outsized reactions to things? Why did I continually need to be told that I was wanted and how much I was loved? Why did I always want so much affection and to be showered with kisses? My mom told me once that I always wanted 100 kisses at bedtime. That's a lot of kisses! Was I trying to make up for lost time? Was I storing them up for a time in the future (I thought) when there might be no more? Was I just plain frightened and needed a sense of security?

Sorting Out the "Story" from the Truth

Some parents hesitate to tell their child they are adopted. This may have been more generational, but I always appreciated the fact that my folks told me from early on and that it was a wonderful thing. Translation: Adoption meant I had been "chosen," that I was "wanted," and they even made it seem, in some way, that it was even better than being *born* into a family. I was special. Well, I can tell you, I was totally onboard with that!

I remember that it made me very happy to think about how they had a choice and that they picked me out of all the little girls in the world! My mother told me she had traveled around the world, and across the ocean, to find me. In this particular circumstance, being different, being adopted, was very cool.

I have a vague memory of one night, crawling into my mother's arms as I asked her to repeat the story of how I came to be adopted. You know, the stormy night thing with the car crash off the cliff. I must have been nine or ten. As she retold the story I began to cry. I couldn't stop. I looked up at my mother and asked her a question that had been troubling me. It was a simple one. When my parents died in the car crash, why didn't anyone from my Greek family take me in? Why didn't anyone step up to take care of me? Why was I unwanted? She held me tight and stroked my hair and said it was because *she* was destined to find me so *she* could adopt me. I kept crying. I think this memory is the root of a deep sadness. That I was unwanted. In trying to be kind, my mother weaved together an origin story, but it left me with unanswerable questions. Why didn't anyone in my Greek family want me? Was I unlovable? Had I done something wrong? And if so, *what* had I done?

The Child Left Behind

The little girl Bess and Jim Maros adopted was left three times. The first time, by my birth mother, who gave me up or was coerced into giving me up. I'll never know. The second time, by an old woman with whom I was in foster care. The last time, by Bess herself, who left Athens thinking she would see me soon in Chicago, but who instead had to return one year later to demand that I be released to her. I have attachment issues.

The Adult Who Remains

Who is she all these years later?

Well, I'm now, officially, a card-carrying-Medicare-gay-woman living in the dry, windy, sometimes hot, sometimes cold, high desert of the Southwestern United States.

In many ways, I'm still that little girl who wanted 100 goodnight kisses each and every bedtime. I still seek approval, but no longer stick around if it's not forthcoming. I want to be loved and also know how to show love, care and affection. I can develop trust with someone quickly, but also can turn off that switch just as fast, if I get hurt or perceive a slight of some kind. I've learned that loyalty is my love language. That's not always easy on my friends and loved ones. I can be quick to feel betrayed. I often feel wronged.

I've had several long-term, committed relationships, but finally, on September 10, 2017, I married for the first time. The attachment issues remain and that means I can be a little sensitive about things. Well, truth is more than a little! I sometimes take offense where there is none to be had. Sometimes I wonder why people don't like or love me when they actually do like me or love me. I wish I didn't set such a high bar, needing so much reinforcement that my friends *really, really* like me, or that my wife and family *love* me enough. Even when I know they do; I seem to require some kind of "proof." I'm getting better, though. I am.

So, with all this said, I guess you could say I'm secure in my insecurities. Overall, I'm a happy Greek American woman, who is as likely to be found cooking up a storm, puttering around my garden, recording my lefty political podcast for activists or walking through the desert hand-in-hand with my beloved.

The journey to this place of contentment has been long and frequently punctuated by anger, sadness and a sense of longing to know more about who and where I came from. That's ok, though, because as we say in Greek, αυτά έχει η ζωή. That's life!

What's in a Name?

About three years ago I obtained my adoption papers from the county clerk of Cook County, Illinois. As I was reading through the legalese and boilerplate text, I saw something. It stood out immediately. The tears came immediately. I had stumbled upon the name of the woman who gave birth to me so many years ago. Her name is Maria Antonopoulos. I read it aloud again and again. Over the next few days, I shared my mother's name with my intimates. I couldn't wait to tell everyone that I came into the world as the daughter of Maria.

She was only 15 years old when I was born. A child herself, she was also my mother. To know her name after all these years felt like coming home, like finding a piece of myself, which seemed to secure my place in the land of my birth, the culture into which I was born.

But sadly, since then, I learned that my birth mother, Maria, had died. When I heard the news, though an intermediary, I sobbed. I had held out hope to meet her one day. I really thought I would because she was so young when she gave birth to me. I don't know how she died. I know nothing about her life or extended family. I don't know the circumstances of my birth, or how and why I was taken from her. I don't know where she lived or how her life unfolded after giving birth to me. I don't know if she got married, had more children or went to university. I don't even have a picture of her. I know her name and, for the moment, that is all and that is *everything*.

Today, I sometimes also think that maybe it wasn't meant to be. I am still processing my feelings of loss. And I am wistful about what might have been. But somewhere in the ether, somewhere out there, I also believe that both my mothers, Maria and Bess, just might be together, comparing notes right now. They were two women who led very different lives, who shared in the joys and sorrows of motherhood, in varying degrees. Maybe both are smiling down on their daughter with pride. Me, Alexandra. Αλεξάνδρα.

Chapter 4

THE SECOND BEGINNING

Marinos/Robert

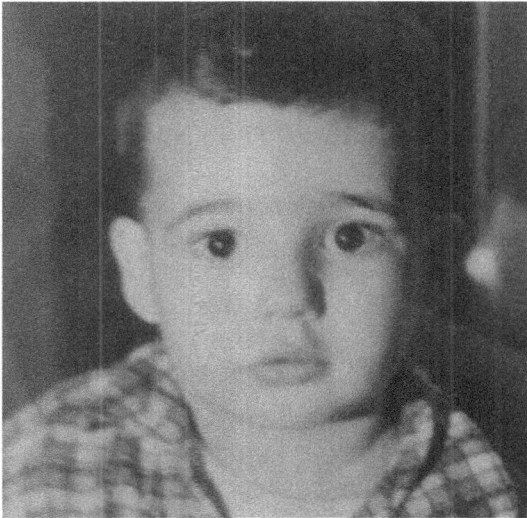

October 1996: Flight from New York to Athens

I met someone once who disliked airports. How is that possible? Air bursting with ions, charging it, making it alive. The most exciting time is the period after the formalities of check-in when all that remains is anticipation. That delicious wait. There is nothing quite like it. Except this time. This wait is particularly hard. The anticipation immeasurable.

We've boarded now and are seated. As you face the back of the plane there I am, fifteen rows back and next to the window on the left side, a vantage point, which I will rue during takeoff, but appreciate once we've stabilized. On my left are my wife, 7-year-old daughter and 4-year-old son.

Waiting to meet us in Athens will be many relatives, among them my twin brother, fraternal not identical (we look nothing alike), my mother, and any number of cousins, aunts, and uncles.

I have extended family in Greece. Quite a large family, actually. What I've neglected to mention, until now, is that three months earlier I did not know any of this family existed. Soon I will meet them for the very first time.

"Robert, please pick up your things, this room looks like a bomb went off."
Typical mother's comment, expecting neatness from her 9-year-old.
My thoughts are elsewhere. "I think Dad looks like Grandma, and his brothers look like Grandpa."
"Sounds right," she agrees.
"It's weird not to look like anyone," I say.
"That's ok, you're special."

Thank goodness that boarding appears to be winding down and we'll soon be airborne. It will be a long flight. There is a preponderance of thoughts trafficking through my mind.

I imagine people to be like buildings. The foundation needs to be solid or the building tips and waivers. So do people. Blood is the most fundamental connection of all. A visceral, subconscious connection, made not of intellect, but of sinew and tissue, both physical and spiritual. The absence of that foundation causes what can be a lifelong pursuit of equilibrium. The presence of love helps to counterbalance the imbalance, but never completely eradicates it. Nothing can.

I hear the doors of the plane being shut and secured, and it looks like everyone is on board and seated. I feel a slight buckling and realize the plane is backing up slowly. For as long as memory serves, I get the most incredible tingling through my gums when I'm genuinely excited about events about to unfold. It's the rush of true adventure, and if I grit my teeth, it tickles beyond description. I have that feeling at this very moment and it never disappoints.

The "fasten seat belt" sign is on and the plane is beginning to taxi toward the runway. The flight attendants are making the usual speech with the usual pantomime, but I never really listen. Taking off is one of those experiences I dread. It's like a giant hand pushing the plane up, right up into a spectrum where you know you have no business being. This time is no exception.

We've finally leveled off, and now I feel myself starting to relax about this flight, at least. The absence of one train of thought has now created a vacuum for another. Now I'll have an eight-hour void to contemplate what might have been as opposed to what is, to try to reconcile somehow a connection with strangers of the same blood, as opposed to those with uncommon origins with whom you share relationships and history.

It's back to the issue of foundation. And blood. The first requires the second. Do you know things with your head or your heart? History and DNA both struggling to find their place.

> *"You come from a line of proud people, people of character and decency." My uncle is in the front passenger seat of the car, looking at me over his left shoulder. My father is driving and I have no recollection of where we are going. I am thirteen years old and remember feeling like a fraud, knowing that I really wasn't a descendant in the one way that truly counts. I wished I was, and my uncle was certainly sincere, but my heart couldn't believe it. I knew it wasn't so. My "foundation" wouldn't permit it.*

Now, here I am in the window seat of row 15 crossing an ocean back to the place of my birth, but with absolutely no memory of it, to see my closest biological relatives, but with no memory of them. Who would imagine?

I'm momentarily distracted by the sight of the clouds below me, a sight that never fails to amaze. I look around and notice that so many are now fast asleep. And again, my minds drifts as I wonder about them. All of them.

It is August of 1996.

I've just returned from work and my wife motions for me to come upstairs to hear a message on the answering machine. She hits the button and a woman's clear and heavily accented voice rings out. "This is Eleni from Greece. I have good news for you and for your case." She goes on to recite her phone number, says thank you and hangs up. A fraction of a moment would bring so much change.

Just a few days before, I had sent a copy of my Greek passport to two extraordinary women in Athens who researched the roots of adoptees hoping for answers. It took 40 years and an article in the *New York Times* on April 13, 1996, a story about hundreds of Greek babies who were sold to families overseas without the consent of their birth mothers. And there was my wife's pioneering spirit and courage, to finally empower and encourage me to delve into my past.

I spent my entire childhood knowing I was adopted and where I was from. It is something for which I will be forever grateful to my parents, that my right to know was respected. I never remember hearing the news for the first time. I was simply always aware. Also, I always assumed that there were very few biological relatives existing. Why I was convinced of this, I have no idea. And the last assumption I had, based on what my parents had been told, was that I was an orphan and had been placed in a Jewish orphanage. I grew up feeling that, had I remained in Greece, I would still be a part of a tiny minority.

It is for this reason that I never really thought of myself as a bona fide Greek. But, in reality, there was no Jewish orphanage and I am Greek through and through.

I couldn't stop staring at the answering machine. I looked at my watch and saw that it was 6:30 p.m., 1:30 in the morning in Greece. The answers were still inaccessible to me. How could I possibly wait until morning to hear what I've only imagined for a lifetime?

I spent the rest of the evening at home, but if you ask me what I did, I couldn't tell you. People have an emotional autopilot when events are too enormous for comprehension. The workings of this faculty are a mystery, but it carried me all the way to midnight. That's when I dialed that long, strange number trying to contact the woman who possessed the details of my past, of my life.

I heard that characteristic European ringing on the other end. On the third one, a man answered in Greek, but the moment he heard an English voice asking for Eleni, he shifted to totally understandable, albeit accented, English, and told me that she wouldn't be in for another two hours. I thanked him and assured him that I would call back. A huge wave of exhaustion, both physical and emotional, washed over me and I knew that I couldn't last a moment longer. I went to bed and somehow fell asleep. But as I drifted off, I asked myself, who are these people that I have waited a lifetime for?

I feel a swaying that's making me so drowsy. Long rides, in this case, a bus ride, always do that. I'm with my parents traveling to Washington, D.C., for my cousin's wedding. My father never really enjoyed driving, and certainly not for five hours, so here we are. The song "Just My Imagination" by The Temptations is running through my head for the umpteenth time. It is the spring of 1971, and at 15, there are so many things I am thinking about, and the tingling in my gums will not stop! A short time later, luggage in tow, we enter the hotel lobby. I see several of my cousins and hasten to greet them. As we're talking, my uncle, aunt and two more of my cousins walk in. And once again, I say to myself, I'm exactly where I want to be and I feel safe, but I don't look like anyone.

It was 6:30 in the morning. I've just dialed that endless telephone number once again. "Hello, this is Eleni," she said with that charming, very characteristic Greek accent. Finally, the one with all the answers I'd been hoping for, after 40 years, poised on the other end of the phone.

"Eleni, it's Robert Lipsky. I got your message last night."
"Yes, yes, how are you? We have good news with your case."
"You can imagine how anxious I am," I admitted. (After all of this time and all these years, I thought to myself.)

I waited nervously for her response while I shifted in my seat in the kitchen, readying the pen and adjusting the paper in front of me. I'll need to physically record my past. I'll need to actually look at it, and read it over and over and over again.

"Yes, of course. Well, we know your mother's name, we know your father's name, and we found out something incredible." In that brief moment when she paused, before she continued, I thought to myself, nothing can be more incredible than what I've just been told.

I had no idea just how wrong I was.

Being adopted, or to be more accurate, given up, means expendable. Not on a conscious level, but deep inside that private place we all have where we muster the courage to face the world, where we define ourselves in the most fundamental way. You do not measure up and never quite arrive. It is a picture that is always distorted, at times dramatically, at other times just somewhat, but never completely clear, never totally right. You are different. You just are.

"You have a twin brother," Eleni said. I looked at the phone for a moment, not processing what I've just heard. "I have a what?" She repeated herself. "You have a twin brother."

Twin. Brother.

I wrote down those two words and as my wife read them, I saw her eyes widen. I was suddenly afraid she was going to faint. If I wasn't sitting, I was afraid of the exact same thing.

"He is a priest in the suburbs of Athens. You are not exact. He has blond hair and blue eyes," Eleni gently explained.

I was staring at the paper in front of me and I could not believe what I was seeing. A fraternal twin brother. A Greek Orthodox priest, a full sibling, who has lived out the past 40 years in a life that I've known nothing about. As I struggled as a 10-year-old, a 15-year-old, a 20-year-old, so did he. Somehow, we were separated and wound up in different orphanages, the details of which remain unclear. My twin was ultimately adopted by a family in Greece, and me by a family in the United States.

How can this possibly be real? I found myself thinking that these things only happen in dreams, and they certainly don't happen to me. I was outside of my body looking in as I continued to record the details of my unknown past.

The hospital, the time of birth, who is older (he is), mother's name, father's name. Is this really happening? I cannot take my eyes off of the paper in front of me.

I was reading, but not quite understanding. It was too big and I found myself breathless. A flood of details commenced. Alexandra Hospital.

At 2:55 in the afternoon. Baptized. Godmother's name. The shadows finally dissipating. A life illuminated.

I wondered just how much of this my children would fully understand. They were so young. On a surface level they did. Their father had found relatives he didn't know existed. But deep down in the soul, did they know that the bedrock had shifted? I wanted them to experience all of this, to drink it, savor this incredible thing happening to us, and to know that even before this discovery, among so many indescribable gifts they'd given me, was the gift of our connection by blood.

I began to regularly correspond with the two researchers, Eleni and Roselyn, and with my twin. It was during those exchanges that I learned more about my brother's life, and how the experience of this revelation affected him. It became evident that, for him, it was not only life changing, it totally redefined his existence. My brother had never been told of his adoption!

He had lived his life certain that the parents who had loved him and cared for him were his "natural" parents. Upon being approached by Eleni and Roselyn, he initially saw no reason for them to meet. They explained the nature of their work and he felt that it had nothing to do with him. He grudgingly accepted a meeting.

The two women arrived at the church with copies of documents in tow. They once again spoke of the research they did, which provided the segue into delivering the message that would change everything. They informed him that he had a twin brother, living in America, and that this brother would love to meet him. He didn't believe it. He explained that he was an only child and was not adopted, that they had to be mistaken. It was then that they laid out the adoption papers on a table before him. As Eleni explained it, he looked down and stared at the papers for a long time. He didn't look up. His breathing became shallower and sweat began to appear on his robe. They asked if he would be willing to meet his brother. In a whisper, he said yes. He also said that he would confirm all of this on his own.

Further complicating the situation was that his adoptive parents had died several years prior. He ultimately would ask extended members of his adoptive family if this was true. They confirmed it. He was surprised how many people knew his story while he had no idea. His relatives told him that his mother, in particular, was afraid to tell him.

Shortly before she died, she had written him a letter. In that letter was something that, at the time, seemed very cryptic and inexplicable. The passage read, "If you ever find out about anything that I've done, always remember that I loved you and adored you." Now he knew what she meant and now he had to adjust to and reconcile a new reality that challenged everything he had assumed to be true about his origins.

For adoptees born in the late 1940s and 1950s, it was not uncommon for parents to conceal the truth from their children. I know of several instances where people found out later in life that their parents were not their birth parents. In my view, it is always better to know. These parents meant no harm and, in their way, felt that they were doing what was best, but knowing is better.

My heart broke for what my brother must have experienced and for what his mother and father experienced harboring that enormous secret. Ultimately, love prevailed. My brother told me that learning the truth made him love his parents even more.

As my brother and I corresponded, the first challenge was language. I spoke no Greek and he spoke no English. I had a neighbor translate all of his initial letters and that also proved difficult. My neighbor, and others who also translated for me, explained that my brother wrote in very eloquent prose, and their English was not strong enough to adequately translate the true gist of what he was saying. But we found a way. Again, love prevailed.

We managed to endure the endless flight to Greece. The impact of the wheels touching down is reality announcing itself. Ready or not, it's coming.

Back then, the plane did not taxi to the terminal. Passengers exited the plane via a long staircase that was wheeled over to the door. We left the plane, walked a short distance outdoors to the terminal building. When it was my turn to exit the plane, I breathed in and immediately recognized the smell of the air. The beckoning of home. Thirty-eight years and a lifetime later, and I still remembered the smell. The scientists were right. The sense of smell brings back the most primal of memories. It was a moment that shook me deep inside, and shakes me still.

I was aware of the layout of the airport from several other adoptees who also had been through the process of looking for relatives. They told me that once you enter the terminal, there will be a ride up an escalator, and there will be plexiglass. Behind that plexiglass will be your past.

As the four of us approached the top, the only thing I saw was empty space. I glanced behind me, and as soon as I did, there was this tremendous commotion: people waving, hitting the plexiglass (which was behind the escalator), and carrying enormous bouquets of flowers. And they were crying. My mother, uncles, aunts and cousins. They were crying because, in their words, "fate took you across the ocean, and now fate brought you back."

My mother carried the pain in her eyes. It was the pain that so many women of her generation carry who gave up their children. It was the pain of being found guilty when no crime was committed, of desperately trying to survive the best they could with what they had. The brutal challenges faced by so many young, unmarried, pregnant women in Greece during the 1950s, and many other countries for that matter, is, for me, unimaginable. I can only hope that, for her, some of that burden was lifted when she saw me again.

The embraces immediately followed. From everyone. Huge bear hugs, lifting me up in the air. My children were passed from person to person, in particular my son, his feet not touching the ground.

We proceeded to a café to sit and catch our breath and to begin the process of starting over. I was blessed that the youngest of my first cousins (there are twelve) taught English in Greece. She was our lifeline in terms of communicating with the rest of my family.

Next, we proceeded to the church to meet my twin brother. My wife and I, our two children, and the two women who connected all of our dots. I sat in the front passenger seat not being able to breathe normally, unable to fathom what was about to happen. I knew from the pictures exchanged what my brother, and all of my relatives, looked like, but now he was about to jump off the screen and land right in front of me.

We entered the church and there he was. We immediately went up to each other and embraced. He was a bit shorter and heavier than me, with the long beard and ponytail of an Orthodox priest. I remember his bright, striking, blue eyes. Despite his imposing appearance, there was a sensitivity and vulnerability about him. And with the help of those indispensable interpreters, we did our best to recap and explain our lives to each other.

It was obvious to me that the universe enjoys occasionally having a laugh at our expense.

While my brother and I were comparing milestones, I, through the interpreter, mentioned the date of my wedding, October 16, 1982. As she imparted this date to him, in Greek, I saw his expression and countenance change. A look of shock came over him. He then quickly spoke to her and she translated his response.

At the very same time my wedding was ending, at midnight, it was 7 a.m. Sunday morning, October 17, in Greece. That was the day he was ordained as a priest. Twin brothers, neither one aware of the other, both celebrating their marriages at the same time. Don't tell me the universe doesn't have a sense of humor. We met my twin and everyone on my mother's side of the family.

In the following few days, we experienced a train of meals, warmth, emotion and just an incredible amount of love. And acceptance. We were engulfed in what my wife called "a tornado of Greekness." And I cherished it.

You cannot rewrite history. You cannot produce a history that doesn't exist. Our travels through life are etched in stone. But there is beauty and peace in knowing.

In having the questions finally answered. And if we are lucky, we both find ourselves having been raised amongst people who love us and then finding those with whom we share common blood. And if you find love there as well, you are blessed beyond.

November 1997: Flight from New York to Detroit

Approximately four months after returning from Greece, in February 1997, I received another call from Eleni. "Robert, sit down. I have some news." I complied, since Eleni's news had a tendency to knock me sideways.

"I just got off of the phone after speaking with your father for an hour." (It is a rarity that adoptees are able to locate both their biological mother and father's family.) I stared at the phone again and had to catch my breath. What I found out that day was that, in addition to a twin brother, I had a half-brother and half-sister. Brother and sister, actually. There is nothing "half" about either of them.

My father and his wife, as well as my two new siblings and their families, all lived in the U.S. During my childhood and the years of not knowing, I didn't envision very much of what my biological family was composed of, with one exception. I always thought that there might be a sister out there, somewhere. I don't know why that was, but the image never left me. It was something in the ether and now, suddenly, that image became reality.

My brother is seven years younger and my sister nine years younger. I began speaking with them on a regular basis. It was a different experience, unencumbered by language. What was familiar was the warmth and love. And the acceptance. We exchanged pictures and I saw that my sister looked very much like the "sister" I had imagined. The universe was playing its games again.

There are also moments when the universe's sense of humor is a bit darker.

My adoptive father had many health issues throughout much of his adult life. He faced them with courage and resolve. I don't believe I could have weathered those storms as gracefully as he did. Toward the end of his life his kidneys failed, and he required dialysis. Ultimately, this damaged his heart as well.

During the course of that February 1997 conversation with Eleni, as she was describing my birth father, she informed me that he was ill. She didn't know the term in English. In her words "he is on a machine that cleans his blood." Immediately, I knew. I knew exactly what she was referring to and I knew the insidious nature of that terrible disease. I grieved for the father whom I had lost, and for the father I now found who still suffered. Some parallels we can live without.

Nine months after that second conversation with Eleni, we were on a plane, once again, to meet biological family we'd never known. The experience of having lived through it once before did not dilute one iota of its wonderment and excitement the second time.

The occasion was the baptism of my sister's twin daughters. Also attending were my brother and his wife, as well as my father and his wife.

I had lamented to my sister, in the course of our many telephone conversations, that I didn't resemble anyone. Jokingly, at one point, I told her, "When you meet me, just say that it's like looking in a mirror." I promptly forgot about that statement. But when I finally met her, many months later, the very first thing she said was "Oh my God, it's like looking in a mirror!" She remembered. Such kindness.

My brother was also very loving. A tough, no-nonsense guy with a gigantic heart, who made me feel as if I was always there, always a part of their lives.

My father was a soft-spoken man, very quiet, but with a huge heart as well. He and his wife sat down with me and mine, and for several hours told us about his life, how he emigrated to the U.S., the experiences he had, and the trials he faced. He wanted us to know his path, to travel it with him as best we could, and I will be forever grateful for the chance to hear his story.

The support of my father's wife was indescribable. She embodied love and family. The relationships that subsequently formed and blossomed probably would not have, without her support, blessing, and encouragement.

And once more, incredibly, on the other side this time, more extended family.

A miracle again.

And yet…

You cannot rewrite history. You cannot produce a history that doesn't exist. Our travels through life are etched in stone. But there is beauty and peace in knowing. In having the questions finally answered. And if we are lucky, we both find ourselves having been raised amongst people who love us and then finding those with whom we share common blood. And if you find love there as well, you are blessed beyond.

June 2021: Postscript

Twenty-five years have passed since the *New York Times* article, the odyssey of newfound family, the "tornado of Greekness." Time has not diminished the magical quality of the entire experience. I still cannot fathom it. I don't think I ever will. I hope I never will.

So many wonderful experiences occurred after the initial meeting of my respective families. My twin and my adoptive mother began corresponding. In one of the many letters exchanged, he told my adoptive mother that he considered the day we were each adopted to be our real birthday. It was an incredible, thoughtful sentiment.

In another instance, my adoptive mother met my birth father's wife. They spent an afternoon comparing ailments, playing cards and just talking and being with each other. Beauty found in the simplest of things.

My birth mother is in communication often and never forgets birthdays and milestones. My siblings and their families occupy an enormous place in my heart. I was blessed with wonderful cousins in my adoptive family and have been blessed once again with so many incredible cousins in my biological family. I correspond with many of them and now with their children as well.

Also, there are the difficult moments that life brings. My birth father died quite a few years ago and I was a pallbearer at his funeral. I was both honored and sad. His wife, my stepmother, died recently and I was a pallbearer again. Again, a mix of emotions. The relationships between mother, siblings, in-laws, cousins, aunts, uncles, nieces and nephews spanning both sides of my "new" family continue with the ebb and flow normal to any family.

But the magic of it all remains.

It is a crime not to acknowledge the blessings bestowed, and so I remain filled with gratitude for all the facets of my life.

For my parents who took me in, raised me, poured everything they had into me and made me theirs. They didn't give me life but gave me a life. They, and all the families who took us in when we were helpless and homeless, are the real heroes. And for my adoptive extended family who never for a moment made me feel different.

For my wife and children who are everything. Simply everything.

For my newfound family that is now not so new, but still wondrous, with your open and accepting hearts, you are a gift that came at a time in life when I would never have anticipated the seismic shift to come.

A common desire I share with all the adoptees that I have met or communicated with is the need to know about our beginnings. Having parts of your past linger in uncertainty and speculation has a corrosive effect on the soul. When I began my own process, the main incentive was a need to, at last, know what happened. To know what took place when my fate was in the hands of others. Next, was the realization that I had no idea what kind of medical baggage I was handing off to my children, and, of course, that was unacceptable.

If I had not found answers, I know that I would have felt and lived with a hole. A bleak void of uncertainty as to who I was, down deep where we harbor our emotional DNA. To finally know, even before I met anyone, brought peace. What I realized was that my life had brought me to a wonderful place. I knew how the latter part of the book turned out and that made me realize that the beginning of the book couldn't hurt me. It was a blessing to know.

And second chances? True. *You cannot rewrite history.* But you can make new history and memories.

When I met my sister and brother, they had small children. My brother's children were very young, and my sister's children were infants. Now, twenty-five years later, my family and I have been a fixture in their lives for the vast majority of *their* lives. And some of them now have children of their own that we have been witness to. Such a blessing and a true second chance.

For those still searching, remember, family is large. If there aren't parents to be found, or siblings, there are very likely cousins and uncles and aunts. The truth is out there and it belongs to you. It is yours to be found, and the quest is truly worth it. Knowledge, even painful knowledge, is empowering.

For my brother and sister adoptees, my brothers and sisters in arms who still have not found the answers they so desperately need and deserve, remember, none of our happiness is complete until the journey is done. I am with you heart and soul. I feel your longing and stand shoulder to shoulder with you always.

For the miracle of finding peace and being gifted second chances, I am grateful.

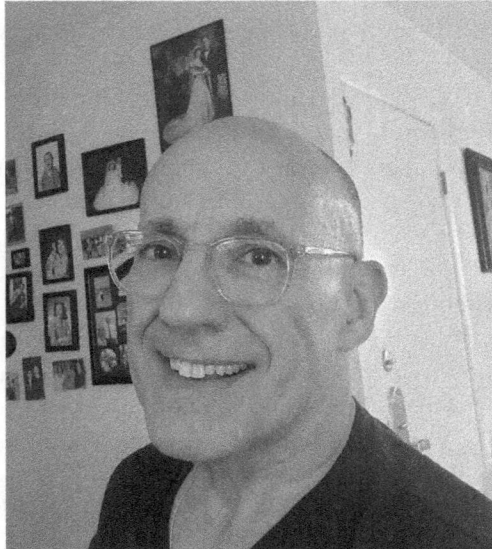

Chapter 5

QUESTIONS OF THE HEART

Panayiota/Paula/Charlie

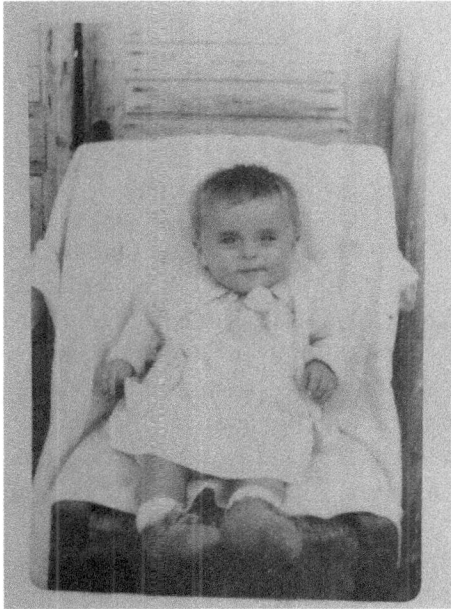

Too many lives. Too many stories. Not enough truth. A lifetime of silent tears. On some days it is completely overwhelming.

I was born in Methoni, Messinia, Greece, in 1955, the second daughter of Evangelia and Emmanuel Diktakis. It is a name well known in Crete for the celebrated Captain Emmanuel Diktakis, known for his bravery, his devotion to family, and love for his homeland. In an epic battle to lead a fight for Cretan land and birthright in 1840, he was slaughtered in the hills and beheaded. His legacy lives on in my birth father's name; he is my ancestor, and part of who I am.

I was not an orphan.

My birth father was in the Greek army, serving in the prefecture near Ioannina. My birth mother, Evangelia, was from a small village not far from there. Apparently, there were many suitors who might have shared a life with her, but she was paired with my birth father by her brother. He was the one who ultimately made a very important and personal decision *for her*. It was a *proxenia*, an arranged marriage. She had no choice in the matter, and so she left her family and returned to Methoni with her new husband.

I was born exactly 14 months after my sister, Sophia. As is traditional, because she was the first daughter, she was named after our father's mother. I was named for my adoptive mother's mother, which perhaps is also traditional. I wonder what name my birth parents would have given me. Certainly, I had a name in the first three months prior to my adoptive mother's arrival in Greece. It is so distressing that no one can tell me what it was.

I find it difficult to believe that Evangelia had six pregnancies after giving birth to me. Knowing this, I cannot even begin to understand the logic in giving me away. Again, I wonder what hold my adoptive mother's cousin, George, had over them. The story goes that George coerced my birth father, and that he, in turn, coerced my birth mother to give me away. Was her desire to give me a better life greater than the pain of relinquishing her child to a stranger? As a mother, I can only imagine the anguish and the persistent thoughts she must have had. Did she make the right decision? I was told that when I was taken from Greece at eight months old, my birth mother was despondent; she did not speak for an entire year and was sent home to Ioannina to heal with her family.

My birth mother finally accepted the pain of her decision and "recovered" from the trauma of having a child in her arms one day and the next realizing that her baby was half a world away. She returned to Methoni from her childhood village home. She began to speak again and she was soon pregnant with another child who would bring even more heartache. The baby was born a healthy infant, but the times being what they were, she died, somehow due to the negligence of the midwife. My birth mother was such a strong woman, and I have nothing but admiration for her resilience and indomitable spirit.

My adoptive mother met my father in high school, but their growing affection for each other was not looked upon kindly by my grandmother because he was Italian, not Greek. They were 22 years old when they were married in a Catholic church, without the blessing and benefit of my grandmother's presence, since she was so opposed to it. My mother was a self-admitted rebel, and she defied her own mother to marry the man that she loved. Ironically, though, my grandmother, once so opposed to the marriage, lived with my parents up until her death in 1946.

My adoptive father was one of five children, and grew up in the Italian section of Chicago. He was a good provider and caretaker, and I believe that is where he concentrated his efforts, while letting my mother do what she did best. For me, he was always and ever my champion, my rock, my support, my refuge. I do know that he trusted my mother's decision-making. She wanted to adopt from Greece and he agreed. I wonder what my beloved adoptive father was really thinking throughout the process.

They decided to pursue an international adoption when they were 40 years old and it certainly was not easy in those days. In the U.S., it would have been difficult because of their ages, I imagine. Somehow, an arrangement was made by George Topouzis, my adoptive mother's first cousin, who was a general in the Greek army. He had homes in Athens and Methoni. In his village home, he arranged for my biological mother, Evangelia, who was pregnant with me, to cook meals for him. And so, the pathway unfolded leading to my adoption.

My adoptive mother, Martha, said that she had many choices when she arrived in Greece to find a baby. She said that she had visited several orphanages in the country and was heartbroken that so many children needed homes. Many would come up to her begging her to take them with her. My adoptive mother always told me that she "wanted to do some good in the world." Was my adoption part of that quest?

In the end, my mother went to the connection that linked her to my birth mother, which was through her cousin. A deal was struck, I suppose, and there were promises made. Martha said she would keep me in touch with and connected to my birth family, which is a vow she kept. I was taken from Greece and from the arms of one family by a stranger who would become my mother. Off we went on a flight to Chicago and a waiting new father.

Who was at the airport to greet me upon my arrival in Chicago? No one has ever told me. Other adoptees have photos of their arrival with excited new family members clamoring around in greeting. I have none. In that era, perhaps society was not so enamored with the concept of preserving every little detail in the form of a photo, as we do today, but it is a bit disheartening to know that I have nothing to help me formulate a memory.

In 1960, my birth parents made the decision to emigrate, bound for a new life in Canada. Relatives of theirs had already made the trek and settled in Montreal. They had an apartment and were employed in the city. What prompted my birth family to leave everything they had ever known, to go to a place so foreign? There was plenty of open land in Canada and opportunity, but they would live in the ethnic ghetto in the inner city of Montreal, sharing the apartment with my birth father's half siblings. It was in November that they arrived by ship, coming through the port of Halifax. How does one gather the strength to follow this path? My birth mother traveled even farther away from her family members in Ioannina, and only saw them once more in her lifetime. Such sacrifice. I have only respect for her. And sadness.

I always wondered: knowing I was in Chicago, why didn't my birth family move closer to me, instead of to Canada? I suppose it is because my birth father had half siblings there and they didn't realize how far Montreal is from Chicago. I do have one precious photo of what I believe to be my birth father's entire family, lined up on the pier in Greece, posing for a farewell memory. The faces of my birth parents and siblings reveal it all. Fear, trepidation, reticence; nothing in their expressions appeared to reveal any joy or anticipation for the journey and new life ahead.

I was almost six years old when my birth family arrived in North America and only a week after their journey, my Mom announced that we were going to Montreal. "Why?" I asked. "To visit your sister." "My sister?" Eyes wide open in incredulity. "I have a sister?" "Yes," she said.

I do remember the flight, a taxi ride, and an arrival at a second-floor apartment in the heart of a very old and crowded city. There was a girl about my age looking at me curiously as we entered through the door. She was my sister, Sophia. And I had two brothers as well: Angelo and the baby, Foti. And there were my sister's parents, my parents. My birth mother was so emotional. She kept kissing me, hugging me, stroking my blond hair. I was not used to so much unabashed expressions of affection. This woman, our mother, could not stop crying. My birth father did not say much. He just sat smiling and nodding as he witnessed the unfolding scene.

My adoptive mother did, indeed, keep her promise to remain in contact with my birth family. After my first visit to Canada to meet them, there were other visits. My adoptive mother brought Sophia to stay with us for a month each summer in our childhood years, to give her a break from responsibility and the ghetto. Sophia would fly to us and we would drive her back to Montreal when the month was up. We would stay there for a week to spend time with them before heading back to the Chicago area for the beginning of the school year. We would always stay in a motel near the airport, since the ghetto apartment was so small.

Sophia tells me that she enjoyed her visits with us so much because my father, Charles, was more of a father to her in the brief times she was with us in those summers than her own father, Emmanuel, had ever been. Eventually, after having three more daughters in Montreal, my birth parents divorced and married other people. Sophia took care of all of our younger siblings; I used to call her the second mother. There were five in all to care for while our birth parents worked nights. She attended school during the day and then was expected to cook, clean, and care for the children, and to keep rats off of them as they slept. My heart breaks for her lost childhood.

As for me, I just wanted to be loved, to fill the void that I carried around all my life, every day of my life. Four parents. Two families. Nothing seemed to fill it. My adoptive mother always said that my birth parents were too poor to keep me and they wanted me to have "a better life." Knowing what I know now, this is not necessarily true. But what better life could there have been than living just steps from the junction of the Mediterranean and Ionian Seas, amidst all of that beauty and promise for beautiful tomorrows? To know that I am a part of the grand history of Greece, the birthplace of democracy. To have descended from a brave warrior who would defend his homeland to the death, against invaders intent on killing, stealing and conquering. There were some feeble attempts on my part to talk about this, but I was met with ambivalence and disinterest, so I internalized and buried the questions and the heartache that I couldn't quite explain to anyone.

I think about my two fathers. The one who was responsible for my birth was never home, so he barely knew his children and they didn't know him. They received no direction from him or advice that one needs from their father about becoming an adult. My adoptive father worked so hard to provide for our little family, and he spent whatever time he could with me. For this and all that he did, I knew how much he loved me.

It is sad that I never really knew either of my mothers. One could not be part of my life due to distance and circumstance. The other was blinded by her own goals for me, not taking into consideration my thoughts or my own aspirations. Throughout my life, she made every decision for me. There were some good, happy moments, but the most important decisions were colored by the conflict of what each of us wanted for me.

Long ago, while studying at the dental school on Marquette University's campus, I met the one great love of my life, that soul mate whom everyone hopes and prays one day to find. My mother made things very difficult from the beginning, doing everything in her power to keep the inevitable from happening. That only made me cling more desperately to the prospect of marrying someone, the only one, who had ever come close to filling the void, completing the missing pieces of my soul. But I was not strong enough to fight her. I knew in my heart of hearts that no marriage would survive my adoptive mother. I believe, truly, that my adoptive mother was afraid that if I married someone who would take me away from all I had ever known with them, that there would be no one to take care of them in their old age. With nowhere to turn, and as the dutiful daughter who was always grateful for being "saved" from a life of difficulty and hardship in Greece, I acquiesced to her wishes and broke my engagement. It broke my heart. I was inconsolable, missing my young Navy pilot-to-be. I was fractured; heart, soul, and spirit. Looking back at it now, it was not unlike the equally painful sacrifices of my (adoptive) grandmother, Panayiota, and my birth mother, Evangelia, who were picture-perfect Greek brides after denying so much of themselves. In this way, we were connected across the generations.

My broken engagement would prompt me to further question the tenuous relationship I had cultivated with my adoptive mother over the years. I never really achieved a close bond with her. I guess it was very difficult for me to forgive her.

I did marry seven years later and the marriage was full of strife, and it was further imposed upon by my caregiving responsibilities for my parents and godmother. The added stress depleted the time I could devote to keeping up a relationship with my birth family. As I approached forty, like my adoptive mother before me, it seemed worthwhile to, perhaps, try to have a child. I thought that a child could possibly, again, fill a void. At least that is what I believed and desperately hoped for.

I had a long career as a clinician. When my full-time faculty position ended, my thoughts turned to what my life might be like in old age without grandchildren to fill my heart and days. Wholeheartedly I threw myself into my work and family responsibilities as wife and caregiver. I had pushed away my feelings about the loss of my biological family and homeland. I valiantly tried to forget the heartache of living without the young man I once had planned to spend my life with. Wasn't it time then to take care of me? A child would bring a new feeling of belonging to my life. A child would fill the void, dispel the feelings of loneliness and loss, and bring hope for the future. That is what I wanted.

A few months short of my fortieth birthday, my daughter was born. We named her Martha, after her maternal grandmother, my adoptive mother, in the Greek tradition. No child was more loved or wanted. When she was old enough to comprehend, I explained to her that she was so unique, because she had eight grandparents who loved her. My husband's parents, my adoptive parents, and my birth parents, and their respective second spouses.

Sadly, though, everything, all of it, was too much for my marriage. My husband was always angry, as my birth father always was toward my birth mother. I believe that, perhaps, he wanted me to be more present for him, but my heart was pulled in too many directions. I had far too many obligations. So, again, circumstances compelled me to do what I never had expected to do, but make the difficult decision to seek a divorce. It was for the best. My heart was too tender.

Other adoptees long for a family that they do not know. I had two families, and yet, still longed for just one that would fill the emptiness of the persistent and perpetual detachment I felt.

At my lowest point, I wondered why I was not worthy of having a family. I have a birth family that I have known since I was six years old. But, except for my birth mother and a sister or two, I feel ambivalence from the rest. I have an adoptive family, but the parents who raised me died many years ago, and my cousins have their own children, their own lives, and are far flung all over the states, so no real closeness has developed there. I had my own family, but now am divorced and single, and my daughter is ready to step off into her own life, planning to be married when the pandemic restrictions fully lift. I could never and would never hold her to the expectations that my adoptive mother had for me in terms of family obligations, because I know how standards set that high can interfere with one's own plans and life. In the depths of my despair, I wonder over and over again what I might have done to warrant a life alone, in solitude with my thoughts and ever-present questions.

All of my life, I never felt as if I fit in anywhere. I lacked the ability to cultivate my own identity. I felt out of place and awkward. I didn't know that I possessed the ability and the power to make decisions for myself. I didn't understand that I had the potential to soar beyond my adoptive mother's sights for me and to attain the life I wanted.

No one in my adoptive family really did anything "wrong" to make me feel the depth of my loss. I think that they were just unaware of what adoption could do to one's soul, and they believed I would naturally assimilate into American life. For the most part, I suppose I have, but every single time I see images of Greece, something inside of me responds to the call of my homeland. It is not esoteric fluff, speculation, or fantasy. One day, before it is too late, I know that I will have to return to the land of my birth.

I do speak with my birth mother every Sunday night on the telephone. She is in her 90s now. She cries when she hears my voice and she tells me that she loves me very much, both in Greek and in English. She calls me *agapi mou*, my love, *psihi mou*, my soul, *chriso mou*, my dear one. I know the pain she has endured. Given the pandemic, it is difficult to travel to Montreal to be with her. At her advanced age this is distressing. I often wonder what it would have been like to be raised by her. Would it be different? More emotional? Would I have felt more connected? Would I have the same sense of obligation that I had toward my adoptive parents? I will never know. However, I do feel all the richer for, at least, having known both sets of parents. Each contributed to my unique footprint on this earth.

If there is a reason for all that has happened in my life, it is unknown to me. Was I supposed to be in a certain place at a certain time in order to have an effect on someone's life? Was I supposed to learn any particular lesson? Teach one? Only God knows.

I have so many unanswered questions, but I have to move forward, one foot in front of the other, and trust that there has to be a reason for me to be here in this place and at this time. I do finally accept that I am enough, and that is progress for my own personal development. Perhaps I should absolve myself of all the worry and guilt I've carried over the years and throw aside the feelings of detachment generated by natural siblings and adoptive family members who have been ambivalent about my journey and what it has meant to me.

I do see a light ahead. I am dreaming of Greece, my homeland. I know that someday I will return. And when I do, I know I will cry; both to mourn what I have lost, and for being able to, finally, come back home and embrace what can be.

Chapter 6

THE SECRET

Pavlaki/David

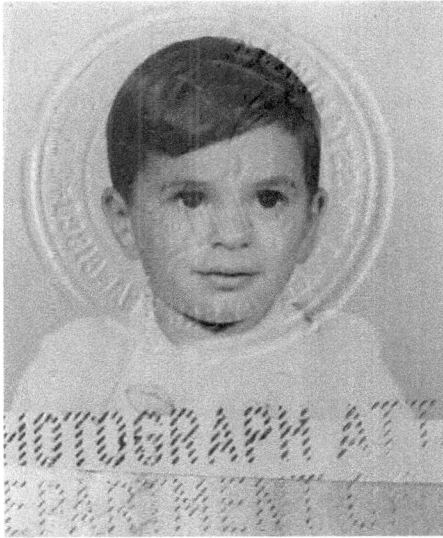

"My sweet boy, my beloved child, my good boy, I would have liked to be keeping you in my arms till I die, to have you near me from the moment you were born, to warm your sensitive heart with my love and affection, but fate was really hard to me and the morals of our country cruel and inhumane. I gave your life from my life and flesh from my flesh, but I lost you, my child, right from the moment you were born, and only great unspoken and incurable pain was left to me. Now that you are a man, I can open my heart to you."

—Athens, January 18, 1984

This is the first paragraph of the first letter that my biological mother, Maria, wrote to me after my wife and I located her in June of 1983. It is so beautiful. I was ecstatic and humbled at the same time by her words.

I always believed my biological mother must have been a good person, and this verified my deepest intuition about her.

Maria speaks no English, and I don't speak any Greek, so Billy Maganiotou, the administrator of the Babies Center Mitera in Athens, translated this letter into English and sent it with the original in Greek. Billy Maganiotou was the administrator who worked with my adoptive parents when they first laid eyes on me on Christmas Eve, 1957. Billy knew quite a bit about me, because my mother, Jean, consistently sent updates as I grew up; about my personality, and about my accomplishments throughout my life.

The second and third paragraphs of the same letter:

"Thirty years ago, a very young girl, almost a child in mind, soul and body, left her village and came to the jungle called Athens. She wanted to work to make a dowry for herself, to make a better living than in the village, where, in those years, life was very poor and difficult. Because of her young age and innocence, she could not understand the dangers around her. She came to Athens and was hired by a family as a housemaid. She was very unhappy, she missed her family, cried a lot, but she kept her work patiently and time went by. She grew up, became a young woman very efficient in her work, and kind. She had beautiful long hair, and the freshness of the village in her face. She was innocent. Maybe all these moved or stimulated her employer, who started to be a nuisance, and so the young girl without even losing her virginity or knowing what exactly was happening to her, she found herself with a baby."

This story, my story is really about my Greek mother Maria, not me. I merely filled in the blanks and answered the questions she had about my life from 1957 to 1983. We led parallel lives, lines that didn't touch until we found each other again. Maria's life was about endurance. She coped with (unknowingly) becoming pregnant against her will at 16, her first child taken from her against her will. She lived with the loss for 25 years, and kept the story a secret for 32 years after our initial contact. Then, finally, she revealed everything to her two younger children, her siblings, relatives and friends, which lifted a very heavy burden from her shoulders.

My biological mother, Maria, was born on Oxi Day, October 28, 1940, in Koronos, Naxos. It was the day when the Greeks refused to let the Italian Army, Mussolini's army, ram its way through Greece.

When the Nazis arrived in Naxos, Maria's father moved the family to the abandoned village of Sifones, the heart and near center of the island. They lived in a small stone house, backed up against a granite wall, with a natural spring running parallel to the pathway that extended the length of the village. Below Sifones was a small, fertile valley where the family raised their food and cared for their goats. Maria's father buried goat meat, covered with salt, in case the Nazis discovered them and confiscated all their food, as was the practice.

In Koronos, over 400 Greeks starved to death during the war years, yet Maria's family survived due to her parents' decision to hide in Sifones. The family eventually moved back to Koronos, where the local elementary school was located, but Maria was only allowed to complete the 6th grade. Her father needed help running the Sifones farm, and only one child was allowed to continue school through the 12th grade, located in the capital, Naxos City, or Chora. Greece continued to suffer, and when Maria became a young teen, she moved to Athens and worked as a live-in maid for a wealthy family. This was not unusual for young women of the time.

Growing up, I always knew I was adopted, and enjoyed this fact, considering myself rather unique. I credit my parents, who realized the value of taking this approach. Plus, everyone else in the family is a blonde or redhead, so it may have been obvious anyway.

Prior to adopting, my parents, Jean and Quentin, were teachers for the Department of Defense, who lived in points all over the world before moving back to the United States. Jean, my adoptive mother, had suffered a miscarriage, resulting from an illness while attending Cal Berkeley. When my parents transferred from Turkey to Spain, they made the decision to adopt. They discovered it would not be possible for them to adopt in Spain, because they were not Roman Catholic, but did hear of a new orphanage opened by Queen Frederica, the Baby Center Mitera (mitera means mother in Greek) in Athens. It was a very modern facility at the time.

Jean and Q (Quentin) flew to Athens, and on Christmas Eve, 1957, toured Mitera. After viewing all the babies, they met with Billy Maganiotou, and were asked if they found the baby they wanted. My mother informed Billy that they had (she always told me I chose them), and by the end of February, took me home to Jerez de la Frontera, Spain. The only request from Billy was to inform the administration when I was baptized, so that my name could be officially documented by Mitera. The nurses at Mitera called me *Pavlaki*, little Paul. Years later, when visiting Mitera, I discovered I was cared for in the green room, which happens to be my favorite color.

My parents taught school in Spain and Morocco for the next five years. Three years after my adoption, Jean and Q returned to the Baby Center Mitera to adopt a second child. They chose a baby boy who was in the same room and crib where they found me. Billy Maganiotou asked Jean if she was sure about adopting again, since, she told her, my mother was pregnant. My mother looked at her quizzically and said she was not pregnant. But Billy informed her that when she touched her arm, she could detect a pregnancy by the softness of her skin. Sure enough, Jean was pregnant! They adopted my brother anyway. Nine months later my mother delivered a baby girl. My parents consistently retold the story of our adoptions and Billy detecting my mother's pregnancy. I never felt any different as an adoptee, and actually enjoyed hearing and telling my friends the story.

In 1963, we moved to Crane, Oregon. We helped my paternal grandparents raise Black Angus cattle, repair and build barbed wire fencing, grow and bail alfalfa. We went out to shoot ground squirrels and to go fly-fishing at every opportunity. I learned to drive a tractor at the age of five and, within a few years, was driving the car to the outskirts of the alfalfa field to hunt squirrels. My grandparents kept a cast iron stove in the house for cooking and heating in winter, and the bathroom was a double-seater outhouse. My dad was the Crane School District principal and I attended a K-8, one-room elementary school. One of the most vivid memories in that school year was the assassination of President John F. Kennedy. Every student was sent home, and I remember my mom being more upset than I had ever seen her before.

The following year we moved to Le Grand, California, where Quentin was hired as an elementary school principal. We lived out in the country, with a dog, cats, chickens, a couple of steers, and a horse named Buck. My parents had two more children, both boys. We lived in Le Grand for seven years. Every summer we traveled to eastern Oregon to help grandpa with the cattle, bailing and stacking hay, and repairing barbed wire fences. After work on the farm, we would travel throughout north America, and up into Canada, seeking the best fly-fishing streams before returning home in time for school.

In 1971, my dad was hired as Superintendent of Parlier Unified School District, twenty minutes south of Fresno, California. We moved after my 8th grade graduation. I had been the student body president, so I was able to read my farewell speech to my friends before departing. We lived south of Parlier, then moved to a home on twenty acres, south of Reedley, California. I attended Reedley High, where I graduated in 1975. When I attended Reedley Junior College, my dad informed us he had been hired as a Superintendent near Stockton, California. I was 18 years old, and informed my parents I would be staying in Reedley. I've been on my own ever since.

While at Reedley, I met Doreen. She caught my eye one day during registration. I introduced myself, and we began meeting each morning in the cafeteria. We dated for a year and half before getting married in 1979, in the Sierra Nevada mountains, a few miles from the entrance to Yosemite.

Doreen was intelligent, beautiful, and adventurous. She was one of the first female firefighters in the area for the Department of Forestry. She set goals and nothing prevented her from meeting them. Doreen was very interested in my adoption story, and we began to plan a trip to search for my biological family. While attending Fresno State, both of us worked while attending college, sometimes two jobs. We saved enough money to begin planning a five-week trip to Europe.

Our adventure began in Spain, visiting the village of Cabra, where Doreen's grandparents were from. We traveled through France and Italy, and we devoted the last two weeks to searching for my roots in Greece. We had no idea what to expect.

Prior to our trip, I had written to Queen Sofia of Spain, who was the daughter of Queen Frederica of Greece, and I told her my story. Queen Sofia had been a volunteer at the Baby Center Mitera as a teenager around the time I was born. I requested a meeting, since we planned on beginning our trip in Spain. We received a reply, and the Queen, while very supportive, was unable to meet with us.

We landed in Madrid and headed out to Jerez de la Frontera to look for friends of my California-based parents, but with no luck. After three days of touring, we caught the train and continued our journey through Spain, France, and Italy, before departing by ferryboat from Brindisi, Italy, to Patras, Greece. It was time to begin my search.

Doreen and I had some unexpected help in locating my biological mother, Maria. My mom's sister married a man whose parents were from the Peloponnese and had settled in San Francisco. James Plessas is my favorite Uncle Jim! He was very excited when my parents adopted me, and when I became a naturalized citizen, he was my sponsor. Uncle Jim and his family have traveled to Greece many times to visit the village his parents were from, and he has kept in touch with his relatives. He contacted a cousin in Athens, we arranged a visit at their home, and gave them copies of my papers. The Plessas relatives were instrumental in my search for Maria.

As one of them was making copies of my documents at the bank where she was employed, a coworker noticed my mother's name. The coworker said she knew someone by that name. They made contact, but the woman was too young to be my mother; however, this woman knew of another woman with the same name, who was my mother, Maria.

The cousin contacted Billy Maganiotou at Mitera, and from there, made contact with Maria. As this was happening, Doreen and I were looking elsewhere for Maria while exploring other parts of Greece. Billy Maganiotou reached us and informed us that Maria was from the island of Naxos. Immediately, Doreen and I caught a ferryboat and made the eight-hour journey.

Upon arriving, we found a local hotel near Agios Prokopios beach, which in 1983 consisted of only a couple hotels. One of the women working at the hotel told me that I looked like a Naxiotis, a man from Naxos! This was uncanny and would occur each time we visited, with most residents having not only the ability to identify me as a Naxiotis, but also able to pinpoint the village of my roots!

The next morning, we headed into the main town, Chora, and noticed a man with very long hair, working earnestly. His name was Lalos and he spoke English. His life goal was to build a hotel and restaurant because his prediction was that the tourist industry would boom one day on the island. (He got that right!) Lalos listened to our story, told us to visit the village of Moni, and find the priest. We rented a moped and to Moni we motored.

Moni is a tiny, one street village. I parked the moped, and we began to walk. Within a minute we noticed a very tall Greek Orthodox priest headed in our direction. He spoke no English. I figured if he heard Maria's full name, and if I could communicate that she was my mother, he would somehow figure it out. The priest listened, looked at the name I had written, pointed to the east, and told us to go to Koronos. We thanked him, and traveled along a beautiful, one-lane road, which wound through the hills toward the east side of the island, as we occasionally yielded to herds of goats nonchalantly crossing the road.

Koronos is a very small, whitewashed town of a few hundred people, on a very steep incline, with a stream running through the center. There are approximately 22,000 steps in the village, and for the most part you are consistently walking up or downhill. In the center of the town was a Greek Orthodox Church. Doreen walked down what seemed to be a major walkway, until we encountered a couple of local people. I began asking questions, using Maria's name, but no one spoke English. We drew quite a crowd, but were unable to get any information at all. We decided to return to Athens and the Mitera orphanage.

Billy Maganiotou was very concerned that we had traveled to Naxos. She said Maria would be very stressed if she knew we were searching for her in the small village of Koronos. I explained that we had limited time and wanted to move on every lead. Billy then revealed that she knew how to contact Maria, with the help of the Plessas cousins, but that it would take time, and told us we should continue to explore Greece. Doreen and I did just that. We traveled to Delphi, Nafpaktos, and then headed out by train to Mount Olympus. We even hiked to the top to visit the Gods. It was magical, all of it, but now we had only a day left before departing for the United States when news came from Billy.

She had contacted Maria, but Maria could not leave the house because she was caring for both of her bedridden parents and her two toddlers, one girl and one boy. By the time Maria was able to call the orphanage to try to arrange a meeting, Doreen and I were headed back to California. We left our address with Billy, who would help translate any correspondence from Maria into English.

Maria and I corresponded for the next six years and sent numerous photos to each other. Several generous individuals in Fresno translated my letters into Greek, and Maria's letters into English. Maria was unable to get the letters translated for herself because it was difficult for her to get out of the house, raising two toddlers, Vasiliki and Michalis, while simultaneously taking care of her ill and aging parents, Emmanuel and Kalliopi. I knew and understood that I was still a secret. The only people who knew about me were Maria's husband, Yannis, and her sister, Marina.

Doreen and I began planning our next trip. In the meantime, we continued to receive beautiful letters from Maria, including this excerpt from one of them:

"Your letter gave me great joy. I feel a secret pride within me that you indeed are a good boy. You have I sense many soulful (psychic) characteristics which has touched me very much. I am pleased to hear that you are contented in your life. I feel rest assured that the foundation screened people thoroughly and places them (children) to god-loving Christians, with that thought in mind, was my only consolation throughout the years. I remember seeing your parents at the time of the adoption. I saw them both from a small distance behind the drawing room of the court. I watched them and felt the desire to run near them, to fall at their feet, to beg them to watch over my child. I have had many meditations and many recollections, my son, and despair from the people throughout my life. I have been crushed spiritually and physically. But I was always comforted with a feeling, a premonition, one secret hope within me that one day you might seek me or I would seek you. I had the fear that you might never be told that you were adopted. You were only a few days old at the time, and I thought that they would never reveal it. Years ago, I gave thought to investigate, only my prayers gave me comfort that this might come to pass. I had that premonition that one day my son would try to find me, and you did. I am happy that you also have brothers and a sister. Your parents should be recognized as saints by our Lord. In my mind and heart, they appear to have been chosen by Him, as good Christians. I beg you to kiss them both for me and tell them that for the rest of my living days I shall never forget them. Thank them, on my behalf for taking such good care of you."

Maria always revealed her thoughts, emotions, and the difficulties she experienced having to give me up for adoption. She told me she thought about me every day, wondering what became of me, what would become of her. She was elated that my wife and I were determined to find her.

In August of 1989, Doreen and I, with two of our friends, landed at the Athens airport. With Maria's address in hand, after trying to hail numerous taxis, none of the drivers knowing the address, a man driving a small green pickup, with benches in the covered bed, said he knew where we wanted to go. It was hot that summer, but the ride was so memorable, even though we found ourselves stuffed in the back of the truck with our luggage. After all, for me, this was a ride that would change my life!

We rode through Athens, and suddenly made a right turn up an extremely steep and narrow street, which reminded me of San Francisco. As we crossed the intersection, I looked out the back window and recognized (from pictures) a short man and woman standing in front of a house. We pounded on the back window of the pickup and told the driver to stop. We piled out of the truck, and unloaded the luggage.

There was Maria, my mother, this woman I had only known from photos and her beautiful letters. We quickly walked toward each other. I cannot describe the beautiful expression on her face. We hugged and hugged tightly, not being able to let go, feeling true love and joy. I felt so happy and was happy *for her*. She hadn't laid eyes on her firstborn since giving birth 25 years ago. She couldn't stop hugging me, kissing me, touching my face, crying tears of joy. Maria then hugged and kissed my wife, as our friends snapped pictures. We went inside, Maria showed us our rooms and we sat down at the dining room table.

Despite not understanding each other's language, we managed to somehow communicate. At one point, nine-year-old Vasiliki walked into the room with a tray of ice cold, tall beers. Everyone popped one open, even the children! Maria started bringing in a fantastic meal, with multiple courses, all prepared in her small kitchen, on a portable two-burner cooker. The food was delicious and it kept coming. I would learn (decades later) that Maria was trained as a chef/caterer.

We had a wonderful time, laughing and talking, even though we could not understand each other. Maria drew me aside at one point and handed me a photograph. The photo was of a wedding party. Maria was in the photo, kneeling, near the bridegroom with members of the family standing behind her. She pointed to a man in the photo and said, "your father." I still have that photo, of course.

The next day we departed with our friends to tour more of Greece, then returned for a second visit with Maria and her family. The second visit was as wonderful as the first and, of course, Maria would often cradle my face in her hands as she grinned from ear to ear. I left Maria, promising to continue our correspondence. It was important to her and to me.

"You gave me great happiness with your coming to Greece. You made me live unforgettable moments. Looking at you feeling proud about my child, my young man whom I was deprived a lifetime. Looking at you I relived all my life and the events that took place during that time, all my thoughts, and all my prayers for this day to come and hold you in my arms once more. The Almighty had mercy on us. I had to keep everything inside me, my thoughts, my expectations, my hardships,

without being able to talk to anyone my whole life. I thank you for everything. I know that it was a hardship and sacrifice for you and Doreen to make the trip. I felt dizzy and disoriented during your stay here. The day you were coming my anxiety and my emotions overpowered me. I was sitting in the armchair and I didn't have the power to stand on my feet and do what I had to do. A long time passed after you left in order for me to get my feelings together and to come to the realization that your coming here and the time we spent together was not a dream, it really happened. Also, David, my happiness is great because, although we didn't live together, your character is very similar to mine. Doreen is in my heart and I love her like I love you. I am very contented and satisfied that you have such a good partner. I wish you to always be happy and always love one another."

—From Maria, 1989

Upon returning to California, I started my new job, teaching high school history. A couple of years later we started our family. Our correspondence with Maria tapered off a bit, with most of our letters and packages sent during Christmas, or when something of major interest occurred. We had two daughters and, as they grew, we began to plan another trip to Greece. We wanted them to be old enough to appreciate the sights, and absorb the situation with my family there.

My parents, very understanding of my interest in discovering my roots, and finding my biological family, supported my endeavor. Yet, at the beginning of my search I could tell they were somewhat hurt. I reassured them of my love for them, but had a need to discover my personal history, discover whether or not my personality matched those I would find, and to see who I looked like. They seemed to understand, and loved the stories and photos I shared. I was also able to share with Maria how my parents felt.

I told my parents that Maria had seen them at a distance at the orphanage after the adoption was finalized. She said she wanted to run to them and throw herself at their feet to thank them for their commitment to raise me. My parents greatly appreciated these stories, especially that one.

In July of 2001, my father passed away. He was a fantastic man, who taught me how to work hard and play hard. We were very close. After his death, my mother happened to watch the movie *Philomena*, about a woman in Ireland who had given up her child for adoption. This movie helped my mom gain a complete understanding of my need to discover my roots, and Maria's desperation to find out what became of her child.

In 2005 we returned to Athens to visit Maria so she could meet our daughters, her only grandchildren. Michalis and Vasiliki were now in their 20s. We were met at the airport by Maria and Michalis. Maria could not stop kissing and hugging my daughters on the ride home. Yannis, Maria's husband, welcomed us with open arms. That night, while eating dinner, Maria hung on to Spenser and Hunter, stroking and hugging them as we ate. I wondered what Michalis thought of these strangers receiving all of Maria's attention that night. They still had no idea who I was to them. We were friends and visitors. Friends of friends. We all kept Maria's secret.

Of course, I wanted my daughters to visit Naxos, so we headed out for an adventurous journey that also included numerous other stops. While in Naxos, though, Vasiliki came to meet us and we had dinner together in one of the many outdoor cafes. Vasiliki's cousin was our waiter, and he commented that my daughters and I looked Greek. To this day I am astounded that Vasiliki and Michalis did not figure out the connection by our physical appearance alone.

For several more years we continued to communicate with Maria, through written correspondence, usually during the holidays. When Facebook came into vogue, we all became Facebook friends, sending pictures of all major events, and yet my Greek brother and sister still did not realize the connection. I had no idea when Maria intended on revealing the secret, if at all. But I was not going to pressure her, or reveal it on my own. It was not my place.

Maria had kept the secret her entire life, sharing it only with one sister and her husband. She had experienced a lifetime of intense emotional ups and downs, and I resolved to leave the decision to her. I was concerned, though, that if she did not tell her children the secret, I would have a hard time later convincing them of our relationship. Also, I was not aware that her older sister knew the story and was her confidante during the adoption process. I knew nothing about Maria's other siblings, how many there were, or their ages. But then something happened on Facebook that prompted the secret to be revealed.

In 2015, Vasiliki was viewing bridal gowns on Facebook, and posted a picture of one in particular. My wife, Doreen, owns a bridal shop, and sent Vasiliki a message, saying that when the time came, we would like to give her a wedding gown as a gift. Vasiliki lived with Maria. (Yannis had passed away several years prior.) Vasiliki told Maria about Doreen's message, and asked why these people in California would offer such a generous gift. Maria began to weep. Finally, she looked at her and said, "David is my son." Vasiliki's mouth dropped open and the room began to spin. She grabbed her mobile phone and called Michalis, who was already in his car, on his way over for dinner. She told him she had very important news, and to pull over. Michalis asked, "Did we win the lottery?" No, she said, but "Michalis, we are not two, but three." Soon after, I received this message from Vasiliki:

"My mother told me, or should I say our mother? Doreen's wedding dress made a huge difference! I'm not only happy, I'm thrilled! Please come and visit us so we

can talk like a family. I can only imagine your life. Please come and spend at least a summer with us. Our mother is getting old and to travel such a long journey. My warmest kisses and hugs to all! Give Doreen a big kiss from me. She gave me today a brother."

In November 2015, Vasiliki informed us that she wanted to visit us immediately. She arrived in Fresno late in the evening, the night before the last day of my school semester, which was a few days before Christmas. Doreen, my daughter Hunter, and I met Vasiliki at the airport, drove her home, and stayed up late into the night, enjoying each other's company, like old friends. Doreen and I had to work the next day, so Hunter spent the entire day with Vasiliki, and they hit it off, becoming very close friends. Soon Vasiliki became Vicki!

For two weeks we traveled the state, including the national parks, major cities, and Vicki's two most desirable destinations, San Francisco and Disneyland! We also got together with my mom and my sister's family for Christmas dinner. My mom was very happy and thought the entire reunion was nothing short of a miracle.

By this time, DNA tests were in full swing. My wife had completed a few family trees, and my immediate family had already received our results. I asked Vicki if she was interested in submitting a sample, and she was very excited to do so. Vicki thought it was hilarious when I said I wanted her to take a DNA test to prove she was really who she said she was.

The following year, I traveled to Greece alone, to stay with Maria, Vasiliki, and Michalis, and to be introduced as Maria's son to family and friends. The very first day relatives began arriving one at a time, grabbing my head with their hands and kissing me on both cheeks, multiple times. Maria's younger brother, older sister, and nephew arrived to see me in the first couple of hours. Her sister sat down in the living room, and with Vasiliki translating, proceeded to share information about my biological father.

His name was Konstantinos Kourmouzas, and he was from a Greek village in northern Turkey, called Renkioi, which is now known as Erenkoy, on the Dardanelles, six miles north of ancient Troy. The family was forced to leave during World War I. He was married and had one daughter.

Maria was the live-in maid for the Kourmouzas family, and when Konstantinos' daughter was married, Maria became part of the dowry. Despite what he did to her, both Maria and her sister described him as a kind man, who had personal problems. It was unclear what he did for a living, but I was told there were no family members alive. Maria never told her oldest brother that she had become pregnant, because, she said, he would have shot and killed her. I was shocked to hear that, considering I had just met a few of her very nice and pleasant siblings earlier that day. Throughout the day I continued to meet cousins. We all looked so very much alike!

In Koronos, we visited Maria's favorite uncle on her mother's side, who was 89 years old. We sat in his modest, tidy living room and she told him the secret for the first time. He was surprised, and just stared at me when Maria finished. He got up, slowly walked toward me, and put his hands on each side of my face, said something in Greek, and kissed me on each cheek. It was very emotional for everyone, especially for Maria. He passed away a year later.

Together, we also visited Komiaki, only a few miles away, a bit higher in elevation, where Maria's husband, Yannis, spent his childhood. The most moving visit, though, was to the abandoned stone village of Sifones, where Maria's family hid from the Nazis during WWII.

At one time, Sifones was an important meeting place for village leaders due to its central location on Naxos. The number on Maria's house, the address, was number 17. (My number in all the sports I had played as a child and young man was 17.)

We walked into a large room, which included a large fireplace, oven, and bed. A storeroom in the back contained numerous large clay pottery pieces used for the storage of food and wine. Maria explained how her mother would bake bread, and how she would sleep with her head on her father's chest, feeling warm and safe there. Immediately outside the house was a trough for stomping grapes, which would drain into large clay pots for the fermentation of wine. She described working in the fields, playing games they invented using the kneecaps of slaughtered goats. Her mother worked in the small fertile valley and gave birth to Maria's brother, soon returning for the difficult work on the harvest. Maria would babysit her infant brother, and her mother would take breaks to breastfeed him throughout her workday. She said her mother was the first vegetarian, because she could not bear to eat their own chickens and livestock. Near the flowing spring water was a large rock where the clothes were washed, and a few steps away was the fig tree under which the family met and talked. Maria's parents not only saved the lives of the entire family by hiding in this abandoned village, they provided a small paradise in the midst of war and the threat of discovery by the Nazis. Visiting this place was one of the most impactful experiences of my life.

I returned home with great memories and stories. A couple of months later, my brother Michalis (Michael) would come to visit us in California. We took him to San Francisco to visit my Uncle Jim, Aunt Eleanor, and two of their four children. My favorite Greek Uncle Jim, who had married my aunt, was very excited to meet Michael, and was able to speak Greek with him, hug him, and basically give him the same welcome I had received when visiting Greece. I taught Michael how to throw a football, and we had long conversations in the backyard late into the evening. He visited my mom, who was elated and said meeting Michael was also a miracle. While in Fresno, Michael also submitted a DNA sample, as Vicki did during her visit.

I returned to Greece in 2019 with Doreen and our daughter, Hunter. (Spenser could not make the trip because of her studies.) The purpose of the trip was to have my immediate family meet dozens of Greek family members and friends. It was a momentous occasion. We stayed near the centrally located Acropolis. Vicki, Michael, and Maria organized a family reunion at a very nice restaurant close to her home in Athens. Luckily, most of the family spoke English. It was wonderful!

At one point, during the reunion, Maria grabbed two of the younger girls who spoke English, with the intent of telling Doreen something very important. She told Doreen that when she gave birth to me, she was still a virgin. Maria said this was because there had been no actual penetration when she became pregnant. Later, during her pregnancy, a nurse at Mitera verified that she was still a virgin. What struck me is how important it was for Maria to share this with Doreen.

One major question did arise on this last trip. Why were we told no one was living on my father's side of the family? I discovered, as a result of DNA testing through Ancestry, that I have relatives on my father's side, who knew nothing of my existence. I made contact and each individual I have spoken with has been extremely interested in my story, and completely accepting of me as a relative, including new first cousins. One cousin actually contacted me first, and filled me in on family history, which contradicts what I had been told previously. I understand and will withhold judgment, but I must reveal my latest discoveries to Maria's side diplomatically and gently.

So, for me, still more secrets. I will devote the same time and energy as I did in locating Maria to locating relatives on my father's side. The door has already opened. I am now in touch with relatives on the Kourmouzas side, who have been open and kind.

I used to think that Doreen and I were very lucky in our discoveries. But I realize now it was not luck. We set goals, we were determined, we asked for help, we did not hesitate to act on leads. We were willing to travel thousands of miles, not knowing what to expect, and willing to accept anything we might encounter. We are open, empathic, and calm toward others, and believe these traits put others at ease. We were patient, but persistent. We believed in what we were doing. We were grateful. We were respectful.

Every adoptee has the right to their personal history, no matter how heart-warming or heart-wrenching it turns out to be. Adoptees want answers, they want to hear the truth, good or bad. The birth mother and families they are seeking must understand that adoptees have gone to great lengths to find them and, hopefully, make a positive connection. The mothers of adoptees, in my opinion, have never stopped thinking about their lost child, no matter how many years have passed. The mothers of adoptees should not feel any guilt. The situation was out of their control, and the societal norms of the time unjustly blamed and punished them.

In my particular case, I noticed the peacefulness in Maria's demeanor once she opened up and revealed her secret to her other children, her family, and friends. She is so happy now. But I'll let her speak for herself, my birth mother, Maria, in a letter she wrote to me before one Easter:

> *"I wake up at night and start to write. As I put the pen in my hand, I hardly know how to start to put into words my whole past 30 years of bitterness, anxiety, and despair, so it takes more than one night to write what I would like to say. Please forgive me for telling you how I feel. I do not have anyone to tell what I have in my heart. I thank you so much for your beautiful words, we have freed each other; and it is a great joy for both of us. A mother's heart longs for her child and never forgets. Please write whenever you can. I hope that soon you will learn a little Greek. I thank the gentleman who translated my letter to you. I wish him the best. I am sending you the picture of your half-brother and half-sister. I wish you all many years of health and happiness. Happy Easter! Please kiss Doreen for me and I pray, my son, that she will give you all the love and happiness that I couldn't give you. Many kisses to all. Your Mother, Maria"*

Chapter 7

A COFFIN FULL OF SECRETS

Sonia

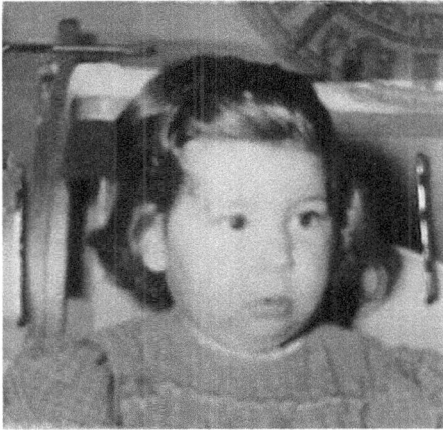

I had always known I was adopted, but it wasn't until I turned 18 when my parents decided it was time to give me my adoption papers. Until that time, I hadn't really been very concerned about my adoption. I am a bit darker than the average Dutchman, and I didn't look like my parents, who were light-skinned Dutch people, but I never was discriminated against or treated differently by my family or friends. I had great parents, loyal friends, and nothing to really think about, or so I thought.

I had never given my adoption papers a thought nor had I wondered what might be contained in them. When my parents presented them to me, I flipped through them, but casually, just out of curiosity. It was a thick document, written in Greek, without an English translation. Suddenly my eye caught the word *'leprosy'* and I sat up a little straighter. I read and reread the text, which stated that my biological mother, at the time of my adoption, was hospitalized for leprosy.

I was utterly shocked and asked my parents for explanations. Leprosy? What do you mean leprosy? How did she get this and where from? It actually still existed at that time? My mother told me that they had no more information than what was in the documents and said that my birth mother had not been present at my final "handing over," because she was in the hospital being treated for the disease. My parents never met her nor had they seen her. I knew then and there that I wanted to go back one day to find out exactly what happened. This was also the very moment when I decided to learn Greek.

I was born in 1959 and was one-and-a-half years old when my parents adopted me in June 1961. They adopted me at the same time as my brother, Peter, who was three years old. Peter is not my biological brother and was from another family in Corfu. Ill and the second youngest in his family, his parents were unable to take care of him. After having spent some time in the care of different foster mothers, he eventually came to the Baby Center Mitera, from where he and I would both be adopted. Peter lived there for only two months.

In the late 1950s and early 1960s, it was fairly easy and "popular" to adopt children from Greece. Over a ten-year period, there were approximately 600 children who came to the Netherlands from Greece. My parents could not have their own biological children and so registered as a couple who wanted to adopt. Within nine months, they were able to adopt two children at the same time.

Prior to our adoption, they were required to stay in Athens for six weeks. My parents said they wanted a boy and a girl. They requested and preferred a toddler and an infant. Once at Mitera, they could, to some extent, choose. One or two children at a time were presented to them, children which the staff thought would suit them well and fit nicely into their family.

Peter had been playing outside in the front yard and saw our expectant parents arrive. He immediately ran to them. A nice little boy, who spoke only Greek, my parents were immediately enamored of him.

I was a little older than an infant, but I was presented to them anyway. My mother thought I was cute, but my father did not agree because of my age. Again and again, other little girls were presented to them, but I remained constantly on their minds. So, in the end, they decided I was also to be theirs. (And boy, did I have a nice father! He was so happy with me. From the time he became my father and for the rest of his life, I became and remained daddy's little girl.)

In Mitera, I had a godmother whose name was Marika Spanoudaki. I don't know why I had her or how she was linked to me, but she was my sponsor as I was baptized as a Greek Orthodox Christian on the premises of Mitera in the presence of my new parents, my new brother, and a number of nurses from the children's home. The *papas* (the priest) dipped me three times up to my neck in a large baptismal font and I was covered in oil until the baptism was a fact.

I was called Sonia, the name that my godmother, Marika, had given to me. But because I would be my adoptive family's first granddaughter, I would be named after my paternal grandmother, Margaretha, as was customary in the Netherlands. So, I would be Margaretha Sonia, but the *papas*, at first, did not accept this because, according to him, Greeks have only one name (no middle name). My parents insisted that everyone has two names in the Netherlands, and the matter was successfully negotiated. But they would continue to call me Sonia, my second name.

I was spoiled rotten at Mitera, and I always seemed to get my way. Peter and I got used to each other very quickly. We played together often. Peter already knew some Greek and was communicating. I had just started talking and was picking up some words, but we had the greatest fun together, while our parents did not understand a thing.

We often played "adoption." Out came all the toy stuffed animals that we had and we each were allowed to pick two. I was somewhat more assertive than Peter, and even though I was younger, often took the lead. But one time, a boy in the playground assaulted me, and Peter came to the rescue. He walked towards us, grabbed my hand and gave the little boy a blow.

While the adoption was being finalized, my parents came every day to Mitera to play with us, to walk and to eat together with us. For hours they pushed me on a swing, well monitored by what they called "the children's police." The caretakers at Mitera continuously watched whether what my parents were doing was "right" and somewhat controlled how they behaved and reacted to us. My parents said they were completely uncomfortable and nervous about this.

After leaving Greece, we lived in Amsterdam for the first ten years, where my father worked for the Shell Oil company. I felt very close to my parents and my brother. When I was seven years old, my father participated in an exchange program and we left for a year to live in New York.

Our house in Brooklyn was not yet fully furnished, so we stayed in a hotel during the first few weeks. Once we moved to the house, Peter and I went to school, and after just a week, we spoke quite a bit of English. At home, our parents spoke to us in Dutch, so that we would not forget the language of our country.

We had a great time in the United States. I did miss my girlfriends back home in the Netherlands, but heck, it was only for a year. Then we came back to our own home in Amsterdam and I immediately picked up where we left off with my girlfriends.

When I was almost 12 years old, we moved to the eastern part of the country. My father had been offered a professorship at the University of Twente, which he accepted. By this time, I had attended four different elementary schools because of the various moves, but fortunately I never had to repeat a year.

Our parents did not want us to forget the English we had learned, which meant that every night at dinner, we spoke English. It didn't even matter whether we had any visitors or not. We had to speak English. In fact, because my parents were so adamant about our learning English, when we would watch television, they would stick Band-Aids on the screen, to mask the subtitles in Dutch. As a result, our friends did not want to watch television at our place anymore. But my parents' efforts paid off! Because I spoke English at home until high school, I obtained an exemption from English lessons in the first year. It was a lifelong benefit, which meant I could work anywhere in the world, all because of my proficiency in English.

I grew up in a very nice family, and Peter and I had a close bond with our grandparents. We were their only grandchildren and we were outrageously spoiled. They continuously doted on us. My grandparents never knew that my biological mother had leprosy. My mother believed that my grandfather would not have accepted me had he known. He was fearful of all kinds of illnesses. I was checked annually for leprosy for the first ten years of my life. Because I did not walk totally upright, my spine had to be checked every year, and so at the same time a check for the existence of leprosy was also done without my ever knowing it.

When I was 11 and Peter was just 13 years old, our parents thought it was time to go to Greece for our summer holiday to discover more about our past. We drove by car to Ancona in Italy from where we took the boat to Patras. From Patras, we drove directly to Corfu to see if we could find Peter's biological parents.

Peter was born in Pelekas, a village on the west coast. Of course, we had no idea where his family lived, but we went to the café, right in the center of the village. Almost instantly people came out of their houses, because our foreign car drew attention. The owner of the café fortunately spoke German, which made it easier for my parents. (My father only spoke three words of Greek, which was definitely not helpful.) In no time at all, the entire square was full of people; we were literally surrounded.

Everyone in the village was, of course, aware of the situation with Peter and his family—that he was given up for adoption. The villagers led us to the home of his parents. There, we found only his father. (Although his parents were still married, they lived separately for part of the year.) Peter's father was so thrilled to see him again and invited us inside. The house was so very, very small. How did they do it, all those children with their parents crammed into such a tiny place? There had been nine of them.

Peter's 98-year-old grandmother also still lived there. She told us she had always known she would see Peter again and said she could now die in peace. Peter's mother lived in Athens with the other children, two sisters and four brothers. Two brothers were in military service. We were given the address and promised his father that we would also go there to visit. After a while we left, while the whole village waved goodbye.

As promised, we later did go to Athens to find Peter's mother. Peter's father had let her know we were coming and we found our way to her home in Piraeus. She also lived in a tiny house, but gave us a warm welcome in her small living room, where the kitchen table was and where she had prepared a bounty of food. She was overwhelmed with joy to see her youngest child again and immediately took his hands in hers to see and feel whether he had the hands of a laborer. But Peter was, of course, still in school, so that was not the case. All her other children had worked starting from the age of twelve. It was a good visit, even though the language barrier was challenging. It was not for another thirty years that Peter would visit his family again.

The following day, we drove to Mitera. My parents had made an appointment in advance. The director still worked there and was very happy to see us again after ten years. Peter and I spoke English well and could tell him about our lives. We got a tour of the place and got to see the yellow pavilion where I used to live. It made a great impression on us. My godmother, Marika, unfortunately, did not work there anymore. I had hoped to see her again. Until I was 11 years old, she had written letters and postcards every year. Suddenly, they stopped coming. I have never been able to find her again. No one knew where she had gone.

In the following years, I did not think much about Greece. I concentrated on school. When I was 21, I had finished all my exams and began working. I occasionally had some boyfriends, but nothing serious. I worked evenings and weekends in a Greek restaurant, Sirtaki, to earn some extra money. It was there that I met the man I would marry a year later. He was French, studied in Enschede, and came to eat regularly at Sirtaki.

When I was six months pregnant with our daughter, Jessica, we decided to go to Athens during the summer holidays. I made an appointment at Mitera because I wanted to show my husband where I came from. Again, we were warmly received and they took us again to the yellow pavilion. There were still so many children, some of whom were older. Not every one of those children was offered for adoption. Some were there because their mothers temporarily could not care for them. Who would come and collect them later? I remember that on the stairs was a little four-year-old, who, I was told, waited every day for her mother. Would she ever come to get her, I thought? The director didn't think so. My heart broke for that child.

Beginning in the 1970s, foreigners could adopt only disabled children. The "healthy" children could be adopted only by Greek couples. Most Greeks are not wealthy and, therefore, could not afford to have a disabled child. (A child would be considered disabled if, for example, the child had a cleft lip.)

While we were talking, the social worker asked us whether we wanted to adopt a child from the home. We had not thought about adoption, but we were quite honored that they offered us that option. I was pregnant at that time and wanted my own biological child, someone who would look like me and would never have to seek his/her biological parents.

I have so much respect for people who adopt, but I knew that I would never do it. Had I not been able to have a child of my own, I would have remained childless. I would not want my adopted child to go through the turmoil that I went through. I am experiencing now what it does to you—to be adopted. Always looking at the past, constantly looking back over your shoulder. Always wondering who your mother is, who your father is, whether you have any brothers and sisters. I was adamant. For my biological child, it will always be clear who her family is.

I also think about what adoptive parents have to go through. Mine provided a nice life. A good life. I lacked for nothing. It could not have been better for me. My parents were highly educated, hardworking people. My father was a professor of chemical engineering at the University of Twente. My mother was a psychologist. *A child psychologist.* It was all the more strange, then, that these parents would be judged about whether they could be good parents. My father was instantly approved, but my mother, at first, did not qualify in their eyes. It was ridiculous. My mom was great. A warm and loving person, always ready to listen. She often would not give me any advice when I asked, not wanting to be the psychologist. My mother was busy, always excited, and she was full of laughter.

So, in my case, yes, adoption proved to be my luck. But there is a downside for the adopters and the adoptees. I often wonder whether adoption is really such a good thing. Is it not much better to let a child grow in his or her own environment? In the 1960s, it was a shame in Greece to be a single mother. The unwed mothers were not spoken to, not helped in stores and mocked by the whole village. Actually, they would have no life, if they decided to keep their child. So, the mothers were forced to relinquish their babies.

I wanted very much to meet my biological parents, to know where I am from. Most adopted children want the same thing. This search often takes years to complete. Actually, your whole life revolves around this. This could be one of the reasons that adoption does not work for everyone. Some kids struggle because they do not know where they are from and from whom. They do not cope well with their adoptive parents, feeling unwanted all their lives. As for me and my brother, however, we were very much wanted. When my mother died, we wrote on her mourning card this text: *"No child is more wanted than an adopted child."* In our case, this was true.

I am Greek-born. Greece is my country. I feel at home there. As you fly into Athens, you can see the beautiful blue sea, the islands with their winding roads and barren vegetation, the beautiful cube-shaped white houses. It is a wonderful feeling to come home, which I do not feel when I return to Dutch soil. But as soon as I step from the airplane onto Greek soil, I can smell the delicious air and feel the warm breeze through my hair.

I'm not a tourist among Greeks. I am one of them. In fact, my daughter always laughs when we get there, because there is always someone who comes to me to ask for directions. "They only do that with you, Mom," she says. "They see that you are Greek." For years I have gone to Greece nearly every summer holiday, visiting various islands and a few times a year I also visit Athens. I *need* Greece as often as possible.

When I was 38 years old, I still had made no move to find my biological mother. But, in the late 1990s, the law changed in Greece. It became possible through Mitera to help me find her, so I wrote a letter asking for help in finding my biological mother.

Within two months I received a letter back, saying that I would receive the help I asked for. I was assigned to social worker Irini Petsa. In just a few months, I received a message that they had found my birth mother, Evangelia. Irini had met with her in front of the hospital where she was treated for leprosy and where she had to go back regularly for check-ups and medication.

Irini wrote that Evangelia was initially stunned and said that she did not want to see me. When she gave me up for adoption, the children's home told her never to come back and search for her child. So, after the adoption, in her mind and heart, she broke all ties with me. Irini also explained that my mother did not look good. She not only had leprosy and was on lifelong medication, but she had breast cancer, which took a toll, even though the cancer was in remission.

At the time of my adoption, she was in the hospital and being treated for leprosy. She stayed there for seven years and met her husband Ippokrates (not my biological father), who was being treated for the same disease. Ippokrates had been transferred to Athens from the leper island of Spinalonga, off the coast of Crete. They were not allowed to leave the hospital during all these years. My adoptive parents, who knew the situation, offered to pay my mother's hospital expenses or to otherwise support her, but Evangelia would not accept anything from them.

I have my own daughter. I cannot imagine that I would ever be able to give her up. How desperate must you be, that you would make the drastic decision to do so. Only after I met Evangelia, when I heard the story about why she had waited so long before she signed the papers to give me away, did I understand.

Evangelia asked Irini whether I could write to her about my life. I had to think about it, but decided to type her a letter that ended up being four pages long. I explained my life from the time I left Greece until the present. Irini translated this letter for her, and I was told that she was very happy to learn about me. But, still, she did not want to meet. More letters followed. She knew more about me than I did about her.

After two more years, in June 2000, Evangelia agreed to meet. The day before the meeting Irini called me to tell me that my mother wanted to cancel. Luckily, Irini was smart enough to say that I was already in Athens, that she could no longer reach me, and that she was really counting on her to show up for me. I had agreed to be there half an hour earlier than the scheduled time so we could talk before Evangelia arrived. The meeting was to take place at 10 a.m.

I had slept badly the night before. I was scared that Evangelia would not come. I felt nervous. After a delicious breakfast at the hotel and a lot of coffee, I got in the taxi and the driver stopped in front of the long driveway to Mitera. I saw two people in the distance standing outside in front of the home. It was my biological mother and her husband, who were already there waiting for us. It seemed like an eternity to walk up to the house, but once there, I ran up the steps and hugged my mom. It was just incredible. Finally, I just stood face-to-face with my mother. What a strange experience, because, in the end, we were strangers to each other. It felt good, though, and was a relief, as we started a conversation.

She was slightly smaller than me and quite heavy. She wore a neat floral dress. She said it was very nice that I spoke some Greek, and I felt proud that I had taken lessons. At least we could talk and not stare at each other in silence.

I shook hands with her husband, Ippokrates. A tiny man, dressed in a suit, he was standing very close in front of me and looked up at me with penetrating eyes. I was taller.

What I did learn was this: Evangelia was very happy to see me. She told me that she had never stopped thinking of me. She told her husband about me, from the first moment she met him in the hospital. He was the only one she ever told. She said she was no longer in contact with her parents, and that her brother had passed away.

Evangelia had only gone to primary school. She could not read or write very well. After elementary school, she worked in the fields, picking olives, where she met my biological father. She told me that when she became pregnant, he left her. Her parents sent her to her brother, Theodore, and his wife, who lived in Athens. Her parents wanted nothing more to do with her and broke off all ties. Her brother, Theodore, and his wife took her into their home. She was 24 years old when she gave birth to me on December 20.

Theodore and his wife could not have biological children and offered to take care of me. They said they would raise me as their own child, with no one knowing the truth about my birth. Evangelia thought about it for a while and said: "If you want my child, then you will have to follow the official way of adoption. I'm not going to give you my child just like that." He did not agree. (I never managed to find his wife. I would have liked to know more about this story, and whether it was really true. Later I would learn that Evangelia told me many lies during our meeting. Was this story a lie, an excuse, for my benefit—that she tried to keep me in the family?)

Seven years after I was born, Evangelia and her husband had three more children, all sons: Giorgos, Yiannis and Kostas. They did not know of my existence and I also did not know of theirs. They are seven, nine, and eleven years younger than me. She told me that she had not told her sons about meeting me. It all had to remain a secret, she said, which I found very sad. She had led a very lonely and secretive life. She had little contact with anyone and she tried to avoid as many people as possible. She, her husband, and three sons, ages 29, 31, and 33, lived in the house together. The boys, now men, had no girlfriends.

What does this say about this family? Sad, I thought. How odd, I thought. Was I missing something, not understanding something? I found theirs a remarkable situation. And I realized that they are my siblings that I might never know.

I had brought a small photo album with me for Evangelia. In it were pictures of me, from the time I left Greece until I was 40 years old. It included photos of my daughter and my husband. She was very happy and enjoyed looking at it, but refused to keep it, as she was afraid that someone would find it. She pulled from it a couple of photos, including one of Jessica, "because she is still my grandchild," she said. Her husband would keep the photos at his office for her.

She had also brought something for me. She put a large plastic bag on the table with all kinds of handmade rugs. These, she said, she had made for me secretly, in the time during our correspondence. The handmade rugs were a present, which a daughter usually receives on her wedding day. I was still her daughter, she said, and she wanted me to have them. I felt incredibly happy and thought it was really sweet that she had done all that work, all while keeping me a secret. With a big grin on my face, I accepted her gifts.

For two hours we sat there talking in the office. I kept looking intently at her and tried to find similarities. I did not think we looked alike. Only our hands were the same. She said that in her family nobody looked like each other. Her sons did not look like her, nor did they look like her husband.

I did feel that I shared some of her personality. My Dutch mother found me a rather sober person and always said I must have inherited that from my biological mother, whom I found a gentle and sensitive woman. But if I did not look like my mother, would I then look like my father? From whom did I get my perseverance, my temperament? I thought to myself that I really had to find out.

Finally, I asked if I could meet with my mother alone, without her husband. He and she obliged, but only for 20 minutes. Even when we were alone, and in the very brief time we had by ourselves, she did not answer all of my questions. It seemed as though she was well-instructed by someone to be discreet, although she told me that I could ask her anything I wanted. I told her that she could too, to which she then replied, "You sent me that long letter. I already know everything about you." Sure enough, I thought, I really did inherit her matter-of-fact way of looking at things.

About my biological father. I really wanted to know who he was, what his name was. She said, "That's not important, because he has left me." Yes, that may well be true, I said, "But you also left me." She admitted that was also true so she told me his name was Nikos and he was from Kalamata. My birth papers stated that he was her fiancé. "Ah, nothing fiancé," she said, "that just looks good on paper. He worked with me in the olive fields and as soon as I became pregnant, he left." She never saw him again, she said, but a few minutes later she told me he was dead. Irini and I looked at each other. Could we believe that? The shame of a pregnancy out of wedlock in Greece was very real. Families were ashamed. Neighbors were ashamed of those families, if they knew you. Greeks talk a lot, they gossip about petty things, but say very little when it comes down to it. About things that are important and serious, they clamp shut.

At one moment during our interview, Evangelia looked at me and said, "In the past I laughed just like you. Now I have nothing left to laugh about."

It was nearing the time they had to leave. They had told their sons that they had gone to the hospital for a check-up, so it would raise suspicions if they stayed away too long.

I had asked twice during our time together to take her picture. One of her. One of the two of us. Both times she refused. Irini also tried to persuade her, but she was adamant. No photos. She was afraid that a photo of us would somehow show up in Athens. Because of my own nervousness, I did not insist and, in retrospect, I should not have asked. I should have had Irini just snap a photo of us while we were talking.

We got up and walked to the exit of the children's home. I had offered to pay for a taxi or bus for Evangelia and Ippokrates, but they refused. I did take a picture of them while they walked away together, arms entwined, down the long driveway. It was from behind. Too far away. Too vague. Looking at them as they walked right out of my life, never looking back, will always be in my memory. What a horrible feeling. With tears in my eyes, I watched them until they had turned the corner. I never saw Evangelia again; these would be the first and last two hours of my life that I saw and spoke to her. Her face, her way of talking and walking; those images will always be engraved in my mind. Years later, though, I had taken another picture of "her." We were not together then either. The photo was of her grave.

From the day I met Evangelia forward, I decided to find out more about her life. Many times, I traveled to Nafplion (where she was born and where I received her birth certificate) and to Kalamata, where she lived before she came to Athens to give birth to me. It took me many years to find out the truth, which was quite different from what she told me. I was also adamant to find my biological father.

In 2017, I took DNA tests with both Ancestry and My Heritage, but no close relatives turned up. Only third cousins, who knew nothing. And then suddenly, in 2020, a close relative appeared on My Heritage. He was really close. A second cousin. My heart skipped a beat and I decided to contact him immediately. He spoke fabulous English and was very helpful. He did not know about my story, but would ask his family. He said he was very close to an uncle, who was then 75 years old.

The uncle recognized my story and was very excited. We talked on the phone and he knew exactly who my father was. My biological father's name is Nikos (my mother told the truth about that), and he was a lot older than my mother. He was not married. He came from a big family and was one of nine children.

When my mother got pregnant with me, he did not want to marry her. He wanted to be free. His mother, my grandmother, offered my mother money to go to Athens for an abortion. My mother did go to Athens, but she gave birth to me instead. Apparently, the family never knew. Later, I was told by my aunts that my mother told everyone she had a miscarriage. She left Kalamata for Athens and nobody ever knew that I was actually born.

My father came from a wealthy family. He owned land and houses, but he did not know how to handle all the money. In the end, he lost his fortune and had to work right up until he died at the age of 72 in 1994 (so my mother told the truth that he was already dead when we met). Three of his sisters were still alive, and the biggest news is that I have eight more siblings—four brothers and four sisters.

Three of my sisters live in the USA. A cousin decided to contact my eldest sister. She was so happy to have another sister. She immediately called all the other siblings and then we spoke to each other through Facebook Messenger. That was a magical moment and, boy, do we all look like each other. The whole family welcomed me and now I have continual contact with everyone.

I met three of my brothers and my three aunts in the summer of 2021. At last, we were all joyous to meet and to be together. I hope one day to meet my youngest sister and another brother in Greece. Three of my sisters were sent to the USA at an early age, so I hope to travel there, too, for a reunion and we can all speak English together!

I am so happy that my siblings all seemed to have led good lives. And I have led a very good life. Everyone has always told me that I should be glad and grateful that I was given away for adoption. I always doubted that and now I realize, I would have had a good life in Greece as well, with my family there.

My search has come to an end and it has been a thrill to see the resemblances between me and my siblings and to get to know them. I know I cannot make up for nearly 60 years without them, but we are all trying so much to learn more and more about each other, and we speak to each other regularly. Knowing the truth about my life gives me joy and peace. I am not restless anymore. I feel so lucky that I was able to find them and, moreover, that they accept me into their families and lives—my life and theirs of no more secrets.

Chapter 8

THE FINAL GOODBYE

Despina/Chris

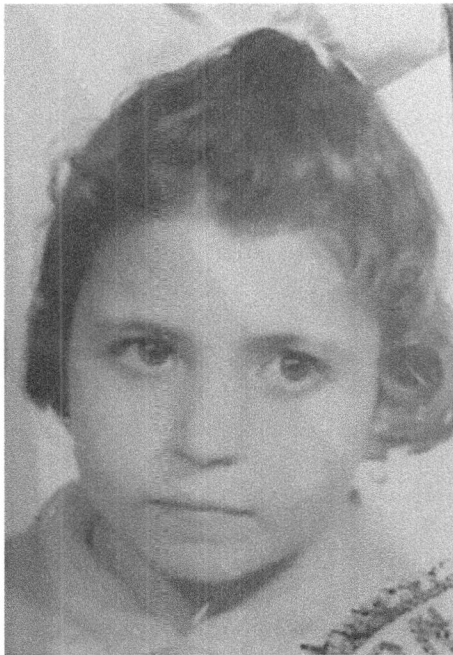

I was born in my great-grandmother's house on January 2, 1955, in Alagonia, Messinias, Kalamata, Greece. I was named Despina after my great-grandmother. My mother was promised that I would receive a piece of land if she would honor her husband's mother with my name.

I am the third-born of four children. However, the fourth-born, who was a baby, was not the one being adopted. I was. At the age of seven, I was adopted by John and Beatrice, an elderly couple from the United States. He was Greek-born and married to an American from the Deep South, ages 72 and 48, respectively. I was not an orphan, but I would be classified as such soon enough. This entire process took about a year and a half.

Being adopted near adolescence, I can recall with vivid detail what it was like to be partially stripped of my culture that was already deeply embedded. I maintained communication with my family back in Greece, and saw, all my life, what it could have been, had I not been adopted. My only solace in my life was that my new father was Greek-born. My village was my whole universe. Would it miss me as much as I missed it? My mother's goal was to relinquish me in an attempt to "benefit" the whole family. I didn't feel singled out. She could have chosen any one of us. But it was me and I was part of a plan my mother had hatched.

It was 1961. The president of the Michigan chapter of American Hellenic Educational Progressive Association (AHEPA) was scheduled to attend a ceremony in Greece, but was unable to make it due to health issues. Instead, my great-grandmother's son, John Anastos, would fill in for him and take the trip with his wife, Beatrice. He had not returned to visit Greece since he was seventeen. He was now nearing seventy.

During their stay, they decided to visit his hometown of Alagonia where he owned a home, which happened to be mine, where I was born and living with my family. This is where it all started.

Upon hearing of their arrival, my mother got her "great idea" for the couple to adopt me. They were older and childless, so my mother thought it was the perfect opportunity for them. She made the offer, which they immediately declined. They felt they were too old to raise a child. But my mother persisted and would not take "no" for an answer. They told her they were leaving for Thessaloniki and, when they returned, would have a final answer.

Over the next few weeks during their trip, John further discussed the idea with his wife, whom he adored. He reasoned with her. He was twenty-two years her senior and had a heart condition, suggesting she would benefit from having a child after he was gone. He wanted to adopt one of the children in our family for the purpose of later taking care of her. Grudgingly she agreed, despite her dislike for children.

They could have chosen any one of us, but the reason they chose me was because of my age and gender. My sister was in diapers. The boys were ruled out because a girl would provide more assistance and nurturing in the future for his wife. John also liked that I was named after my great-grandmother, Despina, who was his mother.

In the summer, John and his wife began filing the paperwork necessary for my adoption. I was not an orphan, and legally only an orphan could be adopted. But in October 1962, the Congress of the United States passed a bill, which rendered me a legal orphan, available for adoption. By December, I was on a plane headed to the United States for a new life and new parents. Just like that.

Thinking back to my life in Greece, I remember the day my mother told us that she was going to have a baby. She would fake being sick so we would do things for her. She always said, she would die unless we did this or that. The day that she gave birth, I was standing in the doorway. The midwife was there, and my mother was in a squatting position, screaming. I was so upset, thinking she was going to die.

Finally, the baby came out, and I always thought that babies came out of your rear end after that day. The midwife told me and my two brothers to take the afterbirth in a little bucket, dig a deep hole in the garden, and bury it. Afterward, make the sign of the cross, she told us.

I was six years old when my mother gave birth to my baby sister. Right after she was born, I got to hold her on the bed. I asked my mother, "Can we name her Maria because all Marias are beautiful." She laughed.

I had two older brothers; one was twelve and the other eight years old. At bedtime, my two brothers slept with my father. Me and my baby sister slept with my mother.

Our village, at least, in my eyes, was a fairytale-like place. Warm fireplaces, farm animals, forests with trickling water coming down from the mountains. It was a place to run free, without rules. No fears of strangers kidnapping you or something horrible happening. Our house was built up high. The first story, at road level, was the barn and next door was a coffeehouse. We were on the road that ran right through the center of the village.

We lived across the street from the church. I witnessed every wedding and funeral that took place, and the smell of the incense emanating from the church made me feel protected; it was inviting, as if it were safe for me to enter.

Sometimes we children would gather at the steps of the church to play with the rocks, our version of jacks. A fun evening in the summertime was when someone from the city showed up with a movie projector. They would set it up and project the image against the church wall across from the house. We were able to see the movie from our small balcony. The movies were in English; nobody understood, but nobody cared because we got to see a movie, a rare opportunity. There was electricity and a phone in the village, but we did not have either in our home.

I was in charge of caring for my baby sister, who was handed to me after being bound. My mother would bind her before she left for work. She made sure to tell me not to unbind her, but I would anyway. I thought to myself, how could a baby be comfortable, not being able to move? I would carry her under my armpit, just as my mother had shown me. This way I would be able to hold her under one arm and still have my hands free to play at the same time.

I remember that my parents stored olives in the living room. Once, I was carrying my baby sister and she would not stop crying so I set her on top of one of the barrels. She fell through and I dove in to get her. The olives spilled everywhere.

I adored my mother. I was an obedient child who always thought that my mother knew best. I was a big help to her when my sister was born. I did everything from changing her diapers to feeding her.

We played underneath the huge oak tree in the village with the other children. We would all run home when we heard our names being called by our mothers. During the cold, winter months there was no heat in the house. My mother would sit next to the fireplace, wearing a long, wide skirt. I would run and hide under her skirt to keep warm. This is also where I would run to hide when I would hear my father yelling at my brothers.

I would go with my parents to the fields, and my mother would flip the horse saddle over and put my baby sister in it. My job was to watch over her. I had a favorite aunt, Aspasia. She lived in the lower part of the mountain. Nature provided what were like steps to make our way down. My mother often sent me down there, back and forth, to get things for her.

The village had everything we needed to survive—cherries, walnuts, pears, and plums growing everywhere. When the cherries were harvested, we carried them with fern leaves for safe transport. Ferns, rocks, water; we used everything there was to use in nature. It was never about money or material things.

We had a carefree, fun life. We hiked, fished for crabs to eat. We had no running water, no electricity. But we didn't need it. We had fresh flowing mountain water right outside our door. We used kerosene lamps at nightfall for lighting.

The calmness and softness I felt as a child was indescribable. How could such a simple thing such as the light thrown off by a kerosene lamp feel so amazing? All of the village children would get together and, with a large piece of cloth, we would carry cheese and olives and go deep into the forest to have a picnic.

We got excited when a pig was slaughtered because we would use the pig bladder as a ball. And we used the pork fat to shine our shoes. There were no refrigerators, so we would keep our cheese in a *touloumi*, which was a goat skin.

My mother cooked over an open fire in our kitchen. There was an outdoor brick oven my mother used for baking bread. She would bake bread once a week. After the bread got hard and stale, we would soften it with water to eat it through the week. Nothing was wasted.

Every so often, a fish truck would come through the village. I would crawl on the back of the truck and fill my underwear with fish and take them home so my mother could fry them for dinner.

One day, my brother and I decided not to go to school. We escaped somewhere to play. My mother knew it, though, because we arrived home too early. She grabbed a handful of *tsikounithes*, stinging nettle, and proceeded to whip our legs as she walked us all the way back to school, swinging the nettle at our legs the whole way. This is the one and only time I can remember my mother punishing me.

By age six, I was able to go to the pasture and bring home the goats. I could light a fire and boil rice for my baby sister. I even fed her. Whatever I ate, she ate. I used my mouth as a food processor, chewing up the food, then giving it to her so she wouldn't choke on big pieces.

Our village was very superstitious. We did not trust doctors. One day doctors came to our school to vaccinate us. I remember their white coats and a basket full of oranges. Each child who was good would get an orange after their vaccine. I was terrified and screamed and cried, but my brother told me to be quiet so that they would give me an orange. Since then, the white coats and white sheets remind me of hospitals. To this day, I still will not put white sheets on my bed.

At school, we were checked daily to see if our hands were clean and we were given powdered milk to drink. I wouldn't drink that milk. I was taught to be wary of anything that I was not familiar with. So, when nobody was looking, I dumped the milk out.

I remember the day my mother told me that she was giving me away. She said I was going to America, like it was up in the sky someplace, like it was heaven. "Look up in the sky where the stars are, that's where America is. When you get there, you will have new clothes, shoes, toys. Your new parents are rich," she told me. She told me to practice not calling her mother any longer. She was preparing me for what was to come.

But there were so many lies. She wanted me to go willingly. My mother began to tell me that she wasn't my real mother, that this American lady gave birth to me, and brought me to the village one day. Now she was coming to take me back home.

The next day my aunt came to the house, and I overheard her telling my mother that what she was planning was a sin in God's eyes. "Whatever you feed the other three is what you feed the fourth child," my aunt told her. I guess they were worried about affording four children. My father, who said very little and never had an opinion about anything, spoke up telling my mother, "Don't give Despina up." She snapped back, "Listen old man, you don't know what you're saying."

While my adoption was being processed, there were preparations to baptize my baby sister. Her godparents had bought and invested in the baptismal clothes; the outfit, candles, a cross. But, when the Americans, my new parents, came to the village, my mother asked them to baptize my baby sister. My mother withdrew her offer to the intended godparents to replace them with the Americans. That day, one of my aunts came to our house, and it took everything she had not to strike my mother. She told her she should be ashamed of herself and accused her of having ulterior motives.

I had never been in a car, a bus, or train until the adoption was being prepared. Now we were getting on buses and trains to Athens all the time to see doctors and lawyers. I had severe motion sickness and these trips would make me very sick.

We would stay with an aunt and uncle when we went to Athens. The wife thought that we were too much like village people, too dirty, to stay in their beautiful home, so we were put up in the maid's quarters. We were not even allowed to use their bathroom inside the house. It really didn't matter anyway because I was afraid of toilets. They had a large orchard with lemons and oranges. That became my bathroom as it was the only place I was not afraid to go.

I was told I had to see a doctor to get vaccinated before I could travel to America. I asked my aunt how big the needle was. She replied, "It's very big, and so big that it's going to come out the other side of your arm." I was already afraid of doctors, and hearing that just made it worse.

We went shopping to pick out the clothes that I would wear to America. My aunt chose underwear for me that would later fit me after I grew some. The shoes she picked out for me were huge and looked like they were meant for boys, but she insisted that we get them. My mother kept whispering into my ear to do exactly as I was told, even if I didn't like it.

That last morning I spent in my village would be forever in my mind. We all woke up early and my mother told me it was time to say goodbye to everyone. I was not coming back, she said.

My father patted my head and smiled. My baby sister had just begun walking, and I was going to miss her the most, since I took care of her more than my own mother. My older brother wasn't usually home much, except to sleep, so I wasn't very close to him. I gathered my belongings and went over to the bed to say goodbye to my brother Yanni. He was two years older than me and we were very close. He was crying and begging me not to leave.

My mother was laughing. She told me, "You should be happy. You are leaving here and headed to a place that is wealthy and full of gold." This meant nothing to me. I already felt like I was the wealthiest person and in the richest place in the world with my beloved family, friends, and relatives.

We all walked to the center of the village where I would catch a ride to Athens with my mother who was taking me to the airport. Tears fell down my cheeks as I climbed onto the bus. The doors closed, and the bus took off.

I ran to the back window and waved goodbye until I could no longer see them. The bus went fast along those twisted mountain roads and I got sick, throwing up along the way. I saw the forest full of ferns and trees and the mountain water trickling down the rocks. That was my last memory, and a painful goodbye.

My mother and I had made this trip to Athens numerous times over the past two years. But this time was different. The last day we spent together in Athens at the house of our rich relatives was the day my mother sat me down outside of my rich aunt's house and told me once more, "Don't ever call me mother again. You can call me Aunt, and your father, Uncle. Your new parents will be called Mama and Papa." I told her that I didn't want to leave. I asked her to go back to court and tell them that she changed her mind.

As always, she laughed as I quietly cried. She kept telling me how lucky I was and that I should be grateful. Also, she said that when I arrived in America, I should kiss the feet of my new parents every day.

I was inconsolable the entire day and through the night. When morning arrived, the maid picked me up and hugged me, telling me she would always think of me and pray for me to have a happy life. I told her, "Maybe I can run away before they take me away." She said, "You must do what you're told. There's no other way out of this, and your mother has already signed papers to give you up." I really loved that maid. She would always make me feel special every time I saw her.

It was time to leave for the airport. They pinned a note to my powder blue coat with my final destination printed on it, in case I got lost. I held my mother's hand tightly. We walked onto the tarmac where a stewardess approached and motioned for me to take her hand. My mother forced my tiny hand from hers. I was being pulled away and my heart was breaking. I was pleading for a way out of this. I yelled for my mother to save me and told her not to cry. She shouted back, "Get on the plane. I will not cry!"

I kept looking back, searching for my beloved mother. I didn't see her. She was gone forever. I sat on the plane crying quietly, looking out the window when a very large man sat next to me. He spoke another language and no one on the plane spoke Greek. The stewardess fastened my seatbelt with a warm smile. I didn't understand a single word she said.

The plane ride took many hours and I didn't eat a thing. I was throwing up and had become very weak. We finally landed in New York, the nice stewardess took my hand and we walked to an office where a man sat at a desk. He greeted me in Greek and I told him he was the first person that I understood. He picked me up and sat me on his desk, and asked me about the plane ride and if I needed anything. He assured me that my trip was almost over and that my new parents were waiting for me at the end of the next plane ride. He hugged me and told me I was going to be alright.

A stewardess then walked me over to a counter full of toys, coloring books and crayons. She pointed to the case and nodded, as if to say, "Which one do you want?" I picked a small, yellow teddy bear. She handed it to me and we walked a bit further where she handed me over to someone else who would escort me from New York to Detroit.

It was nearly Christmas when I arrived in Detroit. Both the pilot and a stewardess walked me off the plane, each one holding one of my hands. I saw my adoptive parents waiting on the tarmac as they called out my name. I ran to them, overwhelmed with emotion. I hadn't seen anyone I knew for a long time. I remembered them from the time they were in the village, nearly two years earlier. My mother had kept a picture of them to remind me who I would live with.

At home, there were Christmas lights everywhere and a tree with presents, which I'd never seen before. My new father turned on the television. I was amazed. The lights would come on in each room with the flick of a switch. I thought I needed permission to turn one on. They showed me my room where there was a beautiful, big doll on my bed. The closet was full of new clothes.

I was worried because I had never slept alone. How was I going to make it through the night, I wondered? They showed me the bathroom and told me to put on the pajamas that were laid out on the bed. I had never owned or worn a pair of pajamas.

Morning came and I met Tasso, who rented a room in my new home. He was a student from Greece, and he became the light in my life. He answered all of my questions about my new life. He showed me the refrigerator and I noticed a glass bottle with milk in it. I asked him how that milk got in there. He explained that it came from a cow and they bring it to a store and we buy it and bring it home. I froze. My fear of cows went back to my village life. There, they would bring the mother cow to slaughter in the main part of the village. The men and the butcher would force the cow to lay down and right there she screeched while they butchered her. I could never drink milk from a cow with that thought in my mind.

With each passing day, a new fear came. My adoptive mother was not fond of children. She did not know how to relate to me. My adoptive father was completely different and seemed to be very happy playing his new role. They took me to a Greek church the week after Christmas and he was eager to show me off. I overheard him tell his friends that I would be starting school. My heart sank and I became suddenly quiet. One of my mother's many lies was that I would visit my new parents for a short time and then return back to my village. I asked my adopted father about this. I was only here for a short visit, right? I am going back home, I said. He grinned and told me that I was not going back to Greece; that this was my new home. I felt empty, abandoned, discarded, and totally lost.

School started and I was sick with fear each night. I was afraid to sleep alone, so I held the teddy bear the stewardess had given me for comfort. I talked to the bear and told him all of my fears. I also started wetting the bed pretty consistently.

I was in a school for foreign-born students ranging in age from seven to eighteen. My teacher was Mrs. Carr and she was like a sweet, loving grandmother. The older kids were helpful and the younger kids quickly took my hand and wanted to be friends. I was sent to another class for about an hour each day to help me to learn English and after six months, I was able to communicate fairly well.

We would often travel to North Carolina to see my new grandparents, aunts, and cousins. They were warm and loving people. My new grandparents lived on a farm, so this felt more like home to me. My grandfather, Oliver, took me to the barn and told me about the chickens, horses, and of course, the cows.

At the dinner table I was to learn table manners. I knew that I did not have any. My mother would make me repeat over and over to "Pass the plate, please." I was never allowed to just say "yes" or "no." It had to be, "yes ma'am" or "no ma'am," always! And if I didn't follow the rules, she wouldn't hesitate to slap me across the face.

I was held back a year at school because of the language barrier. The bullying and humiliation were sometimes unbearable for me. I became stressed and full of anxiety. The class was learning to tell time and I needed help. Every night we sat at the kitchen table and my mother brought a little Baby Ben clock to help me. But she was impatient when I couldn't get it right. She slammed down the clock and shook me. "Why can't you understand," she screamed. She sent me to my room where I wet the bed. I was terrified of what she would do to me next.

The next morning, she saw that the bed was wet again and threatened to tell my friends in school. She told my father to talk to me, and said that she couldn't deal with it anymore. I had eventually built up enough courage to use the toilets at school. But one day, someone jumped on the toilet next to the stall I was in and was looking down at me. I was already afraid of toilets to begin with, but that incident traumatized me to the point that I began wetting myself in school to avoid the bathroom. I went from being a very confident, happy, carefree child to an anxiety-ridden, frightened, depressed little girl.

Doctor visits were terrifying. As soon as we entered the elevator in the medical building, my heart would sink. It took two medical staff to hold me down for a vaccination. My mother stepped in to spank me once when I fought against getting a shot and threw a sucker across the room.

Over the months, during those visits, one doctor decided that I was flat-footed and prescribed an orthopedic shoe that I was forced to wear until I was twelve. They looked like Frankenstein shoes. I was bullied in school over those shoes. Frankenstein shoes, no English, the smelly feta cheese I ate at lunch. The kids had plenty of ammunition with which to tease me.

My mother would come to school during recess to make sure that I wore a slip under my dress, ensuring that there was nothing that could be seen through my dress. Later on, when I had toy dolls, I was not allowed to take their clothes off, and when I did, the doll was to be dressed immediately, so that it was not seen naked.

By the time I was twelve, I had assimilated and grown used to my new world, but still longed for my mountain home. My father, John, had died and my mother became a recluse. She locked herself in a dark bedroom every day when she came home from work. She told me she could not manage without my father and that she didn't know how she was going to care for me.

Our relationship changed two weeks after my father's death, when she was diagnosed with breast cancer. She would need a mastectomy. Before her operation, she asked me, if she died, would I want to go back to Greece. I did not answer. She had just lost her husband and been diagnosed with cancer. I did not want her to feel like I would abandon her.

I became the caretaker, the decision-maker. I did everything and she did nothing, except go to work. I cooked, cleaned, mowed the lawn, and went to the grocery store with my wagon to do the shopping. She had no friends. All she had was me. She cried every day and I became tired and numb to it. I told her there would be better days ahead. She saw that I was a help to her throughout that year, when I was only twelve and thirteen years old, and that John had made the right decision to adopt me. She was grateful for me and asked me what she could do to show me her appreciation. I told her I wanted to go back home to see my family. She granted me my wish, and when I was fourteen, she traveled to Greece with me.

When the plane landed in Greece in the summer of 1969, my feelings were beyond words. I was choked up and could not speak. I was home.

We boarded a train to Kalamata. My brother Yanni was there to meet us, and we hugged each other tightly, never wanting to let go. He told me I was beautiful and all grown up. I had requested that my mom, Beatrice, not come with us to the village on this first trip, so she stayed in Kalamata with some friends while I went with my brother.

Yanni and I traveled by bus to the village and it seemed liked everyone had come to greet me. My mother stood with her hands outstretched toward the sky yelling, *to paidi mou*, my child. She fell to the ground and covered her head, repeating the words my child, my child. All of my friends came to hug me and everyone was crying. My father grinned and patted my head, very quietly saying, "How are you doing, my child," which was typical of him. No emotion.

Once all of the commotion died down, I said to Yanni, "Let's go deep into the woods where we used to play." The tall ferns and the smell of the oregano; everything I missed was there. I felt like the rocks were smiling at me. I was home.

Beatrice came to the village a couple of days later. My other mother, Stavroula, told me to stay away from her now so that Beatrice would not become jealous. And do not call me mother, she said. I became very emotional because it brought back those awful memories from before.

We were scheduled to leave for America in a few days. Beatrice told me she realized how much happier I was in the village than in America. She cried saying it, but told me, you don't have to come back with me. Not wanting to lose me now, she had mixed feelings of both anger and sadness. She had no one left and I knew it.

I went and told Stavroula what she had said. "You are going back to America with your mother. She's old, she won't live long, then you can return," she said. I felt like I belonged in Greece, but I knew I was not wanted. Sadly, I told my mother, Beatrice, that I would be going back to America with her.

On the plane ride home, I had lots of time to reflect on some of the rumors I had heard in the village. I asked Beatrice if they were true; that I was traded for the house that we lived in. She said she didn't know what John had done with the house. I also asked her about my name. She could never pronounce it correctly, so I asked, "Why didn't you just change my name?" She looked at me and said, "I took everything from you. Did you want me to take your name, too?" In my entire life with my mother Beatrice, that was the most profound thing she had ever said to me. I realized then that she knew how I felt.

I know now that the person who truly loved me was Beatrice. She began to look at me with admiration, like I could do anything I set out to do. She thought I was perfect. Even though we had a rough start, she admitted that she did not know how to be a mother. She asked me many, many times for forgiveness, and I did forgive her. She always told me the truth. She was the most honest person I knew, and she thanked me every day of her life for being there for her. And she became the most phenomenal grandmother to my three children.

Beatrice died on November 5, 2009, at the age of 93. I called my mother in Greece to tell her and the only thing she said was, "So, we're all going to die. Did she leave you her money?" I happily told her that there was never any money to be had. But I was so hurt and saddened to realize that Stavroula had sacrificed me, her own child, for financial gain.

Looking back at my adoption, I realize I was a pawn to both sets of parents. Each set had something to gain. I have wondered all these years why my adoption was allowed to happen at all. I was not starving or destitute.

Why would they let someone separate a child from her home and family at my age? My parents failed me. The courts failed me. I was a commodity, a bargaining chip.

I can say that the way I was adopted has made me a very giving person. I am not a taker, and I attribute this to my experience. My children tease me saying that I am the one always trying to save somebody, even though it was I who once needed saving. I was very driven to take care of myself. When I realized that one mother traded me for financial gain and that the other mother was incapable of caring for me after her husband's death, I saw no other way. I had no one to turn to but myself, financially and emotionally. I knew what it felt like to be loved and to have it taken away, leaving me with a sense of loneliness that is with me to this day.

It angers me when people tell me how fortunate I am to have been adopted and brought to the United States. I was given a better life, they say. I feel that they are not taking my feelings into account when they say such things. In Greece, my siblings did very well and my mother and father had a much easier life than I did. All I have ever known is work.

My experience, though, has made me grateful for my life, regardless of all those terrible things I went through. I have three wonderful children who are also givers, not takers. My children know my story very well and they have always tried to give me all the love they know that I lost. We cry together and we laugh together. They are my support and I am theirs. And they are part of my story, which lives on, and has not yet ended.

Chapter 9

UNSETTLED SOUL

Andriana

I'm really not sure when my mom and dad were going to tell me I was adopted. I'm sure it would have been in good time.

But I found out another way. I was at the house of a good friend. They had a daughter who was their foster child. We used to play for hours with our Barbie dolls. One day we went to the kitchen for a snack. I must have been about five or six years old and her mother looked at me and said, "You know you were adopted, don't you?"

When I got home, I ran up to my mom and pointed to her stomach and said, "I didn't come from your stomach?" I remember she just looked at me and said, "No, you didn't come from my stomach. It's true. You *are* adopted." She began to explain saying, "Greece cried out to America and to all the countries of the world that they had starving babies that needed to be adopted. We wanted to adopt a child. We looked through thousands of pictures of all the babies and we found you. We chose you."

This information and the way it was delivered to me changed the trajectory of my life, how I looked at the world, how I felt about my parents. My life was my life, but with a twist. There was so much unknown about me.

After the news broke, my nights in bed were spent thinking about the parents I had in Greece, not knowing anything about them and they not knowing anything about me. I began crying myself to sleep at night, saying over and over to no one there, "I'm here, I'm here now."

My adoptive parents were both Jewish. My father's parents came from Russia and escaped Stalin and communism. He grew up in New York and had a sister, who had two children.

My mother's family was from Minnesota. She was the baby of the family and had two sisters and a brother. My two aunts lived in the San Francisco Bay Area, near to us in the city.

I would not describe us as a typical Jewish family. We didn't go to temple, but we celebrated both Hanukkah and Passover with one of my aunts and her family. On Thanksgiving, we would travel to New York to celebrate with my father's side of the family: aunts, uncles and my cousin.

I had a decent, good, upper-middle-class life, even though my parents were in their mid-40s when they adopted me. It made a difference because they couldn't relate to the younger parents.

My dad worked as a land assessor for the federal government in the Small Business Administration. My mother worked as a secretary for the president of the College of Arts and Crafts in Oakland, California. Both my parents were very much into the arts. My father was an actor and appeared in many plays at the Oakland Civic Theater. I used to work with the prop director. Since I was there for every production all through junior high school, I had memorized everybody's lines. Essentially, I knew entire plays by heart.

My parents taught me good manners and important values in life. I had chores and earned an allowance for all the work I did. I washed the car, mowed the lawn, clipped the hedges, cleaned the house, and did my own laundry. I adored my father, and in the summers, we would travel as a family to Palm Springs, Carmel, New York, New Jersey, Yosemite to camp, and to La Puerta in Baja California. The 1960s were great fun and I have great memories from that time.

On my 12th birthday, I was given a horse. Her name was Patty and I loved her. With the money I earned from my allowance, I paid her board and for any time she needed new horse shoes. Eventually, I also worked at the barn with my friends. We did all the barn chores and would saddle up the horses when people came to ride. At the end of work at the barn, all of us got to ride horses and I would get to ride my Patty, which was the best part of any work day. My friends from those days still keep in touch, even though we live in different states.

When I got a little older, maybe I was 13 or 14, my mom brought me into her room and opened a desk drawer. There were two folders with all the paperwork from my adoption. The papers included my passport, a letter from the King and Queen of Greece congratulating my new parents for adopting me, a picture from the airport when I came to the United States, and a magazine story about my adoption and other adoptions from Greece. The letter from the royal couple also wanted to know how I was and how I was liking my new life in the United States with my new parents.

I learned that I came to my parents at 15 months old. My arrival was delayed because I was malnourished. I wasn't walking yet. I have a dent on my left thigh, which my mother explained was where I got pumped up full of vitamins before I came to the United States. My mother was a vegetarian and made me eat parsley, because she thought it was good for my bones, since I did not come to her in good shape.

As a teenager, I really didn't think about my Greek heritage and that's because I felt like I wasn't wanted by Greece or my Greek parents. And my adoptive parents did nothing to celebrate my ethnicity, my being Greek, in any way. I was a confused kid. It seemed like we weren't Jewish enough, which is why we gravitated to a church called the First Church of Religious Science, where my mom taught Sunday school and where I would later marry.

I did try a Jewish temple in Oakland and I checked out the Greek Orthodox Church, too, which meant very little to me. I was also intimidated by it and wished I had been taught to have some connection to it.

The fact of the matter is, I was a mess. I was angry; I didn't understand what about. I was sad; I didn't know why. I had abandonment issues. Where did that come from? I was rebellious. What was that about? And I was dyslexic. Still am, which makes for such difficulty in so many aspects of my life. Anyway, I was so out of control at one point, around age 15, that I was sent away to a special sleepaway school, which exacerbated all the problems I was having in the first place. My mother just could not handle me.

The school was in La Paz, on the Sea of Cortez. The sea was on one side, the desert was on the other. We were required to wear long sleeve shirts and long pants. It was dangerous. There were rattlesnakes and a herd of bull cows was always roaming around. It wasn't like a regular school. We made bread, we learned to live off the land. We gardened. The school was designed to tame me. And I guess it eventually did.

At 19, I married a very handsome Navy 3rd Class Petty Officer whom I'd fallen deeply in love with. We had a son, who married and gave me two grandsons. These are my only blood relatives.

In the winter of 2019, there was a knock on the door of my condo. It was my neighbor, a nice woman whom I met twice before. She needed help to get to an eye doctor, so I drove her.

On the way back home, we got to talking and I told her I was born Greek. With a look of surprise back at me, she said, "You're Greek? I'm Greek, too!" I told her what I knew about my adoption story and she said, "You really need to know your heritage."

I knew she was right, so I started going to a Greek Orthodox Church with her. She explained what was happening and what it meant. She also explained the culture and the traditions. She was the angel who began to lead me home.

I loved listening to the Greek language and the more I heard it, the more I began to feel peace, to feel like I was connecting to something I had once known, but had forgotten. I even began to cry when I heard the language.

At church, I met another woman who knew all about the thousands of adoptions from Greece. She suggested I do some research on the web and I can tell you that it was a revelation! I had no idea about my own history. There was an entire generation of children, postwar adoptees, who were sent out of the country. And that included me.

This realization rocked my world and turned it upside down. Who was I? Where was I from? Was the story my parents told me a lie? I didn't know what to think, but I did know I was grateful to my parents. They gave me a good life with good values. They wanted me to have a happy life and provided all they could to make that happen. I don't believe they knew what was happening in Greece. I don't believe they thought through that I had a life there and a family before they brought me to the United States. I certainly didn't want to hurt them, but I also knew I deserved to learn the truth about my own life.

I did not look for any relatives in Greece until after my parents died. I do panic about my birth family. Is anyone still alive? Do I have brothers and sisters? Is my mother waiting for me, looking for me? As a mother myself, I cannot imagine giving up my own child and then thinking about that child your whole life. Where is my baby? Who took my baby? Who is caring for, loving my baby? I have cried and mourned the loss of my birth mother and I remain heartbroken over our mutual loss, me for her and her for me. My destiny was changed forever and so was my birth mother's.

I have been searching for my birth family now with the help of DNA sampling. I do know that I am from the Peloponnese area of Greece. I have found some very distant cousins and we have been in touch. I guess I am also waiting for relatives to find me, to reach out.

In my 60s now, I wish that my parents had helped to put more Greek into my life. They knew where I came from. I wish I had been introduced to my ethnicity, to know more about it. I wish I could speak Greek. We were Jewish, but not very Jewish. I am Greek, but was not raised to be very Greek. Now I want to connect with who I was born to be, a Greek woman who happened to be raised by another family, a Jewish family. I want to return to Greece to see where I was born, to see where I spent my early days. As I write this essay, I am realizing, too, that you don't really understand what you have missed until you get older and are able to put things into perspective. Maybe that happens after your parents die. Maybe you are able to see yourself more clearly when you are standing alone, thinking about your life in retrospect.

I will continue to search for who I am for as long as I am alive. My heart goes out to everyone, all my fellow Greek adoptees looking for their relatives. We need answers. I do hope we can find them before time runs out for us and for our birth families.

Chapter 10

THAT'S ALL I KNOW SO FAR

Nikolaos/Nick

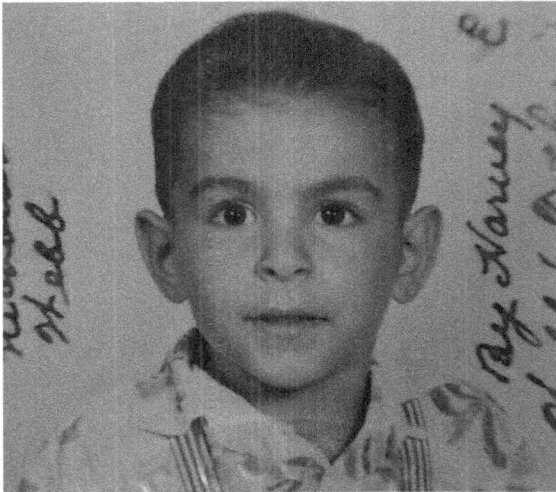

My name is Nicholas Webb and I was born on January 18, 1954. I grew up in the shadow of Disneyland in Anaheim, California, during the 1960s and 1970s. My dad, Harvey, and my mom, Louise, were almost 45 years older than me, which made for a different perspective on how to raise a child, since my other friends had much younger parents.

Mom wanted me to be raised Catholic because she was and her parents were born and raised in Italy and emigrated from there in 1899. Dad was raised in the heartland of America and was Protestant and his family emigrated from England in 1629. His personal belief and "religious" philosophy was,

"Treat others the way you want to be treated." Mom won, though, and I went to catechism. I was never baptized or confirmed a Catholic, but I went to a Catholic church with my friends.

I was an only child and felt a desire to have a sibling, but it never happened. I remember going out to play and not wanting to play by myself, so I would knock on the doors in my neighborhood, homes of my friends, looking for someone to play with.

Early on I realized that I looked a lot more like my Mom than my Dad, so undoubtedly, I felt like I was more Italian than American. My school friends were not as dark as I was, except for my Mexican friends. I played well with others and I liked having a lot of friends, which I did. School was fun and I did pretty well. I was a good student, but I seemed to always get in trouble for talking all the time. As an only child, I guess I was happy to be in the company of other children and so was chatty.

The summer of 1966 brought a surprise that would change my life forever. As I was filling out my paperwork to register for junior high school, there was a question I didn't know the answer to. What is your city of birth?

I asked my parents and my Dad told me that I was from a little country across the ocean. Greece, he said. You were born in Athens, he added. I was already 12 years old and that was not the answer I expected. I started to ask questions.

I knew Mom's family was from Italy and Dad was in World War II. Were they both in Greece when I was born? Well, no. Was mom in Greece while visiting family in Italy? No. Well then, how was I born in Athens, Greece, if mom was never there? Then came the answer I will never forget. "You were adopted, we told you before," my parents said. But I don't remember ever being told, I thought. My mind was trying to comprehend what I had just heard. I loved my parents and I knew they loved me. Because of their love for me, and perhaps because I was a child learning this news for (what I thought was) the first time, I could not imagine anyone giving their child away.

I was so upset with my birth mother. All I could do was focus on how I felt about her. I imagined that I was an accident and not wanted. Actually, I think that was the first time in my life that I felt real hatred. As I look back now, perhaps confusion is a better word. But it hurt, and it hurt a lot to know I was given away by the woman who gave birth to me. I was angry and sad all at the same time and I had no answers. My parents never spoke of it again, and I was left alone to process my feelings about what I had been told.

How did I get through it? I got through it by burying my feelings about my adoption and embracing the fact that I did have good parents. They were completely devoted to my happiness, especially my mom. She did everything for me and when I was in trouble she would always come to my "rescue," whether it was at school or at home or in the neighborhood; she was always there for me.

Dad was strict, but I always felt that he loved me even though I didn't hear many words of love from him. But one time I do remember coming home from a trip to Tijuana, Mexico. We approached the border and had to stop for an inspection of our documents. The border patrol agent looked in the backseat of the car where I was sitting, and asked my dad about me. Undoubtedly, because my skin was darker than my parents, he probably thought I was being smuggled across the border, an illegal immigrant. My dad looked back at me and then at him and said, "That's my son." It was a simple comment, but I felt so proud.

Later, as a teenager, I remember being very upset with them (I don't remember about what), which ended up in a heated discussion. I was about to tell them that I thought they never loved me. As I walked down the hallway, I stopped for a minute to think about what I was about to say. I knew my parents couldn't have children of their own and I knew that they wanted a child and were willing to adopt, even if it meant going to another country. I went back to my room to calm down, realizing that what I was about to say just wasn't true. I held my tongue. Why would I hurt them like that?

When I was in high school my mom gave me a baby picture that had my name in Greek written on the back. I had a foreign language teacher, Mr. Peterson (Anglicized), who was Greek, and he read and translated it for me. My name was Nikolaos Petromelidis, he told me. After almost 18 years, I had a piece of the puzzle to my identity, which was... my Greek name. I also felt more of a connection to Greece because of that name and a great sense of belonging.

About two years later when I was in college, I attended a meeting of fellow students where we shared our life experiences. I only remember one person's story. Her name was Shelley. She was maybe about 19 or 20 years old. She stood up in front of all of us and began to tell us about her life. She had a good family, brothers and sisters, and great parents. But one day things changed.

When she was a teenager, she said, she found herself pregnant. She explained her feelings about being an unwed pregnant teenage mom. She felt that the life within her was precious, and that she would not consider an abortion, but what would she do with her baby? She felt too young to get married, but not old enough to raise and support a baby. Her heart ached. She felt disappointed in herself and bad about embarrassing her parents. She loved the little baby growing inside of her and she didn't want to lose that part of her. She agonized over her decision, but finally realized she only had one choice – adoption. This would allow the baby to have a loving mom and dad who maybe were waiting for a child because they could not have their own; a mother and a father who were prepared for the arrival of a baby, mentally and financially. That was her decision, she told us. She contacted an adoption agency. It was not an easy thing to do, but she knew it was the right thing for her baby. The decision would also give her the chance to move forward and have a family of her own some day when the time was right. Before she delivered her child, and before she knew the gender of her baby, she felt inspired to write her baby a letter. She told her child how much she loved him and how hard it was going to be to say goodbye. She told him about all of her hopes and dreams for him. She told him that she knew he would accomplish great things, that he would be a great husband and father, and that she would never, ever forget him. She would love him forever, she told him, and signed the letter, "Love always, Your birth Mommy." She finished her story by telling us that her baby was born a short time later and that her intuition had been correct. She did have a boy, a beautiful baby boy. She hugged him and kissed him and cried, and then said goodbye, and she cried some more.

I went up and talked to her after she spoke. I thanked her for sharing her experience. I told her I was adopted and that I knew nothing about my birth mom. She told me that because I was offered for adoption, and not aborted, it was proof that my birth mom loved me. I thanked her again and when I got home that night I went to bed and cried myself to sleep, begging my birth mother to forgive me for my feelings of hatred and resentment toward her, and for being so selfish by not considering her feelings. I told her that I loved her and that I would never forget her.

A few years later, in 1977, when I was working in Omaha, Nebraska, my landlady was an older widow named Athena, who had grown up in Greece. When I told her that I was from Greece, she invited me to go to the Greek Orthodox Church with her. I enjoyed going to church with her and her family and learning about my Greek heritage. When her daughter, Helen, came to visit, she told me that she helped bring Greek orphans to the United States in 1952 and all of those babies only went to Greek Orthodox families, and that it was not common for non-Greek families, like mine, to get a Greek baby. That information made me feel like I was destined to be with my parents. Athena and Helen were very nice to me and I enjoyed getting to know them and feeling a little more Greek.

I returned to Anaheim and life went on. I got married to Carla in 1978, and we had two girls and a boy. We later moved to Utah in 1984 where I had a new job waiting and where we had another boy and two more girls. I never thought too much about my adoption since my parents were never very open to discussing it; also, it was very hard to do any research. I never thought of searching for my biological family while my parents were alive, but with the passing of my Dad in 1989 and my Mom in 1993, I felt alone again. Feelings of separation anxiety began to emerge, perhaps much like I experienced as a two-year-old when I left Greece and headed for America. It was time to look for my Greek family. But how?

It was around the same time when I saw a newspaper article online written in the *New York Times*, which was about two women named Maxine Deller and Amalia Balch, who were also adopted from Greece. The article told the story of couples paying one to two thousand dollars, sometimes as much as four thousand dollars, to adopt Greek babies from a man named Stephen Scopas.

I immediately went looking for my adoption papers, which my parents had with all of their important papers. There it was, the name of Stephen Scopas on my paperwork. I was adopted through an organization called American Hellenic Education Progressive Association (AHEPA). Not much information there, except my name, Nikolaos Petromelidis. Birth date: January 18, 1954. Birth country: Greece.

But what was true? What wasn't? What did I believe? I honestly didn't know how to feel, except that I felt lost. Now, with both of my parents gone, I was feeling almost abandoned again.

I had done some genealogy work on my dad's family and had gone as far back as my great-great-grandfather Webb. I contacted some of my extended family and got copies of genealogy records that extend to the 1500s in England. My mom's family was a little harder because her family was from Italy. I was only able to get my grandparents' information and found out they came to the United States in 1899.

Searching for my Greek family was completely different, so I decided to use DNA. I took a DNA test in the fall of 2014. It told me I was Greek, but beyond that which I already knew, there weren't many close relative matches. I went to Salt Lake City to visit the Family History Library and tried looking for my name there, but quickly realized that all the records were in Greek, and I couldn't read Greek. I continued looking online at different Greek websites. I found pictures of the orphanage in Patras and stories about other Greek adoptees who had found parents and siblings, but they knew at least a little something about their Greek families, which aided in their searches. I knew nothing.

It got very depressing, not finding anything, and when I would find a website in English, such as a directory, I never found my last name. It seemed like no one else had it. After so many dead ends, without any information, I just quit looking. After all, I thought, I had a wonderful family, six children who were starting to give me grandchildren, so I embraced what I had and tabled my research. I would start looking again, I knew that, but I felt like I needed a break because I was continually disappointed and grew discouraged while others were being successful.

In the spring of 2015, while online, I came upon an airline manifest with my Greek name on it showing my flight from Greece to New York in July of 1956. That was the first time I found anything about me and my Greek name on the internet. This discovery gave me a glimmer of hope—that there might be more information available than what I had from my parents. I slowly started digging a bit deeper, but my search was sporadic given my full-time job, my family, and other life commitments. Still, though, when I would look for my Greek family, what turned up was the same brick wall.

In 2017, while searching the internet, I found a Facebook group that was dedicated to Greek orphans. I found out I wasn't the only one in my situation. I found other people like me, who quickly became friends. I was encouraged to take additional DNA tests and to upload them to other websites so that I could be represented on several different databases. Currently, I am on seven of them. I have been in contact with seven distant cousins, two in Australia and five in the United States. I continue to get new DNA matches, but no relatives who are really close matches.

It was brought to my attention by one of my Greek adoptee friends to request any and all documents pertaining to my adoption from the Department of Homeland Security through the Freedom of Information Act. In July 2019, I received the results of my Freedom of Information Request (FOIA). I was shocked to see documents from 1956 and 1958, which had my (Greek) first and last name on them. I was also very surprised to see my city of birth as Patras, and not Athens, as my dad had told me. Included were the names of my adoptive parents with their signatures, and the signatures of my aunt and uncle, who served as witnesses.

There was one other document, though, that my parents did not have in all the papers they had saved about my adoption. I had no idea it existed. It was typewritten in Greek and gave the details of my beginnings, my naming and my baptism. I had it translated by one of my DNA cousins in March 2021, who explained that this was "considered" my birth certificate, even though it was not an original birth certificate.

I was an abandoned baby boy. I was taken by the police to the Municipal Orphanage in Patras, on February 3, 1954, at 9 at night. I had a note attached to me, which the police had kept. It said I was born on January 19, 1954, not January 18 as I had celebrated all my life. It also stated that I had not been baptized. So, I was baptized on February 4, 1954, by a Father Nikolaos Galatis and I was given the same first name as him. A woman by the name of Eleni Ntouzalia was present as my godmother and I was given the surname Petromelidis. I have no idea where it comes from.

I had some answers, to be sure, but I also had more questions. The sands of time may have been slipping away, but I launched another plan for finding my Greek family last year at Christmas. I purchased and sent ten DNA kits to Greece with a Greek adoptee to be distributed to anyone in the Patras area who is also searching for a missing family member.

I keep looking, despite the fact that I had a great childhood and great parents, who loved me and whom I loved very much. I keep looking despite the fact that I have a great family of my own; my wife, my children. I keep looking because I was robbed! That's why!

My birth date, my name, my language, my culture and my religion were all taken from me. Everything that makes me what my DNA says I am, Greek, it was taken. But I am using my DNA to find my Greek family. And I am not afraid of what I might find. I am afraid of failing to look. My birth mom made a hard decision to give me up and my adoptive parents made a hard decision to adopt a little boy from Greece. I, my children, and my grandchildren may never know our family in Greece, but I am going to follow the example of my birth mother and my adoptive parents: you make hard decisions and keep looking.

Frontierland, Adventureland, Fantasyland and Tomorrowland may be in Disneyland, but I have experienced each of these at different points in my life. My Frontierland was being born in Greece and not knowing anything about my situation. Where was I born? Why do I have scars on my head, back and leg? My Adventureland was coming to America in 1956 and being raised an only child in Anaheim, California, and experiencing life in the United States instead of Greece. My Fantasyland was thinking I would find my family once I learned my Greek name and that we would have a great reunion. And my Tomorrowland is knowing that it is only through DNA research that I will learn about my family and unlock the last chapter of my story.

Today, I know this: I am not alone. With the love and support of my Greek-adoptee sisters and brothers, I will keep searching. I have my family and friends, and a network of adoptees and Greek DNA cousins that I have only known for a few years, and which continues to grow. All of them are here cheering me on and supporting me. I don't want to let them down or let myself down by giving up and not trying to find out more about who I am.

I know that what you go through will help you get through what's in front of you and I have already gone through a lot. I suspect I will go through more. And even though there are days when I wish I could change some things that happened in the past, my focus is on the future for I know that the future holds the keys to the mysteries of my past.

Chapter 11

GIVEN, TAKEN, NEVER RECEIVED

Yiannoula/Robyn

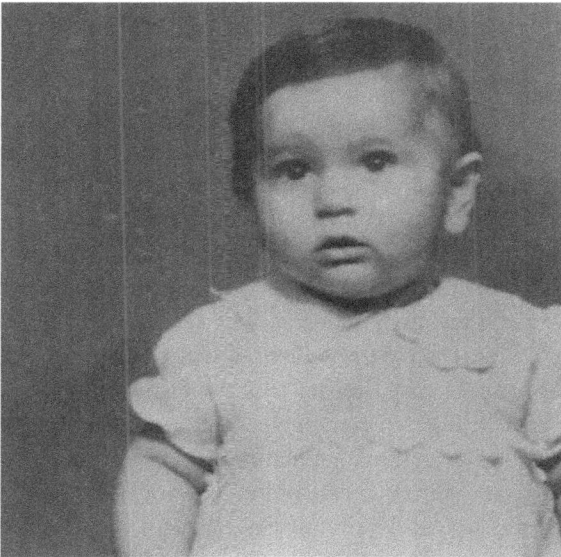

My name is Yiannoula.

I was born of a married mother and father in Messini, Greece, in 1957. My father had accidently fallen into a well after a night of drinking and died there, leaving my mother, Chariklea, a widow before I was born. She was suddenly left with five children to raise and care for all on her own. With the encouragement of an attorney, who was working with the now defunct organization Parents of Greek Orphans (POGO), which helped secure children for couples in the United States, my Yiayia (my grandmother) helped to convince my mother to put me up for adoption. When I was 14 months old, after the preparation and signing of the adoption papers, my mother herself traveled with me from Messini to Athens and reluctantly handed me over to an attendant (a stranger) on a plane. I was flown to Houston, Texas, on November 25, 1958, and was united with an American couple who lived in San Antonio, Texas.

Previously, while my adoption proceedings in Greece were being finalized, my adoptive parents were also in the process of adopting another baby, a newborn from their hometown. My adoptive father had requested a baby boy. His request was not fulfilled. Instead, he received two baby girls: me, from Greece, and an infant from Texas.

The couple who became my parents had lost their only child at the age of 17 months. After what must have been a horrific experience, it was my father's idea to adopt. My mother wanted nothing to do with it. Even though she had lost her daughter seven years earlier, she was still grieving. I was intended to be the most "suitable" match for her deceased daughter. But from the minute I arrived, I can tell you, I also felt like I wanted nothing to do with her. Could I sense her feelings about me?

Growing up, there were no goodnight kisses, no sweet stories and no "I love you" before bed. There was only yelling and screaming. I was never allowed to go to many places and was desperately ashamed of the way we lived. My father was a self-employed house mover. He was always bringing home "stuff" left behind by the previous owners. But on one occasion he brought home a bicycle for me. That bike was my ticket to freedom. I didn't have to ask for a ride to go anywhere now.

As my adopted sister and I grew older, it was clear to me that she was the favored child. My sister was allowed to do anything she pleased, ate better food, and had nicer clothes. I remember that she was allowed to stay home from school because she couldn't get her makeup to look perfect. I wasn't even allowed to wear makeup. Fourteen months younger than I, she eventually turned to drugs, alcohol, and even got pregnant, all very high prices to pay in order to cope with life in our house.

My mother became verbally abusive to me as I reached puberty, which was when I was around ten years old. I had chores to do on weekends before I could go anywhere with friends. One time she told me "You should be grateful we adopted you, otherwise you would still be in the same gutter we pulled you from."

My adoptive parents were flawed people like we all are, I suppose. (Intellectually, I understand that now as an adult.) They were a nice-looking couple.

My dad was an only child whose parents separated when he was just ten years old. He quit school to take care of his mother and learned to drive then, too, in order to cart her around. He was reminded by his own mother that she never wanted to be pregnant again, that she was repulsed by the way she looked when she was carrying him.

My mother quit working when she married my father and I am pretty sure she regretted that for the rest of her life. They had their first child after five years together, but when their baby died, so did that nice-looking couple. I knew she never wanted anything to do with adopting children because she said so.

I do remember a few precious, happy times with them. My mother instilled in me my love for plants and gardening that I have to this day. As a girl, one of my chores was to pull out the weeds in her garden. When my dad was a mechanic and drove race cars, we spent some fun times at the track with other racing families. He also organized reunions with his army buddies once a year over Labor Day weekend. It was one of the rare times I would see my parents happy together. Also, we would take some family vacations together. We would go to different towns and stay at some pretty nice hotels. But those vacations stopped when I was in my early teens.

Those happy times were few and far between. Ours was a dysfunctional family and abusive. How does one feel loved when most of your young life you are told that you came from the trash and will never be anything but trash? I hated that I was adopted and I knew I didn't belong where I was. So much of the time I felt like I had no way out and I so desperately needed one.

I began to gravitate towards anyone who would pay attention to me. I met a young man at school while waiting for the bus to go home. He offered me a ride home and I took it. We spent many afternoons sitting in my front yard where we talked, laughed and became fast friends. One day my friend asked me to leave with him. I hated my home life so much that the choice was easy. I wanted to be loved. I needed to be loved, so I left with him.

That was the worst mistake of my life, and I am very lucky to be alive. I escaped one kind of living hell and wound up in another. This man, my boyfriend, who I thought loved me, turned into my physical and sexual abuser for three months. We lived on the streets for a week until his brother, also an abuser, gave us a room in his apartment.

My boyfriend never worked, but I was forced to wait tables. For hours he would sit at a table at the restaurant where I worked and watched my every move. If I looked or smiled at anyone, I would pay for it in beatings. And in rape. He would hold me down by the neck with one hand, and punch me with the other, all while penetrating me at the same time. He threatened to kill me if I ever tried to leave him. This sick pattern, this routine happened almost daily.

His repeated and futile apologies, after he had his way with me, fell on deaf ears. My ultimate humiliation came when he told his brother he could also use me, sexually, in exchange for the rent payment, which he did.

But it was his brother who told me to leave as soon as I could. So, I ran to the nearest restaurant and hid. While hiding I saw my boyfriend run past and I knew he was looking for me. The manager asked me if I needed help and I asked him for a telephone.

I called my father to come and get me, but he told me he would have to ask my mother, first, if she would allow it. Of course, she said no. He came to get me anyway and took me to a motel close to our house. He brought me clothes and took me to the doctor the next day. To my horror, the doctor told me I was pregnant. I did not want to have a baby so my father scheduled an appointment to have the pregnancy terminated.

When I was finally allowed back in the house, I soon realized that nothing had changed. The abuse, both verbal and physical, once again became intolerable, including from my sister, who had always bullied me. She told me she wished I'd never come back. She called me a whore. I was forced to clean the bathroom every time I used it because I may have brought some "nasty diseases" into the house. Once, when I did need to use the bathroom, my sister forcibly tried to keep me out, but I fought back. The fighting was so intense, the door was broken off its hinges. I needed so badly to get out of the house. Finally, I got a job and moved out a couple weeks shy of my 18th birthday.

I decided to marry my best friend in 1985 when I was 28. We were married for five years. We had a lot of fun, but we partied a lot and I knew it had to stop. After a miscarriage, I decided I wanted a family of my own. But apparently, that was not something that was in the cards for us. The divorce was my decision. I returned home in 1991 for one year to help my father care for my mother. I told my father I didn't want to be there, but that I would stay for him, to help him.

The following year, two weeks after I had gotten married for the third time, I got a call from my father again. He asked that I come back home to help him care for my mother, who had gotten sick again. He was desperate and it was the second time I had ever heard him cry. (The first time was when his mother died.) I really wanted to get out of San Antonio, but I went to help. He couldn't or didn't want to take care of my mother, his own wife. But she had told him, in so many words, that she was not ever going to take care of him, were the situation reversed. She did say to me, though, "I'm sorry you had to come back to take care of me. I'm really amazed that you turned out to be the better daughter." I guess I was.

While she was ill, I do remember a few tender moments when we looked deep into each other's eyes. But the words that really would have made all the difference for me, words of love, were never spoken. I've had to make do with her last, left-handed compliment as I took care of her until her death in August of 1992.

I did finally get out of San Antonio. My husband and I later moved to Connecticut and we started our family. And while my third marriage also ended in divorce, I can say that today I have two amazing children, whom I regard as my greatest achievements. All I ever wanted was to be a good mother and take care of my children; to break what could easily have become a cycle of abuse.

For years, I had been chasing dead end after dead end searching for my birth family. I had always dreamed of finding my way back to Greece, but I had no one to help me. I had been told that everyone there had died, which put an end to that dream as well as an end to any shred of happiness I might have in my life. But one morning, out of the blue, on November 27, 2007, I received a phone call from a man named John in Greece.

John told me that he was the husband of my sister, Sophia. I was overcome with joy, surprise and shock. I thought about how fortunate I was that I could share this joyful news with my children. They would now also learn where I came from and experience the most precious thing in life. Family. But this time, it was *my* family. I would soon learn that I had two sisters, Georgia (who had unfortunately passed away), Sophia, and two brothers, Dimitri (whom I have since nicknamed Taki) and Christos. This is the letter I received from brother Christos (translated from the Greek):

Beloved little sister Yiannoula,
Always good health, that is what I wish for you, too. You cannot imagine the joy that came over me when I learned that you had made great efforts to find out about your parents and your siblings. Many years have passed and the image that comes to mind is from when you were a baby. I would hold you by the hand and take you for little walks. I think of you a lot and I want to see you and be able to talk to you up close, embrace you, and cry tears of joy together. Yiannoula, I was worried every single day about when this would happen, after so many difficult years passed. We will finally be able to meet again and talk up close. Don't ever think I was not thinking of you for all those years that you were gone from me, your brother. When you come, God willing, you will understand how you were being missed. Greece is beautiful. If only you would be able to stay forever, near us, your very own people, your siblings, those who genuinely love you. You were probably too little to remember me. I would hold you by the hand and take you out for short walks until our mother would come home from work. When I lost you, however, you would see what I went through when I learned that our mother had given you away...but let me not sadden you any further. Therefore, I am so anxiously waiting to see you.
With love, Your brother Christos

This was all I had ever dreamed of. To learn what unconditional love is. I found it when I went home to Greece. That is when I found out that my birth mother never really wanted to give me up but, destitute and in despair, she saw no other option. The outcome would have been infinitely better for all parties involved if she had just received a little extra support from family or social services in Greece to help her through the rough patches in life.

My birth mother, Chariklea, was 86 and in a nursing home. She had fallen and broken a hip while I was in the process of getting my papers in order to see her and my whole family. My brothers and sisters did not want to tell her that we had found each other until they knew that I had secured my passport and was really going to be able to come.

As fate would have it, in February 2008, I was able to see her for the first time just a couple of months before she died of a respiratory infection. I looked into her eyes and said, "Hello Momma. It's me, Yiannoula." She was bedridden and very fragile by then, but she realized who I was and kept calling my name. "Yiannoula. Yiannoula." We had no language in common, but we understood each other in the silence of our tears as we kept looking into each other's eyes. I hope she found peace having seen me, knowing I was healthy, before she died.

Having my own children gave me perspective about biological connection and what it means to love and to long for those who come from you. For my own children, I am so grateful. For my own children, I am so happy. They have provided so much joy in my life and they have seen that I am a survivor. But I am a survivor who has lingering pain and scars.

Wishing things could have been different, I still cry every other day. When I found my biological family, I realized, given what Greece was facing, that I might not have survived the poverty in the 1950s. But who knows?

I also learned that a priest who had assisted in my adoption, the attorney who arranged for my adoption, and probably the organization he was working with, POGO, *knew* my adoptive mother did not want me brought into her home. They let the adoption proceed anyway.

Life just wasn't meant to happen any other way than it did for me, I guess. I accept that and understand that I have learned about life in a way that most people do not. Maybe this is the perspective God wanted me to have. Maybe God chose this path for me. And maybe that's what gives me the strength to now share it with you. I do not expect anyone who has not been adopted to fully understand the feelings of one who has. But to all those who have the power and foresight, please do not allow this kind of adoption story to happen to anyone else ever again.

I realize that my story is not over. Since finding my family in 2008, I have wanted nothing more than to go home to where I was born to be with the family who knew me when I left them as a baby. Little did I know that the passport issued to me as an infant was expendable, and was just for one way, which was out of my country. My citizenship from the country of my birth was stripped from me (against my will) after I arrived in the United States.

If I had been able to retain my Greek citizenship and passport, I could have gone home to be with one of my brothers who was diagnosed with cancer and died in October 2020. I could have gone home whenever I wanted to experience my wonderful culture in every season of the year. I could have gone home to experience and learn what it truly means and feels like to be the Greek that I am.

Maybe someday.

Chapter 12

AN ADVENTURE IN IDENTITY

Despoina/Ellen Lori

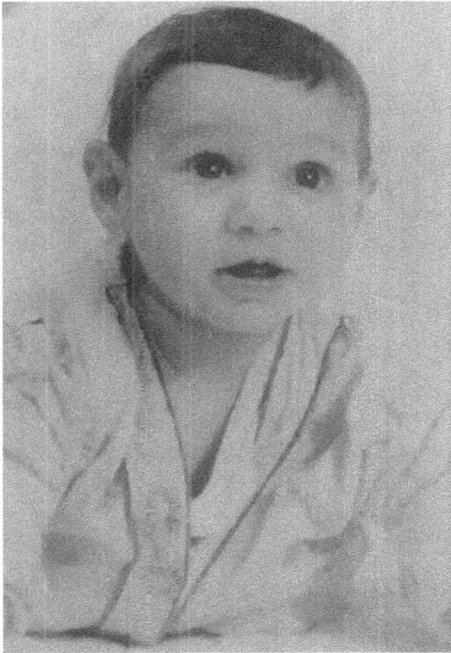

My name is Ellen Rubinstein. I was left in the baby depository at the Patras Orphanage in March 1958. A note was attached to my body that read, "Her name is Despo. She was born 1/5/1958. She likes to eat."

How did I find myself from that orphanage to the United States?

Gilbert and Carole Alexander were close friends of my parents. In 1957, Carole lost a daughter at the age of two to cancer. They did not want to risk another birth and decided to adopt. They knew there were many Greek orphans available, and the cost of adopting a "white" American child was too much money for a middle-class family to handle. Somehow, through a Jewish organization and a reference, contact was made with a woman named Rebecca Issachar, who could secure a child for adoption from Greece. Rebecca Issachar was the sister of a Greek-Jewish lawyer, who would guarantee an adoption from Greece at a reasonable price. Her brother Maurice Issachar, active and prominent in Athens, could handle the adoption process with the Greek courts and have the acquired baby flown to New York in just a couple of months of time. The Alexanders hired Rebecca and her brother. Three months later, a baby girl, whom they named Jayne, became part of the Alexander family. (Jayne and I have remained friends and we have visited each other numerous times over the years.)

After desperately trying for ten years to conceive, my own mother decided to call her friend Carole Alexander to help her make contact with Rebecca Issachar to begin the process of adoption from Greece. Within months, by May 1958, I, too, was adopted with the assistance of Rebecca and her brother Maurice. He, along with several others, was charged with illegal adoption practices in the State of New York one year later. The charges were eventually dismissed because a legal loophole provided that adoption by proxy was considered lawful in the Greek courts.

To be exact, I arrived at LaGuardia airport from Greece on May 26, 1958. Waiting to greet me were my new Jewish family: my parents, both sets of grandparents, my uncle and my aunt. I was given the name Ellen Lori. My family was not particularly observant and I did not have a bat mitzvah, but I grew up firmly in the Jewish culture and with Jewish values. Being an only child, I was fortunate to have made many friends, a by-product of the baby boom generation. The Bronx was a great place to be a child and in which to grow up. I visited the zoo, parks, museums, and beaches. My childhood was truly wonderful.

My adoptive mother told me early on that my given name was Despoina. No last name was mentioned or known. As I grew older, I began to see the differences in my physical appearance from that of the rest of my family. My exotic looks made everyone take notice. I was tall with blue eyes and dark hair. Within my immediate family, I was never treated differently. I was accepted and loved. But as a teenager, my curiosity about who I was, grew. I began to wonder if there was anyone who looked like me or what my biological mother might have looked like. I developed a taste for dark coffee, salt, and olives, which my family could not understand. I attended the Greek Independence Day Parade on Fifth Avenue, hoping that I would find someone who resembled me. I was always hoping that one day I would find someone who looked like me. I even dated a few Greek men thinking it would bring me closer to my identity. None of these ideas ever worked out. My thoughts on being adopted faded into the back of my mind as I concentrated on my education and career goals.

In 1991, my parents retired and moved to Florida. Before they left, they decided to give me my original adoption papers. The envelope contained several pages of Greek writing on rice paper tied together with a red ribbon. Enclosed, too, was a black-and-white picture of me at four months old being held up by a woman. At thirty-three years old, I had never seen a picture of myself from before the time I arrived in New York to my new family. As I held this picture in my hands, I cried. So many questions came flooding through my mind. I knew the picture was taken in the orphanage, but who was holding me? Why did I not have hair? Why were my hands clenched into fists? I sat with this picture in hand and stared at it for what seemed like hours.

This is where and when my search began.

I took these adoption papers to a Greek church to be translated. I was hoping there might be information in the adoption decree that would tell me more about my adoption, but mostly they were legal documents that pertained to the adoption process itself. As had happened in the past, my adoption, once again, took a back seat to my busy, everyday life as a teacher, leaving no indication as to how my life was about to change in a few short years.

The year was 1997. I was told by a friend about an article in *People* magazine that had a story about three Greek-born women, who were adopted and raised in New York as Jews. These women had traveled back to Greece in search of their birth families. My friend figured that I might be interested in the story as well, since the circumstances of my birth were the same. I purchased the magazine thinking that this probably had nothing to do with my life. What a surprise I was in for!

I began reading the article and the first similarity I noticed was the name of Maurice Issachar, who was the same lawyer responsible for my own adoption. Next was a picture of Jayne Alexander hugging a woman who was her birth mother. I was in shock. As I continued reading, I realized that this story had everything to do with my life. The three women who had traveled to Greece were Jayne Alexander, Andrea Friedman, and Maxine Deller. Jayne and Andrea were successful in finding their birth mothers, but the third woman, Maxine, had not been.

They all had help from the Greek government, which made adoption records available to adoptees in 1996. In addition, they had help from an organization that searched in Greece for families looking for children they had given up for adoption years ago. As I studied the pictures in the article, the one woman, Maxine, who did not find her birth family, had a striking resemblance to me. Everyone who read the article and saw the photograph of Maxine could not help but comment on how much we looked alike.

I contacted Maxine and we decided to meet each other. We only lived about 40 miles apart. When we met, she told me about her unsuccessful search in Greece. She said that she would never give up trying to find her birth family. We did look a lot alike, and we were both left at the same orphanage in Patras. We compared adoption papers and they, too, were similar. Maxine's adoptive parents had passed away and she, too, was an only child. She was two and half years older than me and had been adopted at the age of two. She expressed how she thought we looked very much alike. We had the same striking blue-green eyes in common. Maxine thought maybe we were cousins. I found the whole experience surreal. I naively told her we probably looked similar because we were born in the same area of Patras and that many people from that region probably share the same physical traits.

Maxine was on a never-ending quest to find answers about her birth. She set up an adoption support group and started contacting several newspapers and television shows to highlight our adoption stories. Some of the adoptees were legally given up for adoption, but there were many who were sold out of Greece using illegal, black-market channels. Maxine was determined to find the truth.

An unexpected call came to invite Maxine to do a television interview with Maury Povich in 1998. She jumped at the opportunity. The guests on the show were the three women from the *People* magazine article, me, and one more adoptee. The show was willing to perform a DNA test to see if, in fact, Maxine and I were related. I was very nervous to appear on national television, let alone to tell my personal life story. After speaking with my parents and friends, though, I agreed to it. The show was a success, and the DNA test was done.

Four weeks later, a call came from the producer that the DNA tests results had arrived. Feeling very hopeful, but cautious, I told Maxine that it did not matter what the results would be, we will always be a family because of our shared background and experiences. A shock, though. The results came back and showed that with a 99.95% certainty we were full siblings! Same mother and same father! After forty years of being an only child, I had a sibling? It was a lot to digest. After an emotional reunion and joyous congratulations from all around, the reality set in.

Where and how does one begin to develop such a bond with someone who up until then had been a stranger? What was required of me? Do I even know this person? Then the anger of the lost years we should have had also set in. The childhood memories we did not share. And now, the unfamiliar families and life experiences yet to be discovered. These questions and many more absolutely consumed me. Clearly, the only way was to spend time together and establish memories from today, going forward. This began my relationship with my sister, my new sister, Maxine.

Maxine was very experienced with computers. The internet was new, and Maxine was fascinated. After the Maury Povich Show aired nationally, Maxine began receiving emails from several Greek adoptees around the country asking for assistance in finding their birth families. Maxine began setting up a filing system of all those who contacted her. I could not believe how many other adoptees there were who shared the same story. For most of my life, I had understood that I was adopted, but did not think there were other Greek adoptees who had the same experience. For the first time in my life, I felt a real sense of belonging. I now knew others, who share physical resemblances with me and a Greek heritage. Never did I experience such a feeling of inclusion and, finally, a sense of my own community, my people. We formed a support group, and talked for many long nights about being adopted, finding one's birth family, and getting to know other Greek adoptees. The feeling of completeness was so very comforting. Not knowing what I had been missing was both a surprise and a blessing. The next logical thing for me was to finally travel to Greece.

During the summer of 1998, I made my first trip to my birth country. Maxine had a friend who was willing to host me at his home for a month. My excitement was too much to contain. There were so many thoughts that flooded my mind. I wondered if I would remember the smells, or the sounds, or the landscape. Being only four months old when I left Greece, how could this be possible? I had heard, though, from other adoptees that, when they arrived in Greece for the first time, they remembered the smell, and I read that psychologists have proof that the sense of smell is a primal sense which is never forgotten.

The airplane approached Athens and I got my first glimpse of the Greek mountains. I felt serene and at home. I had never traveled alone for such a long distance, but not for one second did I have any fear. I knew in the depth of my soul that I was going home. I had a funny feeling. Even though it was New York where I had spent my life, Greece was my birth home, and my soul knew it. I proudly proved this by showing my Greek passport that I had brought with me. Even my American passport noted my birthplace as Greece. I had every reason to feel like a Greek citizen, and I did. I was not like the other tourists who surrounded me at the airport.

As I went through customs and waited for luggage, I looked around and pondered how many of these people came here for their grand Greek island vacation. I thought about my own life. It felt as if I was regressing to being a child with all the wonderment in my eyes. I thought about the last time I was in this very airport, when my destiny was sealed. I had no control over what was happening to me, the events taking place in my own life at that time. I was a baby passenger traveling to my new American life. I had not been the one who had purchased the ticket. The conflicting feelings, the idea of being adopted and leaving this country, only to return now, willingly, as an adult, paralyzed me for a moment. Soon after, the joy of being in Greece returned as I looked forward to my adventures.

My host met me at the airport with his family and we drove to his house in a suburb of Athens. My senses seemed to be operating at a heightened state. I actively tried to identify the smells I thought I would recognize, but nothing was familiar to me. The air was dry and hot, and my body peacefully enjoyed the gentle, warm breeze as it washed over me. I was feeling a sense of calm as I looked in every direction, down every street and at every tree. Ellen, this is your homeland, I thought to myself.

After Athens, there was no doubt that the first place I needed to go to was the Patras Orphanage. It was a three-hour drive west from Athens. So many thoughts were streaming through my mind, mostly anticipating how I would react to returning to the place where I had been as a baby. Although I had been placed in the orphanage forty days after my birth, it was the only viable, physical place that I could connect to my infant life.

As we drove up the hill, we needed to park the car and walk the long road. A bit nervous, I allowed myself to just go with whatever my heart was feeling. After all, there are no guidelines for processing this experience. Finally, my eyes met the actual building. It is now a daycare for children, but maintains a small museum that acknowledges and honors the building's past. Unfortunately, it was closed for the summer months. My friend and I sat across the street as I stared at the windows. To my surprise, I felt nothing. I did not question my feelings. I just accepted them as they were. I had anticipated a stream of tears and heartbreak, but none came. It was just a building. Strange, I thought, after waiting for so many years, not to have a strong reaction. Many other surprises were yet to unfold that would completely shake me up.

My visit home to Greece was amazing, even though I did not find any leads to my biological family. The remainder of the trip was spent sightseeing and enjoying all Greece has to offer. Meanwhile, Maxine was busy working to connect other Greek adoptees from around the country. She told me that a woman had contacted her, and she thought it was quite interesting because she, too, looked very much like Maxine. This woman was also left in the Patras Orphanage and brought to New York to be adopted by Jewish parents. Her name was Rolene, and she was a one and a half years older than me. Most importantly, she had a document signed by her mother at the hospital where she was born. The document disclosed the mother's name as Nikolitsa Xypolias.

Nikolitsa wrote that she willingly gave her child up for adoption because she was unwed. This was the first time we encountered a legal document with a biological mother's name. Maxine and Rolene agreed to take a DNA test to determine if they were related. If the DNA results delivered a match, then I, too, would be related to Rolene. The DNA results came in and it was, indeed, a match. Rolene and Maxine were half-sisters. This meant that I was a half-sister to Rolene as well. DNA, being a new science, could not show us which half of the parents we belonged to. We all assumed that we shared the same mother and now we had her name, Nikolitsa Xypolias, and now I had not one but two new sisters.

Rolene was a very quiet and shy woman. Both Maxine and Rolene were lesbians, and I had to find a way to understand their lives. Maxine and Rolene had some difficulties in their relationship and I tried to be the calming force between them. The dynamics between the three of us were often strained. Sometimes we did not talk for months. Many times, questions about financial assistance were at the root of the problems. Other times, arguments arose about obligations and requirements of being a sister and what each of us expected from our relationships. It was a turbulent time as we tried to figure it all out. Then a difference of opinion came into play regarding the search for our mother Nikolitsa. Rolene was angry and felt that she had been sold for money. She wanted no part of finding her mother. As for me, I was just curious and wanted to know my family history. Maxine very much wanted to find Nikolitsa and had many questions to ask her, but her wish would never materialize.

Loving Maxine was never easy. She had a passion for life, love, and animals. Her excitement and high spirits were a joy to be around. Everyone enjoyed being in her presence. She could make you laugh just by watching her perform the simplest tasks. Stubborn, manipulative, angry, and moody could also describe her. Maxine was like a ball of fire: you never knew when you would burn being too close to her fire. This dichotomy in her personality was the result of bipolar and addictive personality disorder. Maxine had been in a school for emotionally disturbed children. She attempted suicide while in high school. Alcohol and drug abuse followed her into her adult years. One time, I received a phone call from the police: Maxine was in jail for crashing into a police car while being intoxicated. Another time, she was flat broke, calling and crying to me that she had nowhere to live. My heart was broken for her and for me. From being overjoyed in finding my sister, this was the reality of having this sister. Rolene lived in Minnesota. I lived in New York, so I took on the burden of caring for Maxine. I had to think about how much DNA requires of you as a sister? Was it worth finding out? We never got that far because the inevitable happened. Maxine was found dead at 56 years old from the overuse of her prescription medications.

An identification of the body had to be made. How could I look upon the face of my deceased sister? It would be as if I were to see myself in the morgue. I just couldn't do it. My husband and I both went to the morgue, but it was my husband who identified Maxine. As if this pain was not enough, the State of New York would not release her death certificate or cause of death to me, because DNA results do not constitute proof of sisterhood. What was needed were adoption documents showing that we were adopted into the same family, proving that we were legally sisters. Only then could we claim sisterhood and have access to her documents. But we had not been adopted into the same family, even though we were biological sisters. Even after Maxine's death, what it meant to be DNA sisters haunted me.

Seven years later, I received a phone call that would again be a turning point in my life.

DNA results showed that Rolene was a half-sister and we had the proof of her biological mother's name. When a call came in that a filmmaker from Israel was interested in our story, I was intrigued. The process of documenting these Greek adoption stories became reality after I agreed to participate. We started filming in New York and then traveled to Greece. While in Athens, we filmed all over the city. It was there that we had the opportunity to appear on a Greek television show.

The Light in the Tunnel was a very popular Friday night Greek television program that showcased missing persons and unsolved crimes in Greece. The filmmaker and others were able to secure a spot for me on this show. I had no knowledge that behind the scenes they were hard at work finding the Xypolias family to appear on the show as well. For the producers, the assumption that I was the half-sibling of Rolene, and that her mother was Nikolitsa Xypolias, was enough proof that this was my biological family.

All my dreams came true as I was reunited with the Xypolias family while on national Greek television. They posted a picture of Nikolitsa and my heart stopped. This was the first time I would see a picture of my biological mother. The physical resemblance was shocking. We looked exactly alike! On the stage with me was my cousin Tassos, Nikolitsa's nephew, and his wife. We were holding each other as I cried. After the show, we spent the next days together, piecing together the story of Nikolitsa and her life.

Nikolitsa was a caretaker in a doctor's home in the late 1950s. She became pregnant by the doctor while they were having an affair behind his wife's back. She gave birth to Rolene and promptly gave her up for adoption. The family had little knowledge of this since they lived in Patras, three hours away from Athens where Rolene was born. The family told me that they were not aware that Nikolitsa had had two more daughters. It was odd to think that she had given up three daughters for adoption, but it was not impossible. I spent the remainder of my trip filming the documentary and processing all that occurred. I visited Nikolitsa's grave, her home, and her family. Finally,

I thought I could rest in peace for having learned the story of my life. My soul felt a great sense of peace and comfort for the first time.

But again, a cruel fate would intervene.

Arriving back in New York, I was so excited and could not wait to share this news with Rolene and my adoptive family. Rolene had never felt the need to reunite with her family. I showed her pictures from Greece and the photograph of her mother Nikolitsa. She asked if a DNA test had been performed with this family, and I replied that it was not necessary, because the DNA results gathered from Maxine, her, and me were sufficient. Yet DNA is a complicated science, and so I thought again and decided it was best to re-take the DNA test with Rolene and with this newfound family. The kit was sent to Greece and the DNA test was done by all parties. I waited but did not harbor any doubts about the outcome. Was I wrong? Very wrong.

The results came back. Rolene was, in fact, Nikolitsa Xypolias's daughter. But the Greek family had no relationship to me. There was no DNA match between the Xypolias family and me. Rolene, Maxine, and I probably had the same father, but Rolene had a different mother than Maxine and I. The older DNA test had proven that Maxine and I had the same mother and father by the number of genetic markings that were positive across the DNA lines. Rolene proved to be only a half-sibling, which explains how this all makes sense. The television show in Greece should have performed a DNA test before going on air, but there is no point in looking back at these mistakes and miscalculations. The Xypolias family and I embraced each other and remain close to this day. I will always consider them my Greek family.

My life has been filled with many twists and turns. So much has been out of my control. From my life beginning in a basket with a note attached to my clothing in the Patras Orphanage, to being sent to America. From finding a sister at forty years old, to losing her after only fifteen years of knowing her. To finding who I thought was my birth mother and family, to that being far from the truth. I have lived the full adoption experience, fraught with both elation and heartache as I have searched for my identity.

But in the end, I have come to this realization: My identity is within myself. The person I have come to be, because of my adoption experience, is who I am. Now, my hope is for my soul to be at peace knowing I have explored all possible avenues to learn about my adoption and those I come from. Today there is a quiet place in my heart, knowing that I have found the answers to many of my questions—that is, until I get another call or DNA result.

Chapter 13

BROKEN LINES: A STORY TO TELL

Allison

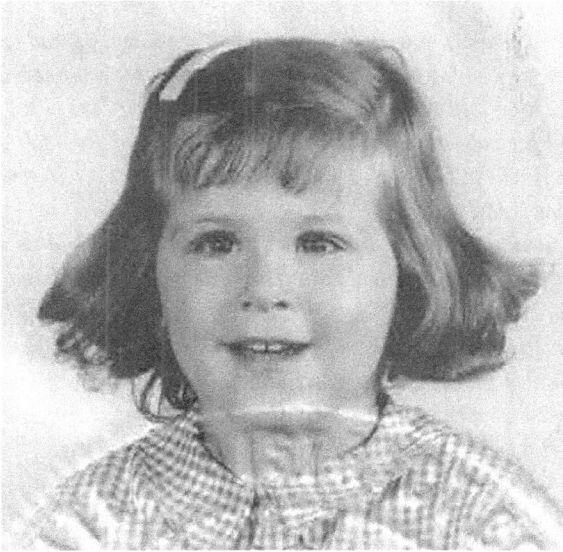

Colorful stories were part of my daily life while growing up in New York City. Everyone living there seemed to have at least one juicy domestic yarn to share with a fellow subway rider or a neighbor on a sitting area bench. Through storytelling, bonds were forged and new friendships made. My family had plenty of their own tales to tell. Yet the stories that circulated in our household never felt like they belonged to me—I couldn't grab them and re-tell them in my own circle of friends. My line of descent was different; my bloodline was unknown. I rejected the sagas of my adopted family and took refuge in those contained in a slim, time-worn volume—the tales of my favorite Olympians.

As a child, I remember crying for poor Demeter whose innocent daughter Persephone was abducted by Hades, the somber ruler of the underworld.

I marveled at the lovely Aphrodite, who was born out of the blood and foam of Ouranos' dismembered body. And, of course, there was Athena, the namesake of that ancient and polluted modern city where I was born, that wise and cunning goddess, who challenged the young and frightened Arachne to a tempestuous weaving contest no mortal could bear. I felt a strange kinship to these mythic deities, but Pandora was my favorite— it is said that curiosity drove her to open wide that coveted box, exposing mere mortals to the dark creatures inside. Like Pandora, my own curiosity and my growing need to find my own family 'ιστορία' (history) eventually led me back to Ελλάς (Hellas), land of light and immortality.

April 1962

Today was the day—the day she would say goodbye to something that had been sheltered deep inside her swollen body for the past nine months, something that squirmed around constantly looking for a place to be, and then came into the world "με τα πόδια"—feet first.

She was denied the opportunity of seeing or holding her tiny boarder. The doctors took the baby while she was still "asleep"—asleep in that trance state so common to mothers giving birth during that time.

The woman was young, only twenty years old. Her mother had accompanied her to Athens, but other family members were far away, working in the fields and factories of their native Thessalia. The year was 1962, over a decade since the Greek Civil War had ravaged the countryside and five years before the oppressive military reign of the "Colonels." The United States was pouring money into the country and the Greeks were slowly recovering from the horrors of their bitter civil war, but poverty was still widespread. Political disarray and a century's long enmity with the Turks was keeping the country from shedding its third-world profile.

Keeping her baby was not an option—her family was poor, she was unmarried, her daughter was "illegitimate." The baby would be given to a "good" family, an American family who would take care of her child and provide more than she could. She signed a form relinquishing her baby, testifying that she was given no money or promise in exchange for giving her child away. Her daughter would have a happy life.

April 1999

The voice on the answering machine recording was hoarse and rough; it didn't sound the way I expected her voice to sound. At the beep I left a message, though I wondered if I had the correct number. I had received it from a private researcher, who had miraculously tracked down my birth family to their native village in central Greece where they were having their Easter celebration. Now they were supposed to be back home in Athens and they were told to expect my phone call.

After leaving the message I waited by the phone in my bedroom, the one with the old-fashioned cord attached to its base. It somehow felt more secure using this one than the newer, cordless model. The old phone was attached and grounded; I clung to it feeling more uncertain than usual. Ten minutes later the loud ring brought me back to my senses. It was the same deep-throated woman whose voice I had heard on the answering machine. "Allison" (she pronounced the "a" like "ah" and the "I" like an "e"), "how are you?" I was surprised she could speak English so well. The accent was thick and heavy as I expected, yet something still nagged at me—the voice was wrong. She asked me questions about myself—what did I look like, how tall was I— and after we spoke for a bit the truth emerged. "Ahleeson," the voice said, "I am not your mother, I am your aunt. Your mother does not speak English. You will call her—I will give you some Greek words to say to her. She is expecting your call."

Before I could do as I was directed, my aunt quickly brought me up to date on "family history." She repeated an age-old story, woven together with those torn and tattered threads that have produced countless cultural variations through the centuries—young lovers, different social class, unsympathetic elders, no dowry.

As we spoke, I tried to digest the details of those distant lives. I formed visual images of people I had never met and places I had never seen. There was much to consume through the coldness and safety of the telephone receiver, and I found myself taking notes in an undecipherable hand. I wanted to capture it all, the missing pages of life before I was born.

Inside my head there was a constant drumming, the sound of the words "no dowry" reverberated over and over. It was all so old-fashioned and unreal to me. Could it be true, could I trust the story this stranger was telling me? My modern American sensibility could not accept that a young woman would be denied marriage because she was poor and didn't have a gift of money or household items for her husband to be! Yes, I had read about such situations in history books, but this was my story, and it certainly did not mesh with the stories I had created for myself while growing up.

My fantasies changed over the years, but they all had one element in common—my birth mother was not poor. As a young teenager who indulged in way too many romance and adventure stories, I spent many hours daydreaming I was a heiress to a long-forgotten family fortune. As I matured into an archaeology student at college, I was certain that my parents were scholars and archaeologists themselves, and could not raise a child because of the travel and hardship required in their profession. These were the type of stories I wanted to hear, not some sorry tale about an impoverished, illiterate woman who could not marry the father of her child because she didn't have a dowry!

Being raised in the 1960s and 1970s, I was indoctrinated with a notion of female independence and I selfishly wanted to have a birth mother who embodied that ideal. On the one hand, I was excited by my new knowledge because it gave me a long sought-after connection to my past. I now knew my beginning, a point of origin, that began before I arrived in the land of cow's milk and plenty. I now could lay claim to those proverbial "roots"—I no longer had to float in mid-air unattached to the surface below. On the other hand, I wanted my newfound family to be people "of consequence," who had power and prestige in the world. I wanted to be a "somebody," and mistakenly thought my missing sense of worth would be conferred on me through my newly found birth line.

Feeling a conflicting sense of disappointment and excitement at the same time, I finally said goodbye to my aunt and prepared myself for my next call—to the woman who ushered me into this world. I was now equipped with two phrases: "Τι κάνεις"—which means "How are you?" and "Σε αγαπώ"—"I love you."

My heart pounded steadily, mimicking the strange ringing bleep of the international phone connection. Finally, a woman answered and I knew it was my birth mother. I felt warmth gently oozing into my upper body. This voice I recognized—it was like mine, high-pitched and thin. She started speaking in Greek, I in English. We both started laughing. Then I tried to utter the strange sounding phrases I had hastily copied down. She replied "Σε αγαπώ, σ'αγαπώ πολύ," I love you, I love you very much, and we laughed some more. Afterwards my husband said he wished he had recorded our "conversation."

June 2000

The flight to Athens was long and sleepless. I was making the same journey I had made many years before, only this time in reverse. After the lights were dimmed, I watched as the airplane monitors showed us how to sleep comfortably while seated. Unfortunately, this is an art I have never mastered. Images of digitized "passengers" floated across the TV monitors, adjusting various seat parts and body limbs into a position designed to encourage a state of twisted relaxation. Ah—if only I had taken more yoga classes! No matter how many poses I tried, I could not get comfortable. Somehow my husband and both children managed to sleep; it was only I who was restless.

By the time we disembarked I was feeling an overwhelming lethargy coursing through my veins. My drowsiness was tinged with a caffeine-high, even though I hadn't imbibed any coffee or tea in the last twenty-four hours. I felt drugged yet hyper-vigilant; my body was an infusion of adrenaline and cortisol mixed together in a somnambulistic cocktail. The air was stifling; a heat wave from Africa was making its way through southern Europe that summer. As we stood and waited in vain for luggage that never appeared, I was sweating profusely, dripping like a goat roasting slowly on an open spit. The carousel went around and around. I was ready to drop.

Even though I was told about my Greek-ness from an early age, I often doubted the veracity of information I received. Frequenting many Greek diners in New York City, I had a hard time believing that those swarthy young men with thick glossy black hair could be of any possible relation to me. I was savvy enough to know that not all people conform to national stereotypes, yet I apparently never applied this understanding to myself. Nor, for that matter, did most other people I knew. With straight light brown hair, hazel eyes, and small chiseled features, no one ever would have mistaken me for a Greek!

In fact, the physical attributes of my DNA remained unmatched for nearly four decades. The brother with whom I was raised was also adopted, and we neither resembled each other nor our adoptive parents, so it was with some astonishment when I opened a package I received from Greece shortly after that first telephone call.

A black and white photo dated from 1963 showed my birth mother in a tall field of Queen Anne's lace, smiling coyly at the camera, her face at a three-quarter angle. I ran and opened an album of my own and took out a picture of myself at eighteen, nearly identical in expression, pose, and facial features. The piercing, yet gentle, look in the eyes, the funny tilt of the nose, the thin lips hesitantly parted conveyed one and the same image—hers and mine.

Now, standing a few feet away from me at the airport in Athens was the woman who gave me my first taste of life. Time had not been kind to my mother—the unhealthy effects of too much tiropita, loukoumathes, and countless bottles of Coca-Cola, as well as years spent under the hot Mediterranean sun had produced a coarser version of that shy young woman in the fields. Her makeup could not conceal the dark circles under her sunken eyes; her skin was lined and wrinkled. But her smile was still sweet, and she welcomed me with thick arms open wide. I felt suffocated in her embrace and awkward receiving her touch. Her upper body was soft, voluminous, and fleshy compared to my physique, yet her skin was the same shade of golden caramel and breathed the same milky scent as mine. I remained within her embrace and she addressed me fondly, "το μωρό μου" (my baby).

During the course of our visit, I met my half-sisters, other aunts, cousins—too many relatives to remember them all. We were introduced to a kaleidoscope of faces and a string of foreign sounding names to accompany them: Nikoletta, Despoina, Efthymia, Kostas. We were showered with gifts, flowers, and φιλάκια (little kisses). In crowded apartments in different parts of smoggy, sprawling Athens, we drank beer, ouzo, and Coca-Cola, and were served heaping plates of pastitsio, galatopita, and melitzanes papoutsakia at eleven o'clock at night. We danced to music and engaged in passionate conversations, which with the help of several wannabe polyglots among us, were at best half understood. We often didn't get back to our hotel apartment until two in the morning, stuffed to the gills and too full of the evening's activities to sleep.

Our mornings were lazy—we often slept in late and enjoyed a simple breakfast on one of the balconies surrounding our rooms. We swam daily at small beaches frequented by grandmothers and children escaping the heat. We ate outdoors at beachside *psarotavernes*, restaurants that served mostly fish, sampling the local seafood specialty of the day. On days when we were feeling more active, we toured monuments where ancient family dramas were enacted thousands of years before us. During our three-week stay our odyssey was filled with snippets of everyday life and adventures. One day when we were in the water swimming, we heard a man yelling at us "παπούτσι, το παπούτσι σας—ο σκύλος!" (shoe, your shoe, the dog!). Turning around we saw a cute little pooch scampering away with my daughter's beach sandal. We all ran after the dog and he ran faster, turning occasionally to look at us and mock our pursuit. We backed off and he promptly dropped the shoe; apparently the pursuit was more exciting than his stolen treasure.

On another occasion, we were in route to ancient Corinth driving a car borrowed from my birth mother's husband, Nikos. The car was a blue Datsun Cherry (which we later renamed the Datsun Lemon) and even though Nikos had reassured us that it was "a good car, runs well," it had no air-conditioning, minimal seat belts, and was beginning to resemble some of the time-worn sites we had been visiting. After an interval of driving at 40–50 mph, we started to pick up speed and the thin sheet of metal that was the engine hood started flapping wildly. We were thankfully not on the freeway yet and were able to pull into a service station. If we had gone any faster, the hood would have flown up in front of us, blocking the view through the windshield. We rummaged through the trunk looking for something to remedy the situation and found an assortment of medical paraphernalia. Nikos was both a smoker and an asthmatic and kept a spare oxygen tank with rubber tubing and other accessories. The tubing was thin but it would suffice; we tied down the cover securely and were on our way.

The days passed by, one by one, falling into a continuum of time unmarked by a regular calendar. Toward the end of our stay I started to relax a little, enjoying the warm breezes at midnight, the outdoor meals, swimming everyday just to keep cool. I started adapting to a slower pace, feeling less annoyed and nervous about crazy drivers, noisy motorcycles, and bad roads.

I gave in to the new rhythms, but was still in an emotional haze, trying hard to simultaneously experience and process all of the new relationships and cultural differences. I wanted to shed some of my American-ness and reclaim some of the Greek-ness that was mine by birth. I wanted to absorb the textures, the sounds, and the light, all of the intricacies of a foreign past that were denied to me while growing up in my middle-class American family.

On the airplane trip homeward bound, I reflected upon what it means to belong to a place. I now had two homes and two histories but could I ever integrate them? While growing up I often felt like I came from "someplace else." Yet now that I had visited and experienced that "someplace else" I was beginning to realize that I didn't truly belong there either—my genealogical lines were cut off too long ago.

I closed my eyes and felt a little disoriented. My mind was cloudy—I'd traveled so far to reclaim something that was lost, yet there was still so much missing. I thought for a while and eventually an image emerged—alongside the broken lines of my birth were beautiful, strong, flowing branches connected to all the people that I held dear to me—my adopted family, my husband and his family, my own two children, and many friends and people who were part of my life. I suddenly realized how fortunate I really was. I also realized that, although my original lines were broken—and they will always be that way—those lines were pieces of a story that was mine to tell.

Chapter 14

AN UNEXPECTED JOURNEY

Mitsos/Merrill

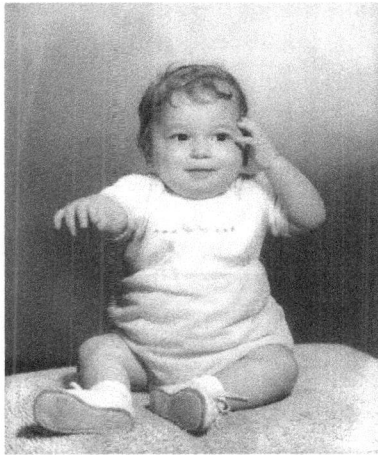

Every journey starts with a first step. A decision, really, to take that first step. To metaphorically move one foot in front of the other. That first step for me was taken on March 10, 2011. It was a cold, overcast, dreary Saturday morning when I typed the words "Patras orphanage" into the search bar. Life is full of unexpected journeys, and this was not my first one.

The past six months had been so difficult. Shirley, my wife of 24 years, had passed away, suddenly, but not unexpectedly, the previous September. We both knew she was sick. Having been a certified nurse's aide in the home health care field for many years, she knew her prognosis. There is no cure for Chronic Obstructive Pulmonary Disease (COPD). I knew that, too. What I didn't know was how soon it would take her. She knew, though, and as I look back, there were signs.

Shirley's death left a void in my life and also gave me time to think about other things, like my own life and where it began. I hit "enter" on the keyboard that Saturday morning in March and that's when everything changed. The first entry came up and was about the Skagiopouleio Orphanage. Was this the orphanage? My orphanage? I clicked on the second entry and it was there I found an article from April 13, 1996, published in the *New York Times* entitled *"Tales of Stolen Babies and Lost Identities: A Greek Scandal Echoes in New York."* The article told the stories of Maxine Deller, and others, in their search for the truth behind their adoptions from Greece in the 1950s. All came from the orphanage in Patras.

"Holy shit! Could I have been a part of this?" I said out loud to no one. I had never heard of this and I quickly became obsessed. The rest of that day was spent searching. There was a website (no longer in existence) published by a Greek adoptee regarding his experiences as an adoptee. On it were pictures of the Patras Municipal Orphanage, an old, decrepit building, long since torn down. There was the link to the Roots Research Center in Greece, an organization aiding Greek adoptees in search of their roots and advocating for the rights of children in foster care.

I rushed downstairs to the basement to retrieve the adoption documents that my parents had saved. It was there that I confirmed it. I, too, was in the Patras Municipal Foundling Hospital (Orphanage). I learned that it was there where my adoptive parents had used the International Social Service (ISS) to facilitate bringing me to them. One thing led to another, and then another. My unexpected journey had begun.

My life was and remains to this day shrouded in mystery. But the "facts" are simple.

I was born on November 11, 1954, in Patras, Greece, and was left on the steps of the Pantanassa Church. From there, I was taken to the Patras Orphanage on November 26, 1954. The note attached to my dirty white and violet clothing said my name was Mitsos, and that I had been baptized. It was the orphanage that decided my last name should be Demetriou. There I was. Mitsos Demetriou, Greek orphan of unknown parentage. This is the only proven statement in this paragraph.

It is more accurate to say that I was born on, or about, November 11, 1954, in, or near, Patras, Greece, and that I might have been left on the steps of the Pantanassa Church. I might have arrived at the Patras Orphanage on November 26, 1954. If there was a note attached to my clothing, it might have said my name was Mitsos and that maybe I had been baptized.

I remember nothing of my time at the orphanage. But the following year, I do know I traveled to the United States, arriving at Idlewild airport in New York City on October 5, 1955. From there it was a train trip to St. Louis, Missouri, with my adoptive parents, Merrill and Rhoda Jenkins, and my new life. A new life that would be far better than anything I could have had growing up in Greece during that time.

I have always known I was adopted. I have no recollection of when my parents told me I was adopted; however, I do remember telling my second-grade class. I would have been old enough to have had some understanding and acceptance of the concept, but not old enough to be scarred by the revelation that I was not my parents' biological child. I was proud to be adopted. It made me special. Or maybe just different. Either way, I accepted it as readily as a child would accept a gift at Christmas. It is part of my identity, but not my whole identity. My parents never emphasized it and, most of the time, I never thought about it.

My adoption was aided by the passage of the Refugee Relief Act of 1953 and facilitated by the ISS. One of their requirements was that prospective adoptive parents (PAPs) had to be vetted and approved by local and/or state child welfare agencies before they could adopt. This process would only happen if the adoption was to be finalized in the United States. It was not a requirement for adoptions finalized in Greece in the 1950s. The Greek courts wanted "assurances" that the PAPs were going to be "fit" parents, but no official reports were required. These "assurances" were often offered by the representatives of the PAPs without any confirmation from governmental agencies in the United States.

The result was that Greek children often went to parents who were unfit and would never have been approved for adoption by child welfare agencies in the United States. The haphazard adoptions led to abuses. Not always, but for those children who were physically and/or emotionally abused, it has led to a lifetime of struggling with the scars left behind. In some cases, the form of abuse was much more subtle, such as being constantly introduced as "our adopted child," with the intended or unintended implication that they weren't a "real" child. This was especially harmful when there was a biological child in the mix who received preferential treatment.

In other cases, it was just the opposite. The adoptive parents were proud enough to announce the arrival of their Greek child in the newspapers. Newspapers of the 1950s and 1960s also show cute little boys or girls standing with their hand on their heart at their naturalization ceremony reciting the Pledge of Allegiance. But some of those children were never told they were adopted. The grandparents knew. Aunts, uncles, and cousins knew. The whole family knew, but the adoption was kept a dirty little secret, never to be uttered, until that one day when it slips out. Maybe now the child is a teenager who hears it from her cousin who overheard her parents talking. Or a young man is told by a well-meaning aunt who just knows it is the right thing to do. Or the child is well into an adult life and is told on the deathbed of a parent, the whole time having lived a lie. Suddenly, the person they thought they were no longer exists, stripped of their identity, and replaced by a stranger. "Who am I?"

My search was never an act of desperation. I had grown up in Spanish Lake, Missouri, a suburb of St. Louis. My upbringing was pretty typical of the middle class at the time. My dad, Merrill Sr., worked during the day. My mom, Rhoda, stayed home. My sister and I went to school. We ate dinner around the kitchen table, and we had to finish everything on our plate.

My sister's name is Cherie. She was born in April 1957. Unlike me, she was not adopted. My folks had tried for years to conceive a child without success. Visits to doctors provided no relief and no clue to the problem. Eventually, they decided to adopt. After I came into their lives, they decided that I needed a sister and started looking to adopt again. But a funny thing happened. My mom got pregnant and nine months later, I had a sister. Our family was complete.

Where we lived consisted of two streets and 25 homes filled with kids my age. Summers were mostly spent outside doing all the things kids do. Running around playing tag. Riding bikes. Playing baseball. One of our streets was a cul-de-sac that had a sewer lid in the center. That was home plate!

My father had no interest in sports, so hauling me around to any little league games was out of the question. But I do have two specific memories of my father and sports. Both involve baseball and both are good ones. One was when I was a young lad and we played catch on the side yard. Normally, not a big thing, but that was the only time I recall that ever happening. The other was during the summer of 1972. He and I went to a St. Louis Cardinals baseball game at Busch Stadium when he had gotten free tickets. We were sitting in our field box seats on the first base line and I asked him, "Who do you want to win?"

"I want the best team to win," was his response.
"Don't you want the Cardinals to win?"
"I want the best team to win."

I could not get him to root for the Cardinals. It could have been worse, though. He was born and raised in New York City. He could have been a Yankees fan! Later in the game he made up for it when a foul ball was hit in our direction. As I sat there with a lapful of food, staring at the ball coming at us, my 6-foot, 250-pound father sprang up, lunged after that ball, and damn near caught it. It was one of the greatest things I ever saw him do, and 49 years later, it still brings a tear to my eye.

Another rite of summer as a kid is getting into trouble. One time, some of us were playing at the construction site of a new home. I jumped from the top of a mound of dirt to a level three feet below and sank knee deep in a puddle of mud. My friends had to dig me out. My mother wasn't pleased when she found out.

There was one other time my mother wasn't pleased. But this time it wasn't anger, it was pain. And it is something I am not proud of. I don't know how old I was, maybe ten or eleven. It was summer, and she and I were out in the side yard. I wanted to do something. I don't even remember what it was, except, at that moment, she didn't want me to do the thing I wanted to do. I got mad. I pleaded. And then I yelled, "You never let me do nothing! You just hate foreigners!" Where did that come from? I had just thrown my adoption in her face, and it hurt her deeply. She started to cry. I knew I had gone too far. More importantly, I knew what I had said wasn't true. I immediately regretted it and started apologizing profusely. "I'm sorry! I'm sorry! I didn't mean it! I'm sorry!" All was forgiven, but I am sure she never forgot it. I know I have not. I learned a valuable lesson that day. I had struck out in anger with the sole intent of hurting and I had succeeded. Also, I had picked the worst person to do it with and to. I felt horrible afterwards and never said anything like that again.

My upbringing was ordinary and typically "American." I played. I went to school. I got in trouble. I watched television. I fought with my sister. I was scolded. But the one thing I never experienced was what it was like to *be* Greek.

My mother was mostly German, and my father was a little bit of everything, including German. Neither one of them had a clue about what it was like to be Greek, so no attempts were made to expose me to Greek culture. Anything Greek I saw was on television, and that wasn't often. But when I did see it, even if I didn't understand it, I felt proud to be Greek.

My unexpected journey began in March 2011, but the seed of that journey was planted in the summer of 1972 in high school. We were sitting around our kitchen table; my sister and a few friends. The details are lost to time, but talk must have gotten around to my being adopted. That's when my mom brought out my adoption papers. It was in those papers that I learned some of the details about my early life.

My memory of that day is that I was left on the doorstep of an orphanage. That revelation did not bother me at all. I actually thought it was kind of "cool" at the time. I had a Greek name! Mitsos Demetriou. (And although it has been spelled at least six different ways, that is the spelling I have used.) My friends immediately started calling me "Mitz," and my mother later admitted that she regretted revealing my Greek name. I believe it was because she feared being marginalized as "not my real mother." Nothing could have been further from the truth. I had one mother.

Certainly, I had a birth mother, but she never mattered. I never thought about her much. But when I did, it was always to try to understand why she did what she did. Why was I here and not there? I did not know the reason, but I believed it had to be a good one, and because of that,

I never felt like I was abandoned. I never asked "Why didn't my mother want me?" I had a curiosity about what happened, but I was also at peace with it. I honestly felt that my birth mother let me go because it was in my best interest.

But in March 2011, when I found that newspaper article and dipped back into my adoption papers, I obsessed the whole day over what I found. The question was what to do now. Where do I go? How do I proceed? Was I sure I wanted to?

It took me eleven days to finally decide to contact the Roots Research Center in Greece. A response came from Mary Theodoropoulou five days later. My naïve expectations were soon going to be tested: I learned that this search was going to be a marathon and not a sprint. But that was okay. I committed to being in it for the long haul.

By the middle of April, something from my adoption papers was confirmed. I *was* left on the doorstep of a church, the Pantanassa Church, in the center of Patras on the Peloponnese of Greece, not at the orphanage. Later, I asked my Aunt Joan what she knew and she, too, told me that my mom had told her I was left at a church.

A month later, I wrote to the American Branch of International Social Service, the ISS, requesting information regarding my adoption. They sent a tracing packet. I filled it out and sent it back. A case file was opened, a case for me. By the end of September, I received notification from my post office that they had a package for me. It was a thick package. That very evening, I began to spend some quality sifting through it.

Much of the file was a collection of correspondence between my parents, the ISS (both American and Greek branches), and various state and federal governmental agencies regarding the procedural minutiae involved in an adoption. Included was the report from the St. Louis County Child Services regarding my parents' competency to adopt. That was an interesting read, but of course, they passed with flying colors. The most interesting things I found were three Greek documents and their official English translations.

The first was the Birth Registration Act No. 1708/1954. (All the information I know about the circumstances surrounding my birth and my arrival at the orphanage came from this document.) It stated I was brought there on November 26, 1954, by someone from the 3rd Police Station and that I was wearing "two vests one white and one violet colour and various rags." A note attached to my clothes said I was baptized and my name was Mitsos. These details were attested to by a janitor, Andreas Fragoulias, who went before the officials and so testified.

The second document stated that the Mayor of Patras, lawful guardian of the "inmates of the Patras Municipal Foundlings Hospital" declared me "adoptable." This was proof of my status as an orphan, as required by the St. Louis County Juvenile Court.

The third document stated that the Mayor of Patras consented to my adoption and emigration to the United States, as was also required by the St. Louis County Juvenile Court. Asking for my adoption file was, by far, the most important step I took in 2011. It gave me information I never had, and a far greater appreciation for what my parents had to go through to adopt me.

There was no movement regarding my search for many months, but finally I received a note from Mary Theodoropoulou dated January 13, 2013. It read: "I have an information about a mother, unmarried who gave birth to a boy, your dates, she was 25 years old, and her surname was Kyriazi." At last! Could there be a real break?

Progress seemed to move at its own pace in Greece. March came and no word. An email I sent came with the response that the Patras archives were closed, the social worker retired, and the Mayor of Patras did not have the money to replace her due to the economic crisis in Greece at the time. Not all was bad news, though. On the March 13, I received a message via Facebook Messenger from a woman named Pam Makos Kirchhoff. She had seen my picture on the website of the Roots Research Center and found me on Facebook. I was touched by her willingness to reach out to help in my search. Pam was the first Greek adoptee I communicated with and her friendship to this day has meant the world to me. She was tangible proof that I was not alone.

Nothing advanced in my search until March 2015, when word came that the city of Patras had hired a social worker and the archives were opening. But it wasn't until August when I met "Tammy," a fellow Greek adoptee originally from Ohio, but living in St. Louis. I found her story, via the Hellenic Genealogy Geek (HGG) Facebook group. Inspired by Pam two years earlier, I reached out to Tammy and it was through Tammy that I met Dr. Gonda Van Steen, who was at the time Professor of Modern Greek Studies at the University of Florida in Gainesville. She was doing research about Greek adoptions for a book that would eventually be entitled *Adoption, Memory, and Cold War Greece: Kid pro quo?* It is a fascinating study of a phenomenon about which little was known. She asked me if I would share my own story and experiences, which I gladly agreed to do. Little did I know the impact Dr. Van Steen would have in my search and on my life.

Gonda became a trusted friend and confidante who has been by my side during my quest, imparting knowledge, offering encouragement and suggestions, helping map plans of action, and allowing me to contribute, in some small way, to her research. Everything I know about the Greek adoption phenomenon, I learned from her, and I am forever grateful. She would be there for the next big step of my journey, a real journey.

In June 2016, I made my first trip to back to Greece since leaving as an infant. I decided to return to Patras for research into my past; a four-day sightseeing tour of a number of ancient sites; down time in Athens to tour and to react to whatever information I might find in Patras; and a six-day island-hopping tour. I arrived in Greece on June 7.

Once I got settled into my hotel, I grabbed my camera and started walking. The streets were narrow. The buildings old. They all seemed identical to one another. The trees lining the streets were filled with oranges. I couldn't help but marvel at where I was. I was in Athens! I was walking the streets of Athens, Greece, the country in which I was born! I had always hoped to return to Greece someday, but for most of my life I felt it was just a fantasy. I had always thought it would be Shirley and me walking those streets together, but fate had other plans. This was not lost on me, and I felt both joy and sadness as I walked those ancient streets alone.

But there was another feeling, a feeling I did not expect. Comfort. I felt comfortable. No fear. No trepidation. No unease. I was walking along the streets of a strange city in a foreign land and I was comfortable. And it was because I was home. This was home and it felt like home. It is a feeling I still remember and cherish.

The next day it was time to get down to business. Several months before my trip, Gonda had suggested we meet with the director of the Greek Branch of the ISS. Quite honestly, I didn't think it would amount to much, but I was soon to learn a new catchphrase: "It doesn't hurt to try." Gonda made the arrangements for us to meet at the office. I walked there and she was already waiting for me. It was the first time I would lay eyes on my friend in person.

The purpose of the visit to the Greek ISS was twofold. It was a chance for me to peruse its "version" of my adoption file, and a chance for Gonda to do research for her book. This visit was a success and well worth the effort. She got greater insight into how the ISS worked in Greece and I got to see pages that were not available to me in my U.S. adoption file.

There was no information regarding my biological family, but I did find one thing that surprised me. Not long after I had arrived in America, the Greek ISS asked for an update on my progress. My folks sent them a photo from a Christmas card taken in 1955, of me and my new family on my first American Christmas. That photo card was still in my Greek file. I had seen this card in photo albums for years, but never expected to see it in Greece. I brought the card home and had digital copies of my Greek file sent to me. We didn't leave until after 6:00 p.m. and we were both gratified as to how things went.

The next day Gonda and I met at Syntagma Square where we took a cab to the bus station for the trip to Patras. After our arrival and check-in at our hotel, we were off to explore. On the agenda was a trip to the Office of Vital Statistics and then to the site of the former Patras Orphanage to meet the social worker. I had been waiting for this encounter for over three years and now my wait was soon to be over. During our walk, Gonda and I strolled past the Pantanassa Church with the very distinctive steps. I don't recall feeling anything necessarily, but I did feel a connection. This was the place, this was the church, these were the steps. I was left right here.

The following day, Mary Theodoropoulou of the Roots Research Center met us at the hotel and we had a light breakfast there, after which we went to try to solve the mysteries of my beginnings. We were off to the Office of Vital Statistics, where the records of the orphanage were held, but accessing them is not easy.

After waiting our turn, Mary did all the talking. Gonda was there to observe. I just listened, not understanding a word. We were told, "The person you want to talk to is not here. Come back in 45 minutes." We did just that, but the results were not much better. Their unwillingness to help, despite my having a power of attorney standing there with me, was punctuated by a gentleman sitting at a desk behind the counter wearing a T-shirt that read, in English, "GO HOME." We walked out of there with nothing more than a copy of the original handwritten version of my Birth Registration. Nice to have, but it was nothing new.

Our next scheduled stop was the orphanage, but we took a detour instead. Mary was not pleased with the response we got at the Office of Vital Statistics and the inflexibility with which we had been treated. It was off to see the Mayor of Patras. To him Mary explained the importance for adoptees to have easy access to their own records. The Greek government, under pressure after the *New York Times* article appeared in 1996, passed a law that required government entities to give adult adoptees access to their records when they asked, but it didn't seem to matter. The mayor listened politely, but in the end, none of it made a difference. We walked out of there with what we had come in with. Nothing.

The final stop of the day was the Patras orphanage. I thought, it was here where I would find out the truth about the name Kyriazi. Was this my bio-family name? I had held on to that name for over three years. It was my one and only clue. But I remembered what Mary had told me. There were no promises. It was only a stab at a clue. Would I get to see my records? No, on this trip it didn't happen.

We walked inside and met with the director of the daycare. "I am sorry. The social worker was not able to make it. She is in a hospital in Athens."

WHAT, I screamed silently to myself. Well, maybe we could look at the ledger anyway. We really didn't need her with us. We could read for ourselves. But the director did not feel comfortable letting us look at a record, even though I had every right to see it. We were denied. Instead, we visited another room that was set up as a "museum" for the orphanage. The most interesting items in it were an original child's bathtub, an upright piano, and a baptismal font. Still, we came looking for answers and found none. The most important part of my trip was also the most disappointing.

Later, in December 2016, Mary did see the ledger we needed to see. That name, Kyriazi, was nowhere to be found. What I had held onto for almost four years was now a dead issue. You could not measure my disappointment, and yet I didn't totally let go of the name. I still wondered from where that name came. I didn't find out until two years later. It seems the former social worker whom Mary had talked to back in 2013 got the name "Jenkins" mixed up with the name "Jennings" and had looked at the wrong entry in the ledger. This is what it means to be a foundling: no name of any blood relative whatsoever. The final nail was put in that coffin.

In April 2017, I was contacted by Gavriil from Igoumenitsa, Greece, regarding his grandmother who, in 1954, had given birth to healthy twin boys in Florina. Several days after their birth, she and her husband were told they had died. The father was given a box, told never to open it, tell no one about it, bury it, and never speak of it again. That is what they did. Sixty-three years later, while researching what could have happened to these children, Gavriil saw my picture on the Roots Research Center website. Based upon when and where I was born, and my resemblance to his uncle, he felt I could be one of those lost children. As we got to know each other and more details emerged, there were things that just didn't fit, the most obvious being that these boys were born on December 10, 1954. By that time, I was already in the orphanage. DNA tells the truth and in early June he sent his grandmother's DNA sample to Ancestry. When the results came in on July 7, there was no match.

Later the same year, plans were already underway for a return visit to Greece in mid-May 2018. This trip I met again with Gonda and four fellow adoptees: Linda Carol Trotter, Maria Heckinger, Ellen Rubinstein, and Sonia Rijnsdorp from the Netherlands. Unlike my last visit, this one lasted only two weeks. It was a busy fourteen days and it started with us being TV and movie stars!

Gonda had been approached by Israeli documentary filmmaker, Ronit Kertsner. An adoptee herself, Ronit was interested in telling the story of the Greek adoptions in the 1950s and 1960s. She had a particular interest in those who were adopted by Jewish couples. Many Greek children had gone to Jewish families in the New York area. Ronit met us in Greece and we adoptees became the subjects of her documentary film project. I found the filmmaking process to be a fascinating experience.

Ronit was also the impetus behind another fascinating experience. She had contacted a representative of the Greek television show *Fos sto Tunel* on Alpha TV. The show's title loosely translates as, "The Light at the End of the Tunnel," and it was similar in format to the U.S. television show *Unsolved Mysteries*. The representative wanted those of us who are still searching for family to appear in a live episode. Both Ellen and I agreed to go on the show. We quickly learned there would be other requirements.

We each had to provide photos at various stages of our life, videotaped interviews with friends and family regarding our search, and a short tape of ourselves explaining what it meant to us to find our roots. These became video segments that the producers would insert into the show. I interviewed my son, my best friend, and a long-time coworker.

Late on Friday night, in May 2018, the cameras rolled, and we were beamed into living rooms across Greece. When the show ended nearly two and a half hours later, my only hope was that somewhere, someone would say to themselves, "You know, I heard a story [...]" or "My grandmother once told me [...]" or "When I was a young girl [...]."

An unexpected benefit from appearing on the show were two follow-up newspaper articles. One was about our appearance on the show. The other one was specifically about my story. Both articles appeared in the *Peloponnisos*, Patras's largest newspaper.

On May 24, a call came and the lady on the other end of the line said, "This sounds like what happened to my aunt." Could this be it, I thought? DNA would provide the answer. The next day Gonda and I traveled to Patras to meet with Vicki in a public park near her home. She was a delightful woman and readily agreed to immediately provide a DNA sample. A few days later, I met with her and her family at a restaurant. They were wonderful, friendly people. The day before I left for home, I again had dinner with the family, this time at Vicki's apartment. These are memories I still cherish.

Three months before my trip I had read a post in a Greek Facebook group about the Patras General Hospital. For a long time, I had felt that some answers might lie in hospital records. That prompted me to do some research. I found out that the records from the old Municipal Hospital are stored at the Patras General Hospital. From there, it was easy to find a telephone number, which I sent to Gonda to find out what she could. The archivist there agreed to meet with us in May. We went to the hospital a day earlier than we planned and I was completely unprepared. I had wanted to put together a list of surnames culled from my strongest DNA matches. I ended up putting together a list of 10 or 15 names right there in the office. The archivist offered to check three names right away. I gave her my top three choices, but there were no matches. We left her with the rest of the list, and she would check those as her time allowed.

A week later the archivist called. "I have a match," she said. Nia. She was 25 years old and unwed when she gave birth to a boy on November 10, 1954. My estimated birthday was November 11. I had more leads for my search on this trip than I had in the previous seven years. Still, it would take two years before there was any resolution related to this lead about Nia.

Later, on the same day of the hospital visit, we went to the Patras Orphanage to shoot more for Ronit's documentary. This was a meaningful visit for three of the four of us. We each spent time as infants and/or toddlers in this place, our orphanage. Particularly meaningful for me was the opportunity to finally see a hand-written entry in the ledger with my name and the date I entered. I couldn't read a word of it, but that didn't make it any less real for me.

When I arrived home, I immediately sent that DNA sample off to Ancestry.com. I got the email two and a half weeks later. "Your results are in." No match. I was so disappointed, and Vicki's family shared in my disappointment when I told them. But I had met a great family, and we are friends to this day.

April 2019 brought another trip to Greece. Gonda and I were to film with Ronit at the Patras Branch of the Greek State Archives (GAK). The brief visit in 2018 had paid off with a big stack of hospital records to look through, but nothing came of it. No names were familiar. No other data fit mine.

Next, we went to the Pantanassa Church. On a whim, Gonda went inside to talk to a priest about me being left at the church all those years ago. During their conversation, the priest offered to speak to the congregation about my case after the Good Friday service the next evening. We went to church that evening and the priest held true to his word.

The church was crowded. It was Easter services, after all, the holiest time in the Orthodox calendar. I was standing near the front of the church. Ronit was filming and, as the priest spoke, her lens pointed at me. The priest said, "He was left here at our church and has been looking for his roots for many years. It is up to this community to help him find his family. He is a part of our community, and we have an obligation to make it right." It was one of the best experiences I have ever had in my life. The only word I can use to describe it is "magical." Little old Greek women, who can't speak a word of English, came up to me afterwards, smiling, patting me on the cheek, and wishing me luck. And, of course, I didn't understand a word they were saying, but I knew what they were trying to tell me.

Word of this service reached a family in Aigio, 25 miles east of Patras. My story sounded a lot like a story from their family and Jenny was willing to provide a DNA sample. As I listened to them telling their story, there wasn't much in the way of hard details that would fit my timeline. I wasn't confident there would be a match, but I took the DNA sample home anyway. I immediately sent Jenny's DNA samples to Ancestry.com. The results came back. No match.

It wasn't until May 2020 when I started thinking about resuming my search. I still had the name that the Patras General Hospital archivist had given me in 2018. In June, I finally posted a brief message requesting information regarding that name to the HGG Facebook group. I got an offer of assistance with names and contact information of the family for which we had been looking.

Gonda called and talked to Irene, the daughter of Nia, whose name we got from the hospital in 2018. Irene was intrigued and offered to help, so she talked to her mother, who had kept the secret of her pregnancy for 65 years. She seemed relieved to finally tell someone. Had we found my birth mother? There were some discrepancies in her story, but we made the decision to send a DNA kit to Greece. Irene would give the sample and if she matched as a half-sister to me, my search would be over.

I received the responses from the Ancestry.com website and looked at Irene's list of matches. My name was nowhere to be found. This was the closest I had ever come to finding a match. Was I becoming so used to disappointment that it didn't matter anymore? I hoped not.

When 2021 came, I was back to where I had started in my unexpected journey which began in 2011. I certainly knew a little more surrounding the circumstances of my birth, but I was no closer to finding an answer to the all-important question: Who was I? From whom did I come?

In early 2021, I had started a conversation with two sisters with whom I had DNA matches. One was on Ancestry, the other on MyHeritage. A couple weeks later contact was made with a gentleman in Greece with a surname that matched theirs. Would this new contact strengthen my connection to that family? DNA samples were collected.

Later in the month, I was contacted by a gentleman who said he was an adoptee, also left at the Pantanassa Church, and he was living in Patras. He felt that we looked alike and might be related. Could he be my brother? Yet again, DNA samples were collected. All negative. From the two sisters and from the man from Patras. No answers from DNA.

Later that month, I thought, what the hell, I ordered a DNA kit for me from 23andMe. I'd never tried that one before. In a few weeks, an email read,

"Your reports are ready." I truly wasn't expecting much, so, imagine my shock when I saw a Petros listed as a first cousin once removed. This meant one of his parents is my first cousin!

We made contact that evening. Before we were done, he was willing to help me in my search and had already ordered a DNA kit for his mother. His mother's DNA results arrived the following May. She did not show as a first cousin, which means Petros and I are related on his father's side. He has already begun the process of contacting family members in Greece to learn what he can, and to find candidates willing to test.

I had now done tests with six families and all results have come back negative. Some of the results I expected, others left me greatly disappointed. But *this* is different. *This* is the closest I have been to the truth about my life. I *know* there is a relationship here. It just needs to be revealed.

My answers, or anyone's answers don't lie in DNA alone. DNA gets you only so far. As strange as it may sound, DNA lacks the human element. It is science. And very good science. But it doesn't measure the love, the heartache, the anger, the sadness, or the joy that can accompany the story of an adopted child lost, or one found.

My unexpected journey is not yet completed. There may be many roads yet to travel. But I am up for it and I remain hopeful.

Chapter 15

TIME RUN OUT

Maria/Mary

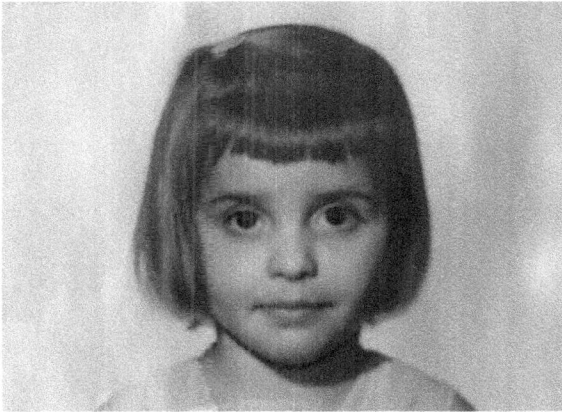

It was another woman who gave me life. Though physically absent, her constant presence came by way of persistent reminders that I was of someone else, from someplace else, an import, brought to the United States to a new, another Greek family.

I was labeled an orphan. An orphan. That was me all my life. But I wasn't an orphan at all. I had a mother, who knew me, touched me, held me. And I had a father, too, who might be out there somewhere. But I wasn't an orphan. I was left. Abandoned. And then signed away to other people.

Wasn't I lucky? She loved me so much that she chose for me a better life. She didn't want to leave me. She had to leave me. Is that even true?

She.

Whoever she was, she was with me, if only for a few precious, painful days, weeks, months. She was with me. She still is.

With me.

My story achieved folk legend status in Gary, Indiana, where I grew up. Not because it was so important, or that I was so important, but because it had been told and repeated over and over again by someone, anyone, who knew the story or was in our lives when I arrived from Greece. I was "special" because I was adopted and I was the adopted child throughout my life. "A souvenir baby," one local newspaper article said about me.

I was left in an orphanage in Athens. Dozens and dozens of babies. Overcrowded. Dirty. Two, sometimes three to a crib, they said. I was the only one awake when a Greek couple had come looking for a baby for their American-born daughter and son-in-law, who could not afford the trip themselves.

They were looking for a baby girl. Up and down the cramped aisles of cribs with steel bars, they gingerly stepped, staring at tiny sleeping faces. But every time they passed where I could catch of glimpse of them, I raised myself up on my two, small, stiffened arms and followed them as if to say "what about me?"

Indeed.

I was wide awake, alert and animated. I watched them back while they watched me. They didn't immediately know whether I was a girl, but no matter. They decided I was the one, despite it. You chose us, Mary, they would tell me.

You chose us.

I was named for this grandmother. Her name was Maria, and called Mary, and so would I also be named Maria and called Mary. My adoptive father wanted me named after her, not after his own mother as is more traditional. He revered his in-laws, my grandparents; they had been so good to him. He was grateful to them for the gift of his first child.

My maternal grandparents felt a special bond with me. They felt a particular responsibility, too, since they had been the ones who chose me, arranged for my adoption, and cared for me on the long journey home aboard the S.S. Olympia, first to Italy, then Portugal, and on toward New York City to dock somewhere in New Jersey. (Ellis Island had been shuttered.)

My grandmother had said they would frequently "lose" me on that ship as the other Greeks coming to the United States would want to hold me, play with me, and would pass me around the deck. I was sick with a fever and a persistent chest infection by the time I met my new parents. To this day, my lungs are vulnerable to pneumonia and bronchitis.

I was held and rocked and cuddled and grew into an insecure kid just the same, afraid to be far from my parents, who had one hell of a time putting me down to sleep when I first came to them. I suppose I had what people now call "separation anxiety." A doctor finally had to instruct my sleep-deprived parents with arms that ached from holding and feet that tired from swaying, rocking and walking, to put me down, to leave the room, shut the door, and to let me "cry it out." I did cry it out, but never learned to self-soothe.

I could never be far from them or my grandparents. I guess leaving my mother's womb, and her arms, to go to an orphanage, then to a foster home, to grandparents, to a ship of strangers, and then, finally, to parents, took its toll in the first year of my life. Later, sleepovers at friends or sleep-away camp were out of the question. Were they going to leave me there and not come back?

At my most vulnerable and emotional, at a loss about what more they could do, my mother would periodically resort to pulling out the adoption papers. "Mary, do you see these important papers?" Yes, I would slowly nod, big, brown eyes soaked with tears waiting to fall, as I looked at her face. "These papers say that you belong to me and to Daddy. Nobody can take you and we are always going to be here. We are always going to be your Mommy and Daddy." I suppose that helped for that one day. Until the next time.

I remember being in the kitchen with my grandparents, the smell of Greek cooking wafting from the stovetop and the oven. My grandfather would have the newspaper spread before him and he would watch me carefully as I set the table for lunch. "My God," he would say in Greek. "You look just like her. As you grow up, you look more and more like her." He was talking about my birth mother. She was small, Mary, he told me. "She was a teenager, frightened and alone. But you *are* your mother. I see her in your face. It haunts me to this day, that image I have of her." I was always touched by this observation, and he said it often. I had often pondered that I looked like no one I knew. But there was someone out there who *did* look like me.

This small, frightened teenager would come every day to breastfeed me at the orphanage, I was told. When she couldn't be there, there were a collection of wet nurses with milk to spare. I have often joked to people that this *must be* the reason I am gay. Early imprinting perhaps? My attachment to women, I suppose, grew beyond the maternal.

My birth mother worked as an *ipiretria*, a maid, a servant for a wealthy man and his family in Athens. He impregnated her, my father did. Consent? Doubtful. A rape? More likely. But she apparently worked as a domestic and lived in his home.

My grandfather said he needed to know what my birth father looked like. He wanted to lay eyes on him, he told me. Like a cop, the designated stake-out in a crime thriller, he waited in a car outside his house. Sunglasses, his signature fedora, a linen, button-down shirt and a cigarette in one hand, the hand with that finger, the middle one that was permanently bent at the first digit. He read or pretended to. He waited.

My birth father. He was handsome, I was told. Dark, short and stocky. An elusive figure in the story of my adoption, who was dismissed as a dishonorable guy. Pay him no real attention, even though I was half of him. Say nothing of the half-siblings who would also be half mine, if there are any. Fathers rarely seem as important or as significant in adoption stories. I wonder about that. Mine had no part in my journey, it seemed. Or did he? What of his knowledge about me? What of his permission, as well, to relinquish me to complete strangers? But if he had abandoned my birth mother, then he had also forfeited his right to decide on my fate. Did her abandonment of me come easier because she had been abandoned, as well, by him?

It was my birth mother, alone, who was summoned to appear before an Athens judge when it was time for me to leave the orphanage. In front of him as witness, a witness to this grand, painful parting, a legal separation, she had to hand me over. Physically hand over her baby. It had to have been the most painful farewell. Or was it? Did she just want to be rid of me? Like a bummer lamb that wanted no part of its offspring?

Can you imagine handing over a child who made her home in your belly, underneath your heart, someone who was *of* you, who came *from* you, to complete strangers? She did, though, and my grandfather promised her, reassured her, he said, that they would not "bother her" and that the baby would not come looking for her, that she could live her life free of this memory.

Free of this memory? Free? Free to do what? Free to go where in the mid-1950s in postwar Greece?

And what if, years later, the "baby" decided otherwise, and did go looking for her birth mother? I did not sign on to this verbal contract, after all. They may have agreed, but I most certainly did not.

My birth mother was poor and had become a mother, who would have nothing to show for it. Except for the shame. The word in Greek is *ntropi*. Presumably she had no one to go to and no place to go. I imagine her disappearing into a battered but recovering city of Athens, maybe to a friend's home, a relative. Or to nowhere, wandering, confused and frightened, trying to figure out what to do. She needed someone to hold her. She needed someone to love her.

Was I in her heart? Did she wonder who would feed me that day? What woman's breast would stand in for hers? What woman's arms would cuddle me? Sooth me? Rock me to sleep so that I could forget that my mother left? Did she think about my life and her absence from it? Did she love me? Did she have that deep, abiding, inexplicable love that parents feel for their children when they look at their faces and into their eyes? Does she miss me? Does she ever think of me at all? Today, all these years later, does she?

She and I, we would lead parallel lives. When I became a teenager, I returned to Greece with the grandparents with whom I had first left. My adoptive mother was happy for me that I would be traveling back to Greece. She was also nervous and asked me if I would go looking for my birth mother.

My mother's question gave me discomfort because I knew she had real feelings about what she was asking. She asked me what I would call her if I did find her. Mom, I said, she didn't mother me. We are strangers. Strangers who shared the same body once, I told her. But my thoughts were calculated. I did not want to hurt her.

Adoptees are pleasers. I have accepted that in myself now. There is a drive to be perfect, not to hurt anyone, to do for, to live up to expectations. Would they leave us if we were, well, human? Flawed? I learned not to share any of the feelings I had about birth mothers and biological family members. Forget about my own well of feelings. I would not hurt her. I would do everything to avoid not hurting my parents, which included actively negating my own feelings.

And it must be said that my adoptive parents gave me the best life possible. So did my grandparents and I am grateful that I was among people who had love in their hearts for me. They could not have foretold what was to come in my life, how or what I would one day feel or think. Or what might be the consequences of their decisions for me and on my behalf. But that is not the point.

I had a past that belonged to me and to me alone and it was rendered useless and unimportant. And what of my birth mother? Could there have been nothing done for her? Did she even have a choice? A chance? Was there any net of support for an unwed teenage mother? We now know the answer is no.

There are things that happen which characterize your life. For me it is my adoption and my fear of abandonment, my perceived and prescribed role to make sure I do not disappoint, and my feelings of not being good enough. Feeling less than. Those feelings were responsible for some of my behavior over the course of my life. It has played over and over again, that tired record, which I actively work at shutting down.

Was I a happy child? Someone who grew into a healthy adult? I do know I carry a load of joy in my heart. I know that's how people read me. Upbeat. Eternally optimistic. Easy to smile and laugh. But I am a deep well of feelings that I have rarely shared because, in the end, who would understand? And on top of that façade and those feelings, there were other challenges, one in particular that I have always said is the least interesting thing about me, but that, nevertheless, resonated with others.

I knew I was gay as early as four years old. I had no words for it. No explanation for it. No ability to express anything about it. But it was and is as much a part of me as my brown eyes. I was born this way. And as I grew from teenager to young woman, I hid it, even though there were many who suspected there was something "not right," something "wrong" with Mary.

And my mother, especially, was displeased with me, how I acted, how I dressed, how I wasn't interested in the things most girls my age *were* interested in. She let me know that I wasn't what she wanted, wasn't what she expected me to be. She wanted me to be someone different, like the other girls she knew and admired. It was not deliberately cruel what she did, how she thought, what she may have said, but it was insensitive and soul-crushing. Never to be good enough. Never to measure up. It took its toll and fed into the narrative of my adopted self. If I revealed my true self, would I be left again?

I was already plenty different. Being gay was, for me, a bridge too far. And so, I led a life of hiding, lying, feeling ashamed of who I was. I dated many boys and men. I behaved as I should have, a Greek girl who would grow into a woman who would attract a Greek guy, to someday have a Greek wedding, make Greek babies and baptize them in the Greek Orthodox Church, just like most of my other friends and relatives were doing.

I tried. I really did. But I was a disappointment. And I didn't want them to think they did anything wrong, that they had damaged me in any way. It wasn't their fault, as if there was any fault to be had.

Ironic, isn't it? The girl with no biological relatives turned out to be gay and would likely not have her own biological children. Is that sad? I don't know. I try not to think about it too much. But I know what it means. I know what it signifies deep in people's psyches. Blood, as they say, is thicker than water. I belong to no one. I can belong to whomever I want. I choose. I find my own connections of the heart. And I do.

I cannot say that I look like anyone, talk like anyone else, nor can I claim any quirky mannerisms that may have resembled or mirrored those of an aunt, an uncle, my grandparents, my brother or my parents. I often felt left out because I *was* from outside the family. I was not a stranger to them, but I was not recognizable by virtue of birth and shared DNA.

When they were tired or fatigued, siblings of my mother and their parents rubbed their eyes and faces exactly the same way. The four brothers Drakos, my first cousins, stand with their arms folded, one hand to their chin, exactly the same way their father and our grandfather did. I experience none of that with anyone.

Layer upon layer of wondering where and to whom I belong. Greek, adopted and gay. That is me. That is all I know.

It was 1973.

My first trip back to Greece was emotional. I remember feeling not like I was going to a foreign country, but that I was returning home, completely comfortable with the relatives and in the chaos of Athens. I felt like this was my place.

And I searched for her. I did. I looked at every face that I passed in the frenzy of that city for someone who looked familiar, for that face that looked just like mine. Was someone searching faces for a girl who looked like them, too? Was she that someone who might recognize my face and see herself in me? "That is my baby. That is my child. I know my own flesh and blood," she might say. Wouldn't she?

My grandmother was comfortable on buses and on trolleys. She got us to the courthouse near Syntagma Square from my Uncle Stamatis's house. She had business to attend to before we would travel to their villages and islands. She had *my* business to attend to. She had a stack of papers with her and at the courthouse, as we waited, a new birth certificate was generated for me. Instantaneously. Just like that. Like waiting at the doctor's office for a prescription or for a new driver's license at the DMV. We waited for a new birth certificate.

This one would be created in 1973. It said so, right there on the paper, and my adoptive parents appeared as if they had been responsible for the birth. The words, *exogamo paithi*, a child outside of marriage, were wiped away forever. That label had bothered my grandmother and she believed it would affect my life, that I would be forever branded by an ugly stigma. If my birth mother's name was listed there, it was wiped away, too, as if she had never existed.

These decisions made for me would come at a price. My adoptive parents would often forget my birthday. They remembered, though, the day I came to them. It was as if what came before, who came before, did not exist. My past was unimportant. Irrelevant. Only the present mattered. I would not need to bother with what may have been the truth 30 or 40 or 50 years ago. This was my life now. Others appropriated my past. Decisions were made *for me* about what I could know and how I could know it. Their lens would be the lens that I, too, was forced to look through. The field of vision was narrowing. I was a teenager and had no power then and no real awareness of what creating a new birth certificate meant. It was done, though. Almost like a new identity. An early version of identity theft.

My grandmother also felt compelled to show me exactly from where I had come. We visited the Baby Center Mitera, the orphanage just outside of Athens that cared for hundreds, if not thousands, of children in postwar Greece. Queen Frederica had been its patron saint.

We arrived with great fanfare. I was a child returned "home" and the people who were now in charge greeted me like a returning hero, having survived who knows what. There was a fuss made. I was shown around and hugged and touched with great affection. At the time, I knew little to no Greek, and so had no idea about the exchange of conversations swirling around me between my grandmother and those in charge of the orphanage.

Did my grandmother know that I had never been there? Was she led to believe that I *had* been there at one point? Or more likely, this display was a charade conducted just for my benefit.

We also visited a woman who had supposedly served as a foster mother, someone who cared for me shortly before leaving Greece. She was kind and appreciative that we had come to say thank you for what she did. I cannot remember if I asked for this past memory tour or if it had been thrust upon me. But I felt on display. It was not that I wasn't grateful. Perhaps it was that I was made to feel different. Again. Always different.

I remember being at a dinner dance at our Greek church in Indiana. It was an event where families celebrated together. Young people sat at different tables than their grandparents, parents, aunts and uncles. I was a young girl. Dinner had been served and my grandmother came to fetch me from the meal with my cousins and friends to meet someone.

Meet someone, I politely asked her? Yes, my grandmother said, there is a couple here who helped take care of you on the ship. On the ship? I paused for a moment. Oh, that ship. Yes, my grandmother pressed, they held you and played with you. We need to say hello. "Mom," I heard my aunt interrupt from the next table, "let her finish her dinner." It will only take one minute, my grandmother said. *Ena lepto*, she said in Greek. And by the hand she took me to a table to meet the people from the ship. As a teenager, you don't want your difference to be accentuated. A spotlight on you. But it was. Again. I would forever be the baby that was brought from Greece and who owed so much to so many.

It wasn't until years later when I realized that my difference as an adoptee should have been discussed and that my past, perhaps, should have been pieced back together, but with me as a participant. What happened to me? How did it happen to me? And I can only imagine what it felt like to have given birth to someone whom you either were forced to relinquish or felt you *had* to relinquish. In my first ten precious months of life, what happened to me? Who had I been and to whom did I belong?

When I left Greece in 1955, I had to be baptized and named before I could leave the country. My grandparents asked a relative, who was a niece of my grandfather. Artemis Makrigiorgiou. She would be my godmother and her husband, Nikolaos, my godfather. I was baptized at the St. Nicholas Greek Orthodox Church in the heart of Athens.

At Greek baptisms it is the godparent or godparents who are central to this religious ceremony. It is the godparents who carry the child, naked, to their baptism, swaddled in a white sheet as the priest takes the child from them. It is the godparents who slather the baby in oil, after which it is held high by the priest and immersed in a gilded font three times. It is the godparents who receive the child, renounce Satan, and carry the child, now dressed in fresh, white garments, around the font with the priest three times.

The mother of the child is relegated to the periphery of the service, until she is summoned to receive her baby clean, blessed, and named. As I recall the deep meaning that marks this ceremony, I have paused to envision that brief moment in my infant life. There was no mother at mine called to receive me from my godparents. In fact, she was not even there. Did she even know I had been baptized and now had a name? Maria.

My wonderful godparents.

She was a pediatrician, he a civil engineer, and as I grew up, I grew to know them and to love them. She and I exchanged letters for years until she got old and lost her sight to macular degeneration. We had shared secrets and became each other's confidantes. A beautiful relationship developed through the post, with pen and on paper, the kind we used to use—thin, onion-skinned paper, lined, and envelopes with red and blue stripes that said Par Avion. Air Mail.

I loved her *very* much. When she learned I was gay, she summarily told her daughter-in-law: "There will be full acceptance." My protector. I knew she would not let anyone mistreat me or be cruel.

My godmother came from the same poor village my grandfather did; Agios Petros on the Ionian island of Lefkada. My godfather came from the island, too, but from another village. That they came from that poor island, during a time of great strife and became professionals, was really something.

Strawberry blond hair and with piercing blue eyes, she was elegant and educated, soft spoken, and kind. She cared for me and by care, I mean time spent with me, showing me Greece, showing me Athens, especially. She wanted me to know my country, love my country and love the city where I was born.

She was a doctor, so we would go to the hospital together. I went with her as she made rounds. I would watch her, intently watch her, as she reassured parents about their children, spoke to nurses and staff, gently giving marching orders for her patients. Afterward, we would jump in a small car, a stick shift, as she deftly maneuvered through the narrow streets of Athens, out of the city and to the sea, to Mati, where the family had a summer home.

I remember the beauty of the evening coming, the quiet of the neighborhood as people were settling in after dinner. She showed me to my room and made sure I would have all I needed. She liked Cat Stevens and liked that his fame drew attention to his Greek heritage. She played his music while we organized the room in silence and made up my bed. The aroma of flowers and the remains of cooking floated in with the wind. The Wind. It is a Cat Stevens song that I will forever associate with her.

I listen to the wind, to the wind of my soul
Where I'll end up, well, I think only God really knows
I've sat upon the setting sun
But never, never, never, never
I never wanted water once
No never, never, never.

My godmother was a loving mother, I thought, and I felt loved by her, too. Those blue eyes. *Galazia*, light blue, in Greek. They were almost translucent. But the way she looked at me when we were talking. It crossed my mind. It did. Φαντασία. It is the Greek word for fantasy. Adoptees fantasize.

I thought to myself, could she be? Why couldn't she be? A poor girl from a poor village, who had gone to Athens and had a child that no one could know about? But they kept that child in the family? She could not be identified as my mother, but she could be my godmother to play a role in my life. It was plausible and the notion drew me ever closer to her.

My godfather was more like me. Gregarious. A big personality. You knew when he came into the room. He was a strong cup of coffee. He, too, wanted me to inhale my homeland. Like a sponge, he wanted me to soak it up, for it to become a part of me. He picked us up from the airport that first time and drove us to the center of the city.

It was revealed slowly as we rounded a curve in the road. At twilight, there it was in all its glory, bathed in light and standing above the city like the proud citadel that it is. The Parthenon on the Acropolis of Athens. He wanted that to be my first image of the city I was taken from. It took my breath away and I'll never forget it. He pulled over and we all stared at it in silence. He turned to me sitting in the back seat of his Mercedes and smiled as if to say, that is yours, too, like it is mine.

Never forget.

My godfather loved the sea like all Greeks do. I had never water-skied a day in my life, but he was determined to make sure that I would learn to do it. He and my godmother and I would motor-boat deep into the Bay of Marathon. She sat with a large sunhat and big sunglasses watching the two of us bond. Smiling, laughing and making sure he was careful with me, she asked him to take it slow.

Take it slow? He had no such speed.

"Get in," he said. "Jump in." And so, I did. He threw me the skis and the line and he explained how to hold the tethered bar and to bring the tips of the skis to the surface of the water. With the roar of the engine, he would pull me up and on top of the water just for a little while until I fell. And fall I did, over and over again, until I didn't anymore. Finally, upright on my skis, steady and to the side of that boat, I was skiing in the legendary Bay of Marathon and I could hear him laugh and shout to me! *"Fourtounes, Maria. Fourtounes!"* Waves, Maria! He would circle back over the wave the boat had created; over the wave it had generated. And he loved that he was the one who gave me this experience.

Fantasy.

Could I see in him my father? Was it crazy to even think so? I was a lot like him, I thought. And his generosity of time and spirit was touching. Not ever moved easily to tears, I cried when I left them. I cried when I left the relatives in our village of Agios Petros on Lefkada. My feelings of connection to Greece and its people were deep and often overwhelming.

I am the little girl adopted from Greece. I am the little girl who came on the ship. I was from nobody and nowhere. Often people ask about my "real" parents and where I "really" come from and to whom I "really" belong. They also never fail to include an addendum, a closing comment about me vis-à-vis my origins.

Like this: "This is Mary's brother. They were adopted." Or "These are Mary's parents, but she was adopted." Or "Mary resembles her mother, *but* she was adopted." Others have negated my feelings entirely, without malice nor any awareness of what they were saying about the reality of my experience, by minimizing my adoption itself. "You were too young to remember anything." As if nothing before mattered at all. Or "You're not really an immigrant. You were a baby." Those folks entirely miss the essence of my existence. It is dismissive.

How could you, why do you feel what you feel, having left Greece as an infant? Why do you agonize about the adoption at all? Your parents are your parents. Your family now is your family. The message, of course, is that you had no past, however brief it may have been, and what came before, doesn't matter.

I get it. I agree that identity is formed as you grow up, where you grow up, how you are raised. This is true. My childhood and teenage years were spent in Gary and Merrillville, Indiana, in a Greco-centric community. My parents are those who raised me, a hardworking, proud union steelworker father and an exceptionally bright, self-educated, executive secretary mother. They were Greeks who spoke Greek. I have a brother, also adopted (who is half Greek by birth), and two nieces and a nephew. I belong to my cousins and my aunts and uncles. "We" originate from Lefkada and Ithaca. But I actually don't originate from there, even though I have claimed them as my own. I *am* different. I *feel* my difference. I don't know a single person I am biologically related to. Not one.

I have often recalled scenes from the movie *The Godfather.* Tom Hagen is the consigliere and "adopted son" of Don Vito Corleone. And there is a discussion about who is really family and who is not. Tom is family until biological son, Sonny Corleone, reminds him that he is not. Tom asserts himself and says during a heated exchange, "I'm just as much a son as you and Mike." Later in the film, when the family is being restructured under a new Don, Tom is dismissed. "You're out, Tom," says the new Don Michael Corleone, coldly. You're out.

Sometimes I feel "out."

I began searching for and claiming my identity quietly in the early 1990s. I didn't want to offend anyone. I didn't want anyone to judge me or question me. My Greek relatives helped me regain my Greek citizenship and I am grateful that I have it. I am proud that I have it. It is who I am. My essence. *Ousia*. It is a Greek word that means essence or substance and stems from the ancient, the feminine present participle of "eimi," which means "I am." But who am I? From where?

My story is not yet finished and details are losing their luminescence. That I know. The romance in the telling of my story is also fading. I was never at the fancy Mitera where I was taken for a tour as a teenager, to see where I was supposedly placed after birth. My grandmother must have known that, wanting to brightly color my life as an infant. She wanted me to believe that I had been in a nicer, cleaner, less crowded place.

But in reality, I was placed in the plain, dusty, public Athens Foundling Home (*Vrefokomeio*) on January 11, 1955. I was small and malnourished. I left it in August of the same year. From there I went to a foster home, managed by Patriotic Institution for Social Wellness and Awareness (PIKPA), a child welfare agency, and then to a private foster home before leaving for the United States with my adoptive grandparents.

That information is helpful and fills in some empty spaces, there is no doubt about that. But what of the circumstances of my conception, where she and I lived, hid out, and the moment when my mother took me to that place. Nine precious days, a snapshot in time, of not knowing where I was, where we were and what she was thinking, or how she felt.

In the records from the Athens Foundling Home, both of my birth parents are named. It is unusual that both parents were included in the records. Would she name a rapist as the father of her baby? Did she love him? Did they have a relationship?

My birth mother knew that I was actively pursuing her, for a meeting, but there was a time that we were "protected" from one another and the process. The social service agency wanted her in counseling and insisted that I have an intermediary because nobody thought I would be able to handle whatever was to be revealed. The intermediary, a psychologist and also an adoptee, thought it was cruel to withhold information that was *about* me, so he shared with me what he was learning as he was learning it.

Didn't they see that time was running out given her advancing age and mine?

From all indications, my mother led a sad and lonely life, and she was estranged from her very large family. She lived in Athens, had never married, and supposedly had no other children. She and I, we were all we had.

She worked as a cleaning lady at a public elementary school and she was overjoyed, shocked, sad, and confused when they told her I had re-emerged. Her first inclination was to see me, but she needed time to process the news. The International Social Service said they were hopeful that a reunion could be arranged. But in 2000, the case manager, a new case manager, wrote back. It was a brief, terse letter. Her message (supposedly) through him was stark and direct.

"I want to let you know that our branch office in Greece informed us that your mother did not want to cooperate with them and make no further contact." The letter asked how I felt. How did I feel? It was a blow. This was not an imagined rejection, but an explicit rejection with no desire to "cooperate." I was not a business deal she was going to have to negotiate. She gave birth to me. I lived inside of her. Quietly, I felt broken inside, and I decided to let it be. In fact, I left it to fester for 21 years. This must be what the notorious second abandonment feels like.

Twenty-one years. The clock was running.

But I came back at it, hopeful that, after two decades, she would have a change of heart. I continued trying to make contact, poking, prodding people at organizations that maybe could help.

I decided to write to her at Christmastime, in the middle of a pandemic. I sent her several photographs of me over the years. I pretended I did not know about her request to, please, just leave her alone. I wrote:

Dear Mother,

Do not worry. Do not be afraid. Your name appears on my birth certificate and I decided to find you and contact you. You gave birth to me on January 2, 1955.

Ever since I was a small child, I knew I was adopted and that another woman had given me life. For this, I am eternally grateful to you and I want you to know that I have never stopped thinking about you.

My family has always spoken of you with great respect, and so you have always been a part of my life, on my mind, and in my heart. I hope you are in good health. I hope you have had some happiness in your life. I hope the memory of me, if any, is not too painful, and I certainly do not want this letter to in any way hurt or upset you.

The parents who raised me are now dead. But there is at least one person in the world with whom I am biologically connected and who may look like me. That is you. In fact, as I grew, my grandfather would often look at me and say,

"You look like your mother." He told me that he had met you. I do not know if this is true, but I hope that it is.

It would be a shame and it would make me so very sad if we never meet. I would love to see you, to talk to you. I want nothing from you, but to know you and to understand how I came into this world and how I got to the orphanage. Please know that I care very much about you and always will.

I wish you a wonderful Christmas and a Happy New Year.

With love and respect,

Maria

There was no response to that letter, a deafening silence that echoed in its own emptiness from across the ocean that separated us. But I would not give up on her because time was not on our side.

In Greece recently, I found what I thought was her apartment building and went to see whether she still lived there. Her last name was on the buzzer, but with a different first initial. Maybe a middle name? Doubtful, but what the hell, I thought. I wrote to her at that address and suggested my cousins as intermediaries.

There was no reply, but as I have since learned, time *did* run out for us.

October 5. It was the date, many years ago, that I came to new parents. But in 2021, it was the date I also learned that my birth mother had died.

Her name was Fevronia Kougoulou. She was born in 1937 in a small village called Elatis in the northern part of Greece. She was 18 years old when she gave birth in Athens, certainly old enough to care for me, had there been someone, anyone, to care for her and for her baby. She died in 2020 during the Covid pandemic, although she did not die from Covid. She was 83 years old.

Ultimately, I know I have to confront the fourth stage of grief, which is acceptance. I am a long way from there. I am upset. I am sad. And I have to admit, there is some anger. Her parents failed her. Her village failed her. Society failed her. And the social services in Athens failed her.

Her shame was too great a burden. She was shunned, ostracized from a large family, instead of being gently brought out from the shadows, so that she could learn to cope and to forgive herself because she did nothing wrong.

My fantasy of a happy reunion will never be. And the possibility of a relationship, of some kind, any kind is lost forever. I wanted to, somehow, give her the love and respect she deserved, and I wanted to make sure she didn't want for anything.

Today the reality is that I will never get to see who looks just like me. I will never know the circumstances of my birth or where we went or how she decided to find her way to that orphanage. I will never hear the sound of her voice, the same voice I heard when I was in her belly. I will not hear any story about how she felt or what she thought about me. I will never feel her embrace.

It is what it is. I do hate that expression, but it is what it is.

There is no chance for us now but until I am ultimately forced to surrender to my unrequited longing and loss, I will continue to search for a piece of her, a tiny shred of her. She deserves it—that someone thought of her, and wanted very much to know her. I hope to acquire the papers tracing her birth, her life, her death, her relatives, anyone who, by extension, carries a piece of me. A precious photo of her at any age. Oh, what I would give.

I went to a church and lit a candle for her. And I will find out where she is buried so that I can leave a stone marking that I was there and to quietly whisper that I came back, that I came back to see her and to say that I am sorry, Mama.

I am so sorry. For both of us.

Chapter 16

TODAY AND AFTERWARD

Mary Cardaras

The estimated 4,000 Greek-born adoptees are among the oldest group in modern history who were exported, en masse, for adoption. What followed was a tsunami of international adoptions. Children traveling, crisscrossing the globe, having been excised from their country of origin, from the arms of their mothers, from orphanages, to the embrace of strangers in points all over the world.

Korea. China. Romania. Vietnam. Ethiopia. Guatemala. Russia. This is to say nothing, of course, about the millions of domestic adoptions within countries that have been problematic and fraught with ethical and moral questions, not to mention legal scandals, in Ireland and the United States.

Although the practice of adoption has been in the public discourse, it was not until the important book, *American Baby: A Mother, A Child, and the Shadow History of Adoption* (Viking, 2021), written by best-selling author and investigative journalist Gabrielle Glaser, aimed a stark spotlight at nefarious adoption practices in the United States, which were widespread and deep. She tells the story of the millions of adoptions in the United States through one single heartbreaking story of a baby whose parents were forced to relinquish him. His birth father had died and he was reunited, just months before his own death, with his mother and sister. His death was one that could have been prevented had he known his medical history years earlier.

Glaser writes, "The United States had little understanding of the possible long-term consequences when it launched a social experiment in which millions of babies were raised by families with whom they had no genetic bond and who knew little or nothing of their inheritance. Closed adoptions of babies born to single women were universally seen as a societal gain, a win-win for the mothers, adoptees, and adoptive couples. Most often they were anything but that."

Glaser began a national conversation about adoption, which seemed to ignite a firestorm of activity that reverberated around the world—in newspaper articles, on television, in other books, on social media, among legal organizations helping adoptees, and for the adoptees themselves, who raised their voices louder than ever for the right to know who they are.

Ireland currently leads the way in terms of the now global fight for justice in all matters of identity. *The Guardian* reported in a January 12, 2022 article that "Ireland will allow adopted people automatic access to their birth records for the first time under new laws the government hopes will end a 'historic wrong', including for thousands sent for adoption in secret by Catholic institutions."

Ireland did the courageous thing, the right thing, by tearing back an ugly veil of secrecy, which had condemned unwed mothers and their babies to "cruelty" and "callousness" in "institutions run by both the state and the Catholic church." The January 2022 article appeared a year to the date when again, according to *The Guardian*, "a judicial commission of investigation published a long-awaited 2,865-page report into a network of 'mother and baby homes' that inflicted abuse and shame—with the complicity of wider society—for much of the 20th century."

Enter the story of the Greek-born adoptees and Gonda Van Steen, a leading scholar in Modern Greek Studies at King's College in London. She had been a quiet weaver, working for years, researching the phenomenon of the thousands of children and babies exported from postwar Greece. She, too, uncovered the iniquitous practices of a prominent Greek American organization, which became a for-profit broker in the baby trade. She got to know the adoptees themselves and the organizations which were involved in those adoptions. She wrote about the operation itself, how adoptions were arranged, by whom, how, and why.

Van Steen's book, *Adoption, Memory, and Cold War Greece: Kid pro quo?* (University of Michigan Press, 2019) was the result of her multi-year research, which didn't stop there. Since 2013 she has been constructing a database of Greek-born adoptees who manage to find their way to her. She has helped them sift through and translate their documents, written mostly in Greek. She has gone with several of them to Greece, acting as translator and navigator of the thick, mostly opaque Greek bureaucratic system to search for paperwork and, if possible, birth parents and kin. In many cases, she has been successful.

She said, "I care so much because children are the weakest and most vulnerable party in any crisis. Let alone children who go under the label of 'illegitimate,' as if even their very existence is placed outside the law and the norm. It's about correcting something for them that went so wrong—and that can still be partly corrected—and at such a small cost of time and effort."

But it wasn't until Van Steen's exhaustively researched book was translated into Greek, by Potamos Publishers in November 2021, that the attention on Greek adoptees was ratcheted up and brought to the light of day, certainly in Greece, and now to an international audience.

There has been an avalanche of stories in the Greek press, in print, and on television and radio, not to mention a number of public appearances featuring Van Steen, that has captured the attention of the Greeks themselves as they revisit their own history and, in some cases, learn about it for the first time.

Many people recalled the wars, which produced such poverty and devastation, ravaging the country, and vaguely remembered the exportation of children. There were some whose families were directly affected because children were taken, some under mysterious circumstances, vanished forever from their homes and parents Always, those people tearfully express an ache in their heart which has not left them in 60 years.

The Greeks have now joined an international effort of millions of adoptees from around the world to find out who they are, from whom they come. They want the practice of secrecy in adoption and in reproductive technology to be stopped now and forever. In the case of the Greek-born adoptees, time is running out. We are aging. Many have died. Many of our birth parents have died. Time is of the essence in opening birth records, finding original birth certificates, baptismal records, and adoption papers, and accounting for each and every one of us. Most of us are searching for birth parents and biological kin.

Now, on a world stage, Van Steen leads the effort for the Greeks in what she calls "Nostos for Greek Adoptees." *Nostos* speaks to the heart of all Greeks, for being rooted in antiquity. *Nostos* is an ancient Greek word as old as Homer. The word nostalgia comes from the word *nostos*, a term we use to describe this longing for our home of the past. *Nostos* means homecoming and *algos* means pain. *Nostos* is the central theme of *The Odyssey*, as its epic hero, Odysseus, finds his way home, over a decade, after the Trojan War.

For Greek-born adoptees it is all about, metaphorically, coming home and to finally connect with who they are, their very essence, their identity. With the help of respected journalist Nicky Liberaki from Mega TV in Athens, who has reported on the plight of Greek-born adoptees, Van Steen formally asked the Prime Minister of Greece, through his former chief of staff, Grigoris Dimitriadis, to form a task force that will address the concerns of the adoptees.

The task force, under the supervision of the government, would sift through the mountains of records in social service agencies, the archives of the former orphanages and in the offices of a number of municipalities, to pair those records with those who seek them. In doing so, Van Steen would continue the building of her database in accounting for each adoptee. Who is who? And what papers does each person have? In many cases, adopted people have no paperwork at all and that presents a particular challenge. But even for those who do not have much documentation, there is always some evidence that they were born in Greece.

Van Steen said, "I always cared about my research, but this time it makes a difference in people's lives like never before. There is an urgency to it, it has to be done, and it has to be done well. I feel as if the cause calls me to task. And rightly so."

Here is the argument of the Greek-born adoptees: The government knows they were born in the country. The state stripped them of their Greek citizenship when they left the country and became citizens of other countries. This was done without the children's consent or knowledge. The now adult adoptees want all their files and records, whatever exists, open and available to them, and they want their citizenship restored.

It is a mantra. Born Greek. Today Greek. Forever Greek.

From a global perspective, these Greek adoptions, which occurred between 1948 and 1975, are only one part of the adoption narrative. Millions of people around the world want their identities fully restored, and their voices are raised and growing louder in books and media interviews, on social media, and in organizations that support and advocate for them.

In the United States, Greg Luce is an adopted person himself, a lawyer, and an adoptee advocate, having founded the Adoptee Rights Law Center, based in Minnesota. "I help adult adopted people navigate legal challenges in obtaining their own original birth certificates, securing U.S. citizenship, and seeking information to which they are entitled. I also work to develop broader legal strategies to challenge existing legal frameworks that operate to deny adopted people basic and fundamental rights of identity," he writes.

A focal point for his work now is the 2021 Adoptee Citizenship Act about which he says, "For intercountry adoptees in the United States, it is critical to assure that they become United States citizens, no matter their age and no matter when they were adopted. This means closing a loophole in current law and then working to ensure that those who acquire citizenship under the ACA have available resources to apply for and secure citizenship that should have been granted to them decades ago. And let's also bring home our fellow intercountry adoptees who have been deported from the United States to countries they barely knew. The deportation of adopted people from the US will remain an open stain on intercountry adoption until we eliminate it."

The protection of and advocacy for adoptees is rising to a new level of urgency and concern. Mia Dambach is the Executive Director of Child

Identity Protection. "In my 20 years experience working on child protection, including alternative care and adoption, I have never seen a greater time where the different international bodies including the United Nations treaty body systems and states have taken to heart the concerns of adoptees," she says.

She wrote, "A few major milestones include the 2010 HCCH Special Commission on intercountry adoption when there was focus on illicit practices, the setting up of a specific working group, the report of the UN Special Rapporteur on Sale and Sexual Exploitation, Maud de Boer-Buquicchio in 2017 on illegal adoptions, and the 2022 campaign led by adoptee organisations to have certain adoptions recognized as crimes against humanity."

As a new organization, Child Identity Protection or CHIP (www.child-identity.org) is building on these initiatives (or working directly with partners) to ensure that, first, the child's full identity is preserved, and second, that whenever a child (or later as an adult) has elements of their identity that are missing and/or are falsified, that CHIP works with relevant actors to restore their identity as required by the UN Convention on the Rights of the Child.

To do this, CHIP has undertaken a number of initiatives, including submitting fact sheets to the UN Committee on the Rights of the Child, raising awareness through its "Experts CHIP in" series, undertaking research, pursuing advocacy efforts, preparing policy briefs and providing technical assistance. One practical example of CHIP's advocacy work is ensuring that Data Protection Regulations are read in a way that gives adoptees full access to all information that is relevant to their identity, even when this may include the personal information of other parties.

At the center of all this advocacy, and in the heart of every single adopted person, is the longing to know who we are, from whom we come, from where, and, to the extent that we can know, what our medical histories tell us about ourselves. This is fundamental.

According to Mariela Neagu, the author of *Voices of the Silent Cradles: Life Histories of Romania's Looked After Children* (Policy Press, 2021), who has done extensive research about the rights of children, "Identity is key to human development for the way in which humans perceive themselves and how they interact with others. It is closely connected to one's agency, belonging, self-esteem, autonomy, and it contributes to young people's resilience and well-being." This is precisely why it is enshrined in the United Nations Convention on the Rights of the Child, which was drafted in 1989.

Article 8 of the United Nations Convention on the Rights of the Child (UNCRC) declares that, "States Parties undertake to respect the right of the child to preserve his or her identity, including nationality, name and family relations as recognized by law without unlawful interference."

And in the second part, that "Where a child is illegally deprived of some or all of the elements of his or her identity, States Parties shall provide appropriate assistance and protection with a view to re-establishing his or her identity."

Gabrielle Glaser, in her groundbreaking work *American Baby*, notes what psychologist Erik Erikson had to say about adolescents and their "essential task" of developing an identity. She wrote, children "rebel against us, but also look to their chief role models, their parents, as they ask questions about who they'll become. Among adoptees who lack access to their personal history, this process is complicated by the knowledge that no matter how they are loved, wanted and wished for, they understand that a crucial part of them is lost." This results in "confusion, shame, feelings of abandonment, embarrassment and low self-esteem."

Identity. It is the beginning. It charts our course. It is everything.

May this collection from these aging, but still fighting Greek-born adoptees, serve as testament to what it has cost them, what has been restored for some of them, and what can be lost forever.

Surely it is much too high a price to pay.

For any child.

ACKNOWLEDGMENTS

First and foremost, to the essayists, my fellow Greek-born adoptees, my brothers and sisters: Chris Anastasiou, Robyn Bedell, Maria Heckinger, Merrill Jenkins, Robert Lipsky, Alexa Maros, Allison Murray, Andriana Nickerson, Ellen Rubinstein, Paula Sabbia, Sonia Rijnsdorp, Nick Webb, and David Wright. Your courage in telling your stories, some of you having to relive many painful memories, is no small thing. You have my enduring appreciation and admiration.

Thank you to author and poet Andrew Mossin, another brother adoptee, who graciously agreed to write the Foreword for this collection. He is a gentle soul and knows how much I love his writing.

Thank you to Dena Poulias. I can never tell my own adoption story without now talking about you. You were the one who started me on my own out-of-the-fog adoption realizations and storytelling.

To Gonda Van Steen for her research and tireless efforts in helping us get what we deserve, *Nostos** for Greek Adoptees. It is an honor and a privilege to work by your side in this endeavor.

Gabrielle Glaser, for her open heart, her kind heart, and whose understanding and empathy have been a well of inspiration. Finding you again is a gift that I will cherish forever. Thank you for recognizing me.

My gratitude and appreciation for Greek journalists Nikos Konstandaras, Nicky Lyberaki and Katerina Bakoyianni for helping to bring the Greek adoption story to light. And to Greek human rights lawyer Vasilis Sotiropoulos for his efforts in helping Greek born adoptees get open access to all their adoption records.

To my two mothers. I cannot mention one without the other. They never knew each other, but, through me, are forever connected. I know the mother who raised me would have been quick and eager to fully embrace the mother who brought me into the world.

---

* *Nostos* means homecoming.

Dad, I never took any wooden nickels, as you always advised. You were my guy, always there to hold me and to make me laugh whenever you knew I needed to feel safe.

Yiayia and Pappou, I think about you every single day. You shifted the entire trajectory of my life. You took me into your arms and into your hearts.

Thank you to my lifelong friends from Gary, Indiana, Beth Pappas Orfanos and Pam Bianchi Schrode, who have been by my side for over 50 years, and to all my friends from home who now know me just a little bit better, after all these years.

To my family in Indiana and those scattered in points all over the United States, you had a big hand in shaping who I have become. To my family in Greece; in Athens, in Lefkada, in Andros; you always make me want to Greek dance!

To my biological family, we've only just begun. Thank you for helping me put together the pieces of my young life and the reason for my existence at all.

To advocates and activists Greg Luce and Shawna Hodgson, thank you for your expertise and for your loud, strong adoptee voices. You teach me things every day about what the fight means and what it is all for.

To Mia Dambach and Mariela Neagu, new friends and colleagues, who I work with now on an international stage for the rights of children to their identities.

Thank you to my boys, Harrison and Nicholas, for making me laugh all these years and for their understanding about my own personal struggles. To Francesca for her devotion and support in my doing what she knows I need to do.

To C.J., thanks for always being at my feet, my shadow; for always reminding me when it's time to eat, to play, and to walk.

And to the person who looked at the manuscript last, my editor, proofreader, and fellow adoptee, born in the United States but with Canadian biological roots, the intrepid Janine Baer, for her interest, care, and sensitivity in our lived adoptee experiences.

ABOUT THE EDITOR

Mary Cardaras holds a PhD in Public and International Affairs at Northeastern University in Boston and is Associate Professor and Chair of the Department of Communication at California State University, East Bay, where she teaches political communication, journalism, and documentary film. She has spent over 40 years producing and writing news and is an Emmy award-winning documentary film producer currently working on a series about young people around the world who are taking the effects of climate change on the environment into their own hands. She is also building The Demos Center for the study of democracy, citizenship and civic engagement at the American College of Greece in Athens. Cardaras is the author of *Ripped at the Root*, the extraordinary, true adoption story of Dena Poulias, who was stolen from Greece as a baby.

RESOURCE LIST

International Organizations in Support of Adopted People

Child Identity Protection (CHIP), *Advocates for Laws, Policies and Practices to Uphold Family Identity. Based in Geneva.* www.child-identity.org. *Animation:* https://www.child-identity.org/en/about-us-bottom.html. *Talks by Experts:* https://www.child-identity.org/en/resources/experts.html.

Intercountry Adoptee Voices (ICAV), *To Educate, Support, Connect, Collaborate, Galvanise and Give Voice to Intercountry Adoptees from around the World.* https://intercountryadopteevoices.com/.

List of adoptee-led organizations by country or continent of origin. https://intercountryadopteevoices.com/adoptee-led-groups/country-of-origin/.

International Agreements about Adoption and Identity

United Nations Convention on the Rights of the Child (UNCRC) (1989)

Article 7

The child shall be registered immediately after birth and shall have the right from birth to a name, the right to acquire a nationality and, as far as possible, the right to know and be cared for by his or her parents.

Article 8

States Parties undertake to respect the right of the child to preserve his or her identity, including nationality, name and family relations as recognized by law without unlawful interference. (https://www.ohchr.org/en/instruments-mechanisms/instruments/convention-rights-child)

Hague Convention on Intercountry Adoption (1993)

Protects children and their families against the risks of illegal, irregular, premature or ill-prepared adoptions abroad. https://www.hcch.net/en/instruments/conventions/specialised-sections/intercountry-adoption.

US Department of State, https://travel.state.gov/content/travel/en/ Intercountry-Adoption/Adoption-Process/understanding-the-hague-convention.html.

Greek Adoptees

Organizations

Greek Born Adoptees (based in Australia), https://www.facebook.com/groups/ 245212812166190.

Greek Orphans Seeking Answers (GOSA), *Adoptees Who Want to Search for Their Greek Roots*, https://www.facebook.com/groups/225165427849789.

Roots Research Centre (based in Greece), *Promotes the Rights of Children in Alternative Care and the Rights of Adult Adoptees*. https://www.roots-research-center.gr/en/home/.

Online Reading about Greek Adoption

Cardaras, Mary, "Demanding What Belongs to Us: Our Greek Identity," *The Pappas Post*, 7 June 2021. https://pappaspost.com/demanding-what-belongs-to-us-our-greek-identity/.

Cardaras, Mary, and Gonda Van Steen, "Bring Them Back!" *The Pappas Post*, 16 June 2021. https://pappaspost.com/opinion-bring-them-back.

Kitroeff, Alexander, "Greece's Forgotten Cold War Orphans and America's Complicity," *The Pappas Post*, 5 May 2021. https://www.pappaspost.com/greeces-forgotten-cold-war-orphans-and-americas-complicity/.

Books about Adopted People and the Politics of Adoption
Adoptee reading

A catalog of books written by adoptees along with other adoption-related books recommended by adoptees (http://adopteereading.com/).

Briggs, Laura, *Somebody's Children: The Politics of Transracial and Transnational Adoption* (Duke University Press, 2012).

Briggs, Laura, *Taking Children: A History of American Terror* (University of California Press, 2020).

Cardaras, Mary, *Ripped at the Root* (Spuyten Duyvil, 2021).

Forero-Hilty, Abby (editor), *Decoding Our Origins: The Lived Experiences of Colombian Adoptees* (CreateSpace, 2017).

Glaser, Gabrielle, *American Baby: A Mother, A Child, and the Shadow History of Adoption* (Viking, 2021).

Ja, Janine Myung, Michael Allen Potter, and Allen L. Vance (editors), *Adoptionland: From Orphans to Activists* (Draft2digital, 2014).

Joyce, Kathryn, *The Child Catchers: Rescue, Trafficking, and the New Gospel of Adoption* (PublicAffairs, 2013).

Kim, Eleana J., *Adopted Territory: Transnational Korean Adoptees and the Politics of Belonging* (Duke University Press, 2010).

McGettrick, Claire, Katherine O'Donnell, Maeve O'Rourke, James M. Smith, and Mari Steed, *Ireland and the Magdalene Laundries: A Campaign for Justice* (I.B. Tauris, 2021).

Mossin, Andrew, *A Son from the Mountains: A Memoir* (Spuyten Duyvil, 2021).

Neagu, Mariela, *Voices of the Silent Cradles: Life Histories of Romania's Looked after Children* (Policy Press, 2021).

O'Connor, Susan Harris, Diane René Christian, and Mei-Mei Akwai Ellerman (editors), *Black Anthology: Adult Adoptees Claim Their Space* (An-Ya Project, 2016).

Oh, Arissa H., *To Save the Children of Korea: The Cold War Origins of International Adoption* (Stanford University Press, 2015).

Redmond, Paul J., *The Adoption Machine: The Dark History of Ireland's Mother and Baby Homes and the Inside Story of How Tuam 800 Became a Global Scandal* (Merrion Press/Irish Academic Press, 2018).

Ross, Loretta, and Ricki Solinger, *Reproductive Justice: An Introduction* (University of California Press, 2017).

Shawyer, Joss, *Death by Adoption* (Kindle edition) (Cicada Press, 1979, 2014).

Trenka, Jane Jeong, Julia Chinyere Oparah, and Sun Yung Shin (editors), *Outsiders within: Writing on Transracial Adoption* (University of Minnesota Press, 2021; first published 2006).

Van Steen, Gonda, *Adoption, Memory, and Cold War Greece: Kid pro quo?* (University of Michigan Press, 2019).

Symposium on US Adoption

Adoption, family separation & preservation, and reproductive justice

Symposium reflecting a range of lived experiences related to adoption, including adopted people, birth/first parents, and adoptive parents, edited by Gretchen Sisson (https://blog.petrieflom.law.harvard.edu/symposia/adoption/).

United States-Based Organizations

Adoptee Rights Law Center

Gregory Luce represents intercountry adoptees who have been adopted by US citizen parents, who often have significant issues related to their own US citizenship (https://adopteerightslaw com/citizenship/).

A map of the 50 states and the District of Columbia detailing their birth certificate access laws (https://adopteerightslaw.com/maps/).

Adoptees United (AU)

A national organization with an unwavering commitment to equality for all adopted people, sponsoring events that work to change the narrative of adoption while centering adoptee lives and experiences (https://adopteesunited.org/).

Alliance for the Study of Adoption and Culture (ASAC)

Promotes understanding of the experience, institution, and cultural representation of domestic and transnational adoption and related practices such as fostering, assisted reproduction, LGBTQ+ families, and alternative kinship formations (https://www.adoptionandculture.org/).

Adoption & Culture is the journal of The Alliance for the Study of Adoption and Culture (https://ohiostatepress.org/AdoptionCulture.html).

American Adoption Congress (AAC)

An international organization devoted to family connections by providing the needed education for all members of the adoption constellation as well as those professionals within adoption, foster care and assisted reproduction (https://www.americanadoptioncongress.org/).

Bastard Nation

Advocates for the civil and human rights of adult citizens who were adopted as children, working to end a hidden legacy of shame, fear and venality (https://bastards.org/).

Concerned United Birthparents (CUB)

Provides support for all family members separated by adoption; resources to help prevent unnecessary family separations; education about the lifelong impact on all who are affected by adoption; and advocates for fair and ethical adoption laws, policies, and practices (https://concernedunitedbirthparents.org/).

www.ingramcontent.com/pod-product-compliance
Lightning Source LLC
Chambersburg PA
CBHW030650270326
41929CB00007B/289